Unknowable, Unspeakable, and Unsprung

Unknowable, Unspeakable, and Unsprung delves into the mysteries of scandalous behavior – behavior that can seem shocking, unfathomable, or self-destructive – that is outrageous and offensive on the one hand, yet fascinating and exciting on the other. In the process, this anthology asks fundamental questions about the self: what the self is allowed to be and do, what must be disallowed, and what remains unknown.

Clinicians strive to know their patients' selves, and their own, as fully as possible, while also facing the inevitable riddles these selves present. Covering topics ranging from trauma, politics, the analyst's subjectivity, and eating disorders and the body, to self-revelation, secrets, evil, and boundary issues, a distinguished group of authors bring the theory, practice, and application of contemporary psychoanalysis to life. In doing so, they use psychoanalytic perspectives not only to illuminate struggles that afflict patients seeking treatment, but to shed light, more broadly, on contemporary human dilemmas.

This collection offers not a unified voice, but rather the sound of many, each in its own way trying to articulate the indescribable, the unwanted, and the off-limits. It is a book that raises more questions than can be answered, complicates as much as clarifies, and contains the essential paradox of trying to talk about aspects of clinical and human experience that can never be fully seen or known. *Unknowable, Unspeakable, and Unsprung* offers invaluable reading to interested mental health professionals as well as to anyone intrigued by the secrets of the self.

Jean Petrucelli is director/co-founder of the Eating Disorders, Compulsions and Addictions Service, faculty and supervising analyst at the William Alanson White Institute, adjunct clinical professor at the New York University Postdoctoral Program in Psychotherapy and Psychoanalysis and the Institute for Contemporary Psychoanalysis, and editor of five books.

Sarah Schoen is faculty and supervising analyst at the William Alanson White Institute and the Eating Disorders, Compulsions and Addictions Service, adjunct clinical professor at the New York University Postdoctoral Program in Psychotherapy and Psychoanalysis, and writes and teaches about contemporary clinical controversies.

PSYCHOANALYSIS IN A NEW KEY BOOK SERIES

DONNEL STERN
Series Editor

When music is played in a new key, the melody does not change, but the notes that make up the composition do: change in the context of continuity, continuity that perseveres through change. Psychoanalysis in a New Key publishes books that share the aims psychoanalysts have always had, but that approach them differently. The books in the series are not expected to advance any particular theoretical agenda, although to this date most have been written by analysts from the Interpersonal and Relational orientations.

The most important contribution of a psychoanalytic book is the communication of something that nudges the reader's grasp of clinical theory and practice in an unexpected direction. Psychoanalysis in a New Key creates a deliberate focus on innovative and unsettling clinical thinking. Because that kind of thinking is encouraged by exploration of the sometimes surprising contributions to psychoanalysis of ideas and findings from other fields, Psychoanalysis in a New Key particularly encourages interdisciplinary studies. Books in the series have married psychoanalysis with dissociation, trauma theory, sociology, and criminology. The series is open to the consideration of studies examining the relationship between psychoanalysis and any other field – for instance, biology, literary and art criticism, philosophy, systems theory, anthropology, and political theory.

But innovation also takes place within the boundaries of psychoanalysis, and Psychoanalysis in a New Key therefore also presents work that reformulates thought and practice without leaving the precincts of the field. Books in the series focus, for example, on the significance of personal values in psychoanalytic practice, on the complex interrelationship between the analyst's clinical work and personal life, on the consequences for the clinical situation when patient and analyst are from different cultures, and on the need for psychoanalysts to accept the degree to which they knowingly satisfy their own wishes during treatment hours, often to the patient's detriment.

For a full list of all the titles in the Psychoanalysis in a New Key series, please visit the Routledge website.

Recent titles in this series

Vol. 32 *The Age of Perversion: Desire and Technology in Psychoanalysis and Culture* Danielle Knafo and Rocco Lo Bosco

Vol. 31 *Unknowable, Unspeakable, and Unsprung: Psychoanalytic Perspectives on Truth, Scandal, Secrets, and Lies* Edited by Jean Petrucelli and Sarah Schoen

Vol. 30 *Trauma and Countertrauma, Resilience and Counterresilience: Insights from Psychoanalysts and Trauma Experts* Edited by Richard B. Gartner

Vol. 29 *The Purloined Self: Interpersonal Perspectives in Psychoanalysis* Edgar A. Levenson

Unknowable, Unspeakable, and Unsprung

Psychoanalytic Perspectives on Truth, Scandal, Secrets, and Lies

Edited by Jean Petrucelli and Sarah Schoen

Routledge
Taylor & Francis Group
LONDON AND NEW YORK

First published 2017
by Routledge
2 Park Square, Milton Park, Abingdon, Oxon OX14 4RN

and by Routledge
711 Third Avenue, New York, NY 10017

Routledge is an imprint of the Taylor & Francis Group, an informa business

British Library Cataloguing in Publication Data
A catalogue record for this book is available from the British Library

Library of Congress Cataloging in Publication Data
Names: Petrucelli, Jean, editor. | Schoen, Sarah E., editor.
Title: Unknowable, unspeakable and unsprung : psychoanalytic perspectives on truth, scandal, secrets and lies / edited by Jean Petrucelli and Sarah Schoen.
Description: Abingdon, Oxon ; New York, NY : Routledge, 2017. | Series: Psychoanalysis in a new key ; 31 | Includes bibliographical references and index.
Identifiers: LCCN 2016022524| ISBN 9781138689008 (hardback : alk. paper) | ISBN 9781138689015 (pbk. : alk. paper) | ISBN 9781315537931 (e-book)
Subjects: LCSH: Psychoanalysis. | Psychotherapy. | Scandals—Psychological aspects. | Self-destructive behavior.
Classification: LCC RC506 .U55 2017 | DDC 616.89/17—dc23
LC record available at https://lccn.loc.gov/2016022524

ISBN: 978-1-138-68900-8 (hbk)
ISBN: 978-1-138-68901-5 (pbk)
ISBN: 978-1-315-53793-1 (ebk)

Typeset in Times New Roman
by Swales & Willis Ltd, Exeter, Devon, UK

For my grandmothers and my mother, Lonnie, who inspired my love of a good meatball

J.P.

For my mother, Marthe Whitcomb, who experienced more than her share of the ugly and the sublime

S.S.

For our dear friends, colleagues, and patients

J.P. and S.S.

Contents

About the editors

Jean Petrucelli, Ph.D. is a clinical psychologist and a psychoanalyst, director and co-founder of the Eating Disorders, Compulsions and Addictions Service (EDCAS); fellow; supervising analyst; teaching faculty; Conference Advisory Board (CAB) chair and founding director of the EDCAS one-year educational certificate program at the William Alanson White Institute for Psychotherapy and Psychoanalysis. She is an adjunct clinical professor of Psychology at the New York University Postdoctoral Program in Psychotherapy and Psychoanalysis, and the Institute for Contemporary Psychology; associate editor for *Contemporary Psychoanalysis*; and member of The BODI Group, conducting research on the intergenerational transmission of body image and embodiment.

Dr. Petrucelli is editor of the books: *Body-States: Interpersonal and Relational Perspectives on the Treatment of Eating Disorders* (Routledge, 2015); *Knowing, Not-Knowing and Sort-of-Knowing: Psychoanalysis and the Experience of Uncertainty* (Karnac Books, 2010); and *Longing: Psychoanalytic Musings on Desire* (Karnac Books, 2006) and co-editor of the book *Hungers and Compulsions: The Psychodynamic Treatment of Eating Disorders and Addictions* (Rowan & Littlefield/Jason Aronson, 2009, 2001). She specializes in the interpersonal treatment of eating disorders and addictions and lectures at colleges, universities, institutes, psychoanalytic societies, and treatment facilities nationally and internationally. She is in private practice in New York City.

Sarah Schoen, Ph.D. is a clinical psychologist and psychoanalyst. She is a supervising analyst and teaching faculty for psychoanalytic candidates at the William Alanson White Institute, as well as supervisor, faculty, and

Steering Committee member of White's Eating Disorders Compulsions and Addictions Program. She is an adjunct clinical professor of Psychology at the New York University Postdoctoral Program in Psychotherapy and an invited speaker at Columbia Psychoanalytic University Center for Psychoanalytic Training and Research. Dr. Schoen teaches and writes on the topics of working psychoanalytically, contemporary perspectives on narcissism, gender, and relational psychoanalysis. She is a former fellow of the American Psychoanalytic Association and former supervising psychologist at the Bellevue/NYU Program for Survivors of Torture. She is on the editorial board of *Contemporary Psychoanalysis*, and has a private practice in New York's Flatiron district.

Contributors

Mark J. Blechner, Ph.D. is training and supervising analyst at the William Alanson White Institute, and adjunct clinical professor at New York University (NYU). He has published three books: *Sex Changes: Transformations in Society and Psychoanalysis* (Routledge, 2009), *The Dream Frontier* (Routledge, 2001), and *Hope and Mortality: Psychodynamic Approaches to AIDS and HIV* (Routledge, 1997). He is the former editor-in-chief of the journal *Contemporary Psychoanalysis.*

Steven Botticelli, Ph.D. is on the faculty of NYU Postdoctoral Program, co-chair of the Independent Track; contributing editor, *Studies in Gender and Sexuality* and *The Division/Review*, co-editor with Adrienne Harris of *First Do No Harm: The Paradoxical Encounters of Psychoanalysis, Warmaking and Resistance* (Routledge, 2010). He practices in the West Village in New York City.

Judith Brisman, Ph.D. is the founding director of the Eating Disorder Resource Center in New York City. She is co-author of *Surviving an Eating Disorder: Strategies for Family and Friends* (3rd edition, Harper Perennial, 2009) and she is on the editorial board of *Eating Disorders: The Journal of Treatment and Prevention.* Dr. Brisman is an associate editor for the journal *Contemporary Psychoanalysis*, and is on the teaching faculty for the Eating Disorders, Compulsions and Addictions Service (EDCAS) Teaching Faculty at the William Alanson White Institute. She has published and lectured extensively regarding the interpersonal treatment of eating disorders and is well known for her expertise in running training seminars and presentations.

Philip M. Bromberg, Ph.D. is a training and supervising analyst of the William Alanson White Institute, and adjunct clinical professor of Psychology at the NYU Postdoctoral Program in Psychoanalysis and Psychotherapy. He is emeritus co-editor-in-chief of the journal *Contemporary Psychoanalysis* and an Editorial Board member of *Psychoanalytic Dialogues* and *Psychoanalytic Inquiry*. Dr. Bromberg is most widely recognized as author of *Standing in the Spaces: Essays on Clinical Process, Trauma, and Dissociation* (Analytic Press, 1998); *Awakening the Dreamer: Clinical Journeys* (Analytic Press, 2006); and *The Shadow of the Tsunami and the Growth of the Relational Mind* (Routledge, 2011).

Sandra Buechler, Ph.D. is a training and supervising analyst at the William Alanson White Institute and faculty for EDCAS. She is a supervisor at Columbia Presbyterian Hospital's internship and postdoctoral programs and at the Institute for Contemporary Psychotherapy. A graduate of the William Alanson White Institute, Dr. Buechler has written extensively on emotions in psychoanalysis, including papers on hope, joy, loneliness, and mourning in the analyst and patient. Her books include: *Clinical Values: Emotions that Guide Psychoanalytic Treatment* (Analytic Press, 2004); *Making a Difference in Patients' Lives: Emotional Experience in the Therapeutic Setting* (Routledge, 2008); *Still Practicing: The Heartaches and Joys of a Clinical Career* (Routledge, 2012); and, most recently, *Understanding and Treating Patients in Clinical Psychoanalysis: Lessons from Literature* (Routledge, 2015).

Jack Drescher, M.D. is a training and supervising analyst at the William Alanson White Institute; clinical professor, New York Medical College, and adjunct professor, NYU Postdoctoral Program in Psychotherapy and Psychoanalysis. Author of *Psychoanalytic Therapy and the Gay Man* (Routledge, 2001), he has edited more than a score of books dealing with gender and sexuality. He served on the DSM-5 Workgroup on Sexual and Gender Identity Disorders and is a member of the World Health Organization's Working Group on the Classification of Sexual Disorders and Sexual Health revising the ICD-11.

Kenneth Eisold, Ph.D. is the past president, International Society for the Psychoanalytic Study of Organizations, and former director of the Organizational Program at the William Alanson White Institute. He is a practicing psychoanalyst as well as organizational consultant and has written extensively on the psychodynamics of large systems as well as on the organizational dimension of psychoanalysis. He is the author of *What You Don't Know You Know* (Other Press, 2010).

Daniel Gensler, Ph.D. is director of training, Child Adolescent Psychotherapy Training Program at the William Alanson White Institute; co-author of *Relational Child Psychotherapy* (Other Press, 2002), and has published a dozen articles and chapters in the professional literature. He is in private practice in New York, NY and Great Neck, NY, doing psychotherapy, psychological testing, and supervision.

Mary-Joan Gerson, Ph.D., ABPP is an adjunct clinical professor, clinical consultant, director of Advanced Specialization in Couple and Family Therapy, NYU Postdoctoral Program; supervisor, National Institute for the Psychotherapies; founding president of Section VIII – Couples and Family Therapy of Division 39 of the American Psychological Association. She is the author of *The Embedded Self: An Integrative Psychodynamic and Systemic Perspective on Couple and Family Therapy*, 2nd edition (Routledge, 2009), as well as many articles on psychoanalysis and couples therapy, coping with chronic medical illness, and adult development.

Anton Hart, Ph.D. is former fellow, training and supervising analyst, and faculty of the William Alanson White Institute, supervisor in the White Institute's Intensive Psychoanalytic Psychotherapy Program, at Teachers College, at Columbia University, and at the Derner University of Adelphi University. He is faculty at the White Institute's Eating Disorders, Compulsions and Addictions program, the National Institute for Psychotherapies, the Institute for Contemporary Psychotherapy, and he teaches a seminar in the Department of Psychology at Mount Sinai St. Luke's/Roosevelt Hospital. Dr. Hart is on the Editorial Board of Psychoanalytic Psychology and Contemporary Psychoanalysis. He has written and taught on mutuality, disruption, safety, otherness, and diversity and is the author of a book in press (Routledge) tentatively entitled *Beyond Oaths or Codes: Toward Relational Psychoanalytic Ethics*. He has served as associate co-producer for, and was featured in, the documentary film, *Black Psychoanalysts Speak*. He is in private practice in New York City

Irwin Hirsch, Ph.D. is faculty and supervisor, Manhattan Institute for Psychoanalysis; distinguished visiting faculty, William Alanson White Institute; adjunct clinical professor and supervisor, NYU Postdoctoral Program in Psychotherapy and Psychoanalysis; and faculty and supervisor, National Training Program, National Institute for the Psychotherapies. He is the author of over 80 journal articles and book chapters, the Goethe Award-winning book, *Coasting in the Countertransference: Conflicts of Self-Interest between Analyst and Patient* (Routledge, 2008), and *The Interpersonal Tradition: The Origins of Psychoanalytic Subjectivity* (Routledge, 2015). Forthcoming, is a book co-edited with Donnel Stern: *The Interpersonal Perspective in Psychoanalysis: Selected Papers, Volume 1* (Routledge).

Sheldon Itzkowitz, Ph.D. is an adjunct clinical associate professor of Psychology and Clinical Consultant at the NYU Postdoctoral Program in Psychotherapy and Psychoanalysis, guest faculty, the Eating Disorders, Compulsions, and Addictions Program of the William Alanson White Institute, and on the teaching and supervisory faculty of the National Institute for the Psychotherapies training program in psychoanalysis. Dr. Itzkowitz is an associate editor of *Psychoanalytic Perspectives* and a former president of the Division of Psychoanalysis of the New York State Psychological Association. He is in full-time practice in Manhattan, where he practices psychoanalysis and psychoanalytic psychotherapy, and provides clinical supervision for mental health practitioners. Dr. Itzkowitz has presented his work with extremely dissociated individuals both nationally and internationally.

Sue Kolod, Ph.D. is a supervising and training analyst, faculty, and is on the Steering Committee and faculty member of EDCAS at the William Alanson White Institute. She is co-editor of the blog *Contemporary Psychoanalysis in Action*. Dr. Kolod has written numerous chapters and articles about the impact of hormones on the psyche. Her work also focuses on the impact of hormones on sexuality. She maintains a full-time private practice in Brooklyn and Manhattan.

Emily A. Kuriloff, Psy.D. is a training and supervising analyst, faculty, and member of the EDCAS faculty at the William Alanson White Institute, and editor for special issues and former book review editor for the journal *Contemporary Psychoanalysis*. She is the author of the book, *The Holocaust in Psychoanalytic Theory and Practice* (Routledge, 2014).

Edgar A. Levenson, M.D. is a training and supervising analyst of the William Alanson White Institute; adjunct clinical professor of Psychology, NYU Postdoctoral Program; author of numerous articles and the books: *The Fallacy of Understanding* (Routledge, 1979), *The Ambiguity of Change: An Inquiry into the Nature of Psychoanalytic Reality* (Basic Books, 1983), and *The Purloined Self: Interpersonal Perspective in Psychoanalysis* (Contemporary Psychoanalysis Books, 1991). He was the 2006 recipient of the Mary S. Sigourney Award for recognizing distinguished contributions to the field of psychoanalysis.

Paul Lippmann, Ph.D. is a training and supervising analyst, former faculty and fellow and past president of the William Alanson White Psychoanalytic Society. He is founder and currently on the board of local Division 39 of the American Psychological Association (Western Massachusetts and Albany Association of Psychoanalytic Psychologists). He is founder of the Stockbridge Dream Society. He was formerly faculty at the NYU Postdoctoral Program in Psychotherapy and Psychoanalysis. He is the author of *Nocturnes: On Listening to Dreams* (Analytic Press, 2000). He is in private practice in Stockbridge, Massuchesetts.

Susie Orbach, Ph.D. is a psychoanalyst, writer, and activist. She co-founded the Women's Therapy Centre in London. She has a practice seeing individuals and couples. She is a member of the UK government's Expert Panel on Body Confidence, the UK convener of www.endangeredbodies.org, and the author of 13 books, including *Fat is a Feminist Issue* (Paddington Press, 1978; Berkeley Books, 1982), *Hunger Strike* (Norton, 1986), *On Eating* (Penguin, 2002), and *Bodies* (Karnac, 2009). Her latest book *In Therapy* is from the BBC Radio series of the same name. She lectures and broadcasts extensively worldwide. She was visiting Professor at LSE for 10 years, had a column in *The Guardian* and has been profiled in national and international newspapers including *The NY Times*.

Adam Phillips is a psychoanalyst, essayist, and visiting professor in the English Department at the University of York. Since 2003 he has been the general editor of the new Penguin Modern Classics translations of Sigmund Freud. He is also a regular contributor to the London Review of Books. Author of many books, including *On Kissing, Tickling and Being Bored* (Harvard University Press, 1993); *On Flirtation*

(Harvard University Press, 1994); *The Beast in the Nursery* (Knopf Doubleday, 1998); *Going Sane* (HarperCollins, 2005); *Side Effects* (HarperCollins, 2006); *On Balance* (Farrar, Straus and Giroux, 2010); *Missing Out: In Praise of the Unlived Life* (Farrar, Straus and Giroux, 2012); co-author with Leo Bersami, of *Intimacies* (University of Chicago Press, 2008); with Barbara Taylor, of *On Kindness* (Farrar, Straus and Giroux, 2009); and with Judith Clark, of *The Concise Dictionary of Dress* (Violette Editions, 2010). Most recently, he is the author of *Becoming Freud: The Making of a Psychoanalyst* (Yale University Press, 2014).

Melissa Ritter, Ph.D. is a Supervisor of Psychotherapy and faculty member at the William Alanson White Institute, Clinical Adjunct Faculty at City College and Adelphi University, founder and former Chair of the White Institute LGBTQ Study Group, and Co-Editor of *Contemporary Psychoanalysis in Action*, a blog under the auspices of *Psychology Today* and *Contemporary Psychoanalysis*.

Susan Sands, Ph.D. is on the Faculty at Psychoanalytic Institute of Northern California; Clinical Faculty of the Psychology Department, UC-Berkeley; and is in private practice in Berkeley. She has treated individuals with eating disorders for more than 25 years, including 5 years in the Eating Disorders Clinic, Psychiatry Department, Stanford Medical School. She has published, taught, consulted, and presented widely on the subject, as well as on dissociation, unconscious communication, female development, and aging.

Andrew Solomon is the author of *Far From the Tree: Parents, Children and the Search for Identity* (Simon and Schuster, 2012); *The Noonday Demon: An Atlas of Depression* (Simon and Schuster, 2001), and a novel, *A Stone Boat* (Simon and Schuster, 1994). He is a writer and lecturer on psychology, politics, and the arts; and an activist in LGBTQ rights, and mental health. He is the winner of 14 national awards, including the 2001 National Book Award, a Pulitzer Prize finalist, and a *New York Times* bestseller, now published in 22 languages.

Donnel B. Stern, Ph.D. is a training and supervising analyst and member of the faculty at the William Alanson White Institute in New York City; and adjunct clinical professor and clinical consultant, NYU Postdoctoral Program in Psychotherapy and Psychoanalysis. He is the author of three books from Routledge: *Unformulated Experience: From Dissociation to Imagination in Psychoanalysis* (1997); *Partners in Thought: Working with Unformulated Experience, Dissociation, and Enactment* (2010); and *Relational Freedom: Emergent Properties of the Interpersonal Field* (2015). He is the founder and editor of a book series from Routledge, Psychoanalysis in a New Key.

Don Troise, LCSW is a supervisor, training analyst, and on the faculty for the Institute for Contemporary Psychotherapy. He has published articles in *Psychoanalytic Dialogues* and *Contemporary Psychoanalysis*. He is in private practice in New York City.

Steven Tublin, Ph.D. is a training and supervising analyst at the William Alanson White Institute, and adjunct clinical professor, NYU Postdoctoral Program in Psychotherapy and Psychoanalysis, and serves on the Editorial Board of *Contemporary Psychoanalysis*. He is an associate at Upstart Logic, an organizational consultancy, and in private practice in New York City.

Acknowledgments

We owe thanks to many people for bringing this book to life, and we are lucky to have such creative and inspiring chapter authors who have contributed their talents and experiences to this project. This collection originated in a conference entitled, *Unknowable, Unspeakable, and Unsprung: Navigating the Thrill and Danger of Living Amidst Truth, Fantasy, and Privacy*, sponsored by the William Alanson White Institute, and held at the Mount Sinai Medical Center in New York City.

This was an experience in which a multiplicity of voices cohered in a dynamic exchange of ideas that spoke to our theme in ways unanticipated at the genesis of the conference. The Conference Advisory Board (CAB), of which I (JP) was chair, created this event, and the editors would like to acknowledge and thank the CAB members for their tireless efforts in brainstorming and producing a symposium of this magnitude. They are: Seth Aronson, Lori Bohm, Grant Brenner, Jacqueline Ferraro, Elizabeth Halsted, Maria Nardone, and Jonathan Wormhoudt. In particular, Maria and Jacqueline went above and beyond the call of duty in fine-tuning, from soup to nuts, all the details involved in creating this scrumptious stew for so many palates, and Maria's dedication and energy in procuring sponsorship were invaluable. We are also indebted to key members of the Institute's administrative staff, Richard Herman, Marisol Pitre, and Elizabeth Rodman, who were vital to the execution of our vision. A thank you also goes to the Institute's Board of Trustees and to the Council of Fellows.

We would not be where we are now if it were not for the incisive wisdom of our mentors, analysts, and teachers over the years. We want to thank them for their continued guidance, enthusiasm, and unwavering support for the projects they have also inspired.

Our loved ones, kids, spouses, parents, and siblings, alive or with us in spirit, are always a felt part of everything we do as we live, breathe, spin, and become *sprung* and plugged into all new ventures. They are the bedrock of our creative urges – our riverbed – and they make all the pain exhilarating and worthwhile.

We thank Don Stern for his continued mentoring and his inclusion of us in his prestigious book series. Our publisher, Kate Hawes, has once again given me (JP), and for the first time, my brilliant colleague and co-editor, Sarah Schoen, the privilege of joining the Routledge family. For this, we are eternally grateful.

And lastly, we wish to thank our patients who inspire us with all that is human.

Introduction

Jean Petrucelli and Sarah Schoen

Like a riverbed that shapes the flow of waters, a conference harbors the flowing dynamic of intertwined currents. Long after conference day comes and goes, once the tumult and drama quiet, one hopes that the papers and presentations that form the riverbed will continue to reverberate and ripple. The river – the bubbling hubbub of conference day – may demand our attention, but it is the riverbed that we ultimately want to explore: what is it that holds, that shapes, that anchors, but that also hides the river's treasures?

This book, an edited anthology of the papers that made up the conference, entitled *Unknowable, Unspeakable, and Unsprung: Navigating the Thrill and Danger of Living Amidst Truth, Fantasy, and Privacy* (otherwise known to its contributors as U3, borrowing from the band U2 but adding an "intersubjective third") originated as an idea about scandal. We, as psychoanalysts, have a unique perspective both on why it is that people behave in ways that are shocking, at odds with their public identities, and appear from the outside to be strikingly self-destructive, and on why it is we love to watch them. At the heart of any scandal is a mystery, the mystery of the self: what the self is allowed to do and be, what must be disallowed and disavowed. As clinicians, we are always striving to know our patients' selves and our own as fully as we can while also facing the inevitable riddle of those very same selves.

The members of the Conference Advisory Board committee, at the William Alanson White Institute, including one of us (JP) as chair, hoped that in creating and producing this event, we would be able to bring this far-reaching topic – what we can and cannot know, speak, or fathom – into a more experience near place. As the conference committee explored the question of scandal – of what it is about those events that are outrageous and offensive, yet fascinating and titillating – they found themselves thinking more broadly about the many things we have difficulty talking about openly, both in and out of the consulting room. Like a sudden shift from calm waters to rapids, the conference's topics burgeoned: sex, lies, gossip, politics, the body, obesity, privacy, failure, stuck-ness, the uncanny, mortality, violence, and otherness, to name just a few. And we (the editors) have tried to harness these currents and some of their many treasures and bring them to you in this anthology.

Medusa became the river's muse, as she is a mythical being at once unmistakably identifiable and ambiguous. She wanders through territory belonging to life and death, male and female, order and chaos, and the visible and the invisible. Medusa has long fascinated psychoanalysts. Freud argued that she was "the supreme talisman who provides the image of castration – associated in the child's mind with the discovery of maternal sexuality – and its denial" (Freud, 1922). It took analysts quite a long time to acknowledge maternal sexuality, and it seemed right, somehow, to redefine Medusa's meaning in contemporary psychoanalytic terms: as an icon for speaking the unspeakable in a world of ambiguity – a world in which beauty and ugliness can quickly become either figure or ground; as a symbol for the dangers that can unfurl as we get lost in the timelessness of the unconscious; as a representation of the experience of having parts of ourselves (states, desires, actions) that feel like alien creatures – threatening, and beyond conscious control.

From multiple vantage points, the authors in this collection explore the enigma of people – our patients, our selves, and our psychoanalytic ancestors, whose pasts still haunt us all. In doing so, the authors invite you, the reader, to risk your own encounter with what's been silenced or hidden, as they attempt to articulate the unknown, the unspoken, and the *unsprung* – chancing the uncoiling of Medusa's snakes. In keeping with our Levensonian quest to attend to "what's going on around here" (cf., Levenson, 1985) – and, as you will see from the plethora of chapter topics, that is *pretty much everything*[1] – we invite you to find your own something in this everything, and "pursue the particular" (Levenson, 1988).

This volume is comprised of eight sections and 26 chapters. Part I opens with papers by the conference's keynote speakers, Adam Phillips and Andrew Solomon. In Chapter 1, *The Unforbidden*, Phillips questions whether unforbidden pleasures have something more to tell us, or at least something else to tell us, about pleasure than do forbidden ones. He muses that, were this to be true, a lot of things that we have taken very seriously would seem less serious, and he argues that the tyranny of the forbidden is not that it forbids, but that it tells us what we want.

Chapter 2, *Far From the Tree*, by Andrew Solomon (and adapted from Solomon's book of the same name) explores the experience of parents who are markedly different from their children. Solomon draws on his own experience of being the gay child of straight parents, and goes on to talk about deaf children born to hearing parents, children with developmental and psychical disabilities born to parents without these struggles, and the like. Throughout, Solomon examines the fine line between illness and identity, and the ways in which it is often our differences that can bring us closer. Both Phillips' play on how the prohibited defines the permissible, and Solomon's take on how differences create opportunities for connection are themes that run throughout this diverse collection of papers.

Part II, *The Traumatic Field: Psychoanalytic Growth and the Growth of Psychoanalysis*, has chapters by Philip M. Bromberg, Donnel B. Stern, Don Troise, and Jack Drescher. In Chapter 3, Bromberg examines the mutually personal nature of the psychoanalytic relationship as it emerges in the clinical experience of enactments that relive developmental trauma. Such experiences, on the one hand, offer the potential for healing and growth. On the other hand, because such enactments are also personal for the *analyst*, they have the potential to become seriously problematic. Bromberg describes how, under certain affectively laden circumstances, the analyst's capacity to maintain the "impossible duality" of his analytic task – to stay fully connected to, and able to reflect on, his patient in *both* the reality of the enactment *and* the reality of her "real-world" roles – is compromised.

In Chapter 4, Stern explores the links between the post-structuralist concept of interpellation, which conceives of the organization of experience into binary opposites (e.g., in the work of Saussure, Derrida, and Althusser), with the interpersonal and relational conceptions of dissociation and enactment. Stern elaborates this link in the service of broadening and deepening the field between patient and analyst.

Troise, in Chapter 5, argues that psychoanalytic doctrine and its alterations over time can be viewed as translation and transformation of the traumatic past. In this way, the analytic field may be regarded as a traumatic field. Troise illustrates how the theories of Freud and Sullivan represent two opposite responses to trauma: Freud's organized by dissociation, Sullivan's by affiliation. These two poles, in turn, create a spectrum along which most psychoanalytic theories can be located.

From his vantage point as a scholar in the field of sexuality and gender and as the adult child of Holocaust survivors, Drescher, in Chapter 6, also takes up the impact of trauma on the development of psychoanalysis and the question of whether psychoanalysis is a traumatized field. In reflecting on his parents' trauma, Drescher extends his discussion of the intergenerational transmission of trauma to include the concept of "hierarchies of suffering," in which victims, both real and imagined, are compensated by a morally superior high ground.

Part III, *Utters from the Gutters: Political Loyalties and the Clash of Deeply Held Values in the Consulting Room*, has chapters by Steve Tublin, Steven Botticelli, Kenneth Eisold, and Melissa Ritter. In Chapter 7, Tublin takes up an often-neglected treatment dilemma: how do analyst and patient address or fail to address the presence of clashing political loyalties? Tublin highlights the risks in either instance, noting that a failure to address this particular transference–countertransference matrix can, in some dyads, result in a deadening inauthenticity. Alternately, broaching this provocative topic demands that both participants be willing to question the values they hold most dear.

In Chapter 8, Botticelli continues to elaborate the hurdles in negotiating differences between patient and therapist in deeply embedded aspects of identity. He addresses the complex differences that can characterize participants in a gay male therapy dyad, describing the impasse arising from a gay male patient's refusal to be ushered into the happy, healthy, twenty-first-century-style homosexuality seemingly achieved by his therapist.

In a moving personal account, Eisold, in Chapter 9, reflects on his unusual experience working with a number of oil traders who came to him to consult about their financial losses. Rather than emphasizing the potential threat of irreconcilable differences between himself and these unlikely consumers, Eisold describes how his work with the traders gave him an opportunity to revisit his childhood experiences of being taunted and bullied. In this context, he transforms the envy he once felt of boys who were freer than he was to play and fight into a gratifying and reparative experience of inclusion, identification, and empathic connection.

Usefully complicating and elaborating our understanding of female, heterosexual therapy dyads, Ritter, in Chapter 10, takes up the analyst's countertransferential response to two patients' seemingly regressive adherence to traditional roles and rituals in romantic relationships. Ritter emphasizes both the analyst's and patients' distinct psychological configurations as contextualizing their different relationship to feminism and gender performance, and she emphasizes the clinical value of self-examination and judicious self-disclosure.

Part IV, *Stuck in the Middle with You: Encounters with the Analyst's Subjectivity*, has chapters by Sarah Schoen, Sheldon Itzkowitz, and Irwin Hirsch. In Chapter 11, Schoen asks us to ask ourselves: what makes us think of one patient as "analytic" and another one not? Using a clinical example, she examines enactments in which the analyst unconsciously avoids substantive involvement with patients likely to entail contact with her most disavowed aspects of self. In particular, Schoen probes the role of frequency given the contemporary emphasis on the emergence of enactments as central to therapeutic action.

In Chapter 12, Itzkowitz investigates the influence of the analyst's subjectivity from the perspective of a clinician with expertise working with extreme dissociative disorders. He offers a clinical example that illustrates the complexity of transference–countertransference matrices occurring on different levels of consciousness for both patient and therapist. And finally Hirsch, who has contributed much to the discourse on the influence of the analyst's subjectivity, gives us Chapter 13, in which he argues that, in general, the ways in which analysts both theorize and engage with patients is primarily a function of personal proclivity and aesthetics. Rather than emphasizing the problems that can arise as the result of the analyst's personal engagement, Hirsch argues that individual analysts are likely to be most helpful to their patients when they work from positions to which they are passionately committed.

Part V, *Body Tyranny: Hyperawareness and Hyperdeadness with Eating-Disordered Patients*, is made up of chapters by Jean Petrucelli, Judith Brisman, Susan Sands, and Susie Orbach. This section opens with Petrucelli, who, in Chapter 14, illustrates the way in which the analyst's willingness to access and share her own vulnerability can help eating-disordered patients reclaim their own disavowed longings and needs, rather than continue to detour them into their body and control them via their use of food. Using a personal story and two clinical vignettes, Petrucelli illustrates how fear, courage, shame, and the mutuality of affective and bodily experience characterize our work with these patients, and how a safe and real therapeutic relationship can ultimately allow them to re-enter the world of human relatedness.

In Chapter 15, Brisman takes up how, with the weight-preoccupied patient, a focus on eating and food gives the patient a voice, but can also hide her from sight. Brisman illustrates how the goal of treatment involves making space for both the patient's concrete food- and weight-centered language and the therapist's language of analytic exploration. Sands, in Chapter 16, also explores the therapist's struggle to stay connected to the eating-disordered patient's perspective without losing her own. She elaborates on the ways in which the eating-disordered patient repudiates need and desire. Sands goes on to describe an enactment characteristic of work with anorexic patients in which the patient's dissociated longings evoke, and are evoked by, the analyst's dissociated neglect.

In Chapter 17, Orbach argues that the relational origins of development are as critical to our experience of our bodies as they are to our experience of our mental and emotional lives. She explores how bodies today are increasingly troubled and illustrates how clinicians can reflect on and make use of their body countertransferences to expand their understanding of their patients' troubled corporeality.

Part VI, *On Being Naked: Self-Revelation, Secrecy, and Shifting Truths*, has chapters by Mark J. Blechner, Sandra Buechler, Sue Kolod, and Paul Lippmann. In Chapter 18, Blechner examines how the official condemnation of sexual contact between patients and therapists is not universal and/or can coexist with more private, sentimental views in which certain of these relationships are condoned or accepted. Blechner suggests that bridging the gap between public and private perspectives could lead to a more open dialogue about, and more consistent approach to, sexual boundary violations.

Buechler, in Chapter 19, explores ways we do and don't tell the truth by looking at what we do and do not say to patients, particularly early on in treatment. She encourages us to think more complexly about the valuing of authenticity and openness in some contemporary psychoanalytic circles, noting ways that timing and tact still matter when it comes to answering patients' questions about where treatment will lead. In particular, she highlights the time it takes for the therapist in training to develop a personal sense of when to wait and contain, which can be just as challenging as offering "answers" or risking confrontation.

In Chapter 20, Kolod brings us back to an exploration of scandal and the ways in which its onlookers often oscillate between reactions of disgust and fascination. She uses a clinical example of working with a man accused of child molestation to take up these countertransferential responses, as well as to explore the therapist's intermittent need to "really" know an accused patient's guilt or innocence. Kolod also describes the way in which such responses diminish as the patient becomes a fuller human being with whom the therapist establishes a real connection.

Lippmann, in Chapter 21, takes on psychoanalysis itself as the scandalous patient, exploring several of the darker features of psychoanalytic practice and institutional culture. Although aware that the diminished status of psychoanalysis makes it challenging, Lippmann encourages us to look honestly at ourselves so as not to deny our personal or our field's flaws. Indeed, he suggests that this may be the very thing that allows us to have a voice once again in the broader cultural milieu.

Part VII, *Unsafe Surprises: Evil, Mortality, Diversity, and Other Strangers,* has chapters by Edgar A. Levenson, Emily A. Kuriloff, and Anton Hart. In Chapter 22, Levenson argues that contemporary psychoanalysis, with its emphasis on the nurturing aspects of relatedness, may err on the side of denying the underbelly, the uncanny aspects of our patients' and our own experiences. Evil, Levenson notes, becomes the absence of good, rather than an inherent force of human nature, as was more openly acknowledged in our psychoanalytic ancestors' times.

Kuriloff, in Chapter 23, confronts the contradiction between the quintessentially psychoanalytic goal of expanding awareness and how psychoanalysis' history, so intimately intertwined with the Holocaust, means that this awareness necessarily confronts us with shock, upset, and evil. In Chapter 24, Hart addresses another contradiction in psychoanalysis: the field's need and desire for diversification on the one hand, and its resistance to it on the other. He explores some of the obstacles to genuine dialogue on racial, ethnic, and socioeconomic differences, while persuasively arguing that such dialogue is crucial if we are to move beyond the scripted ways we are taught to talk about these loaded aspects of identity.

Part VIII, *Silence and Privacy: Negotiating Boundaries between Public and Private – In and Out of the Consulting Room,* has chapters by Daniel Gensler and Mary-Joan Gerson. Gensler, in Chapter 25, addresses the predicament of the therapist working with adolescents who are capable of mutual engagement, but do not talk about their experience. He conceptualizes their silence as arising from the dissociation of a more related state that the therapist has the potential to activate. And finally, in Chapter 26,

Gerson relies on both her expertise in individual and couples treatment to ponder the essential difference between privacy and secrecy. In doing so, she takes up ways that privacy and secrecy have been eroded given the influence of the internet, and she maintains that the psychotherapeutic relationship remains a bastion of both.

In the end, this is a collection of papers that raises more questions than can be answered, that complicates more than it clarifies, and that contains the essential paradox of trying to talk about aspects of clinical – and human – experience that can never be fully seen or known. This volume offers not a unified voice, but rather the sounds of many, each in its own way trying to give voice to the indescribable, the unwanted, and the off limits. But we hope, in its sprawling, expansive flow, that we have managed to bring you some of what makes up the riverbed, and that we have invited you to think, say, and see things that perhaps were not possible before.

Note

1 Despite the surfeit of riches in this anthology, we nevertheless regret the absence of those wonderful presentations from the conference that could not be included.

References

Freud, S. (1922). Medusa's head. In: *The Standard Edition of the Complete Psychological Works of Sigmund Freud*, Vol. XVIII (1920–1922) Beyond the Pleasure Principle, Group Psychology, and Other Works. London: Hogarth Press, pp. 273–274.

Levenson, E. A. (1985). Chapter 4: The Interpersonal (Sullivanian) Model. In A. Rothstein (Ed.), *Models of the Mind: Their Relationships to Clinical Work*. New York: International Universities Press, pp. 49–67.

Levenson, E. A. (1988). The pursuit of the particular – on the psychoanalytic inquiry. *Contemporary Psychoanalysis*, *24*: 1–16.

Part I

Keynote addresses

Chapter 1

The unforbidden[1]

Adam Phillips

> *To define . . . is to distrust.*
>
> Laurence Sterne, *Tristram Shandy* (1999)

Part 1

We may live in the aftermath of the myth of the Fall, and the even longer aftermath of the myth of Oedipus, but the first traffic lights were invented in the United States after the First World War. The traditional mutual accommodation travelers had been making to each other on their bikes and in cars and carts was replaced by a set of lights. "Its purpose," the anthropologist James C. Scott writes, "was to prevent accidents by imposing an engineered scheme of co-ordination" (2012, p. 81). Partly through pressure of numbers and the proliferation of vehicles, and partly through the new scientific and bureaucratic fantasies of efficiency and productivity, familiar forms of co-operation gave way to a new, technologically implemented set of rules. People's practical judgment was delegated to a red light. They had known when to stop, but now they were being told when to stop.

But in 2003 in Drachten in the Netherlands, Hans Monderman, a "counter-intuitive traffic engineer," proposed the removal of traffic lights in the interest of what he called "shared space." Once put to the test, the results were extraordinary, leading to a series of what were called "red-light removal schemes" across Europe and America. "He began," James C. Scott writes,

> with the observation that when an electrical failure incapacitated traffic lights, the result was improved flow rather than congestion. As an experiment, he replaced the busiest traffic light intersection in Drachten, handling 22,000 cars a day, with a traffic circle, an extended cycle path,

> and a pedestrian area. In the two years following the removal of the traffic light, the number of accidents plummeted to only two, compared with thirty-six crashes in the four years prior. Traffic moves more briskly through the intersection when all drivers know they must be alert and use their common sense, while back-ups and the road rage associated with them have virtually disappeared. Monderman likened it to skaters in a crowded ice-rink who manage successfully to tailor their movements to those of the other skaters. He also believed that an excess of signage led drivers to take their eyes off the road, and actually contributed to making junctions less safe.
>
> (Scott, 2012, pp. 81–82)

It is, of course, in many ways a suggestive experiment, and not incidental that Scott uses it in his book *Two Cheers for Anarchism* (2012), anarchism being one of many traditions of antinomian thought, at least in the West. For us, people questioning the rules – wondering both what a rule is, and what it is to follow a rule; wondering what morality really is, and why moral obligations matter – it is the news that stays news. We are always tempted to ask, as Sterne does in *Tristram Shandy*, "Is a man to follow rules – or rules to follow him?" It has become second nature now for many people to think that rules, even in their most extreme versions, or particularly in their most extreme versions when they become taboos – may always be no more and no less than human artefacts. Gravity may be more fundamental than justice, but our morality doesn't need to have the gravity of gravity. We are inevitably exercised about where we draw the lines, the kind of lines we draw, and to whom we delegate the drawing of lines. Killing people is not forbidden, but killing certain people is; torture is not forbidden, but torturing certain people is, and sometimes how we torture them is; sex is not forbidden, but certain kinds of sexual activity with certain people is, and so on.

But attending to the rules can mean inattention elsewhere. When it comes to the forbidden, we are not supposed to let our minds wander. We are supposed to be utterly gripped, and in the grip of the law. The forbidden is by definition defined, is indeed always already defined. Whether one is conscious or unconscious of the definition, it is in principle knowable. Acculturation – adaptation – means living as if one knows what is forbidden. Psychoanalysis, the theory and therapy that organizes itself around forbidden desire, adds that we can be both conscious and unconscious of what is forbidden. When what is forbidden becomes blurred, or vague, or ambiguous – or even contested – something is being done to the forbidden. It is being re-described. The forbidden, by definition, should not be subject to re-description. And yet we know that this is what keeps happening to forbidden pleasures: they keep being reconsidered. We are more and less ambivalent about the forbidden than we want to be. "A Fundamentall Law in every Commonwealth,'' Hobbes writes in *Leviathan* (a book Freud quotes in *The Interpretation of Dreams*), "is that, which being taken away, the Common-wealth faileth, and is utterly dissolved; as a building whose foundation is destroyed . . . a Fundamentall Law is that, by which subjects are bound" (Hobbes and Pogson Smith, 1909, p. 334). It is clear to Hobbes that the only foundations that we have are our Fundamentall Laws; that we are the kind of creatures that, without these so-called Fundamentall Laws, will be in a war of all against all – in endless uncivil civil wars. And this presumably is the logic of the forbidden – of the Fundamentall Law. It is deemed to be that without which we cannot live, or cannot live the lives we most want (or have been persuaded to want); that by which we are bewitched by the analogy of having foundations; of there being something upon which everything depends. These two things – the Fundamentall Laws and the foundations – go together. *Leviathan* is a book about what we might be wanting, what we might be thinking and feeling. It is a book, that is, about what we might be doing if we were not paying full attention to these Fundamentall Laws.

In Monderman's traffic experiment, which is not about revising a fundamental law but is nevertheless suggestive, there are fewer accidents because people are more attentive to what they are doing, more alert. It is as if the rules make people less sentient – as if something is handed over to the rules and implicitly to the rule makers – making people behave automatically or as sleep walkers, or as people less inventively competent than they in fact are. An excess of signage led drivers to take their eyes off the road, and actually contributed to making junctions less safe. There is more flow than congestion: traffic moves more briskly but this cuts both ways. It is more "efficient," but it increases mobility. Once movement is no longer forbidden by a red light, the unforbidden pleasures of co-operation, and its attendant talents, reveal themselves. And it is perhaps worth remembering Deleuze and Guattari's use of a similar analogy in *Anti-Oedipus*: "The prime function incumbent upon the socius [the society]," they write, "has always been to codify the flows of desire, to inscribe them, to record them, to see to it that no flow exists that is not properly dammed up, channelled, regulated" (Deleuze and Guattari, 1972, p. 33). The forbidden is pictured here as a controlled flow. Whatever it is that flows threatens to get anywhere and everywhere.

If Monderman's experiment (and Scott's parable) is about "red-light removal schemes," it is also, by the same token, about the more or less impeded, regulated, formulated flow of something or other. The question becomes: what kind of flow does the red light think it is organising? What is the catastrophe the red light assumes it needs to avert? Something, after all, has to be done to desiring, to pleasure, to make it forbidden; it has to be described in a certain way (forbiddingly, intimidatingly). The forbidders have their reasons.

But what Monderman's experiment revealed, whether or not it is representative, was that there were fewer accidents, virtually no back-ups or road rage, more fluency and flow, less congestion. And, most interestingly for my purposes, more co-operation with other people and more attentiveness to them, the two things going together. Again, Monderman likened it to "skaters in a crowded ice-rink who manage successfully to tailor their movements to those of the other skaters." It is a picture, however idealized, of sociability as akin to an unwilled choreography. And the idea of tailoring here – "tailor[ing] their movements to those of the other skaters" – is genial. As with the skaters there is an attempt at – a shared project of – minimizing frustration and antagonism, and a realistic one (it actually happens at the skating rink, not just in someone's mind).

For people who like the language of early infant observation this is not a million miles from the kinds of attunement witnessed between mothers and their infants when things go well enough. It can be linked with the Boston Change Process Study Group's (2005, 2007) salutary point that what matters is not that things go wrong between the mother and baby – how could they not? But what matters is how they are repaired. One of the things forbidden to the drivers by the red light was a way of working things out with the other drivers. These drivers and skaters and tailors and anti-Oedipus's and mothers and babies are having to make it up as they go along – not, of course, from scratch but in the actuality of their immediate circumstance together. However rule-bound their behaviour – and however pastoral a view promoted by this example – each of these figures is having to acknowledge that whatever else they are doing, they are experimenting. And the forbidden is clearly where the experimenting is supposed to stop.

Part 2

> *The attribution of value to mere conforming behaviour, in abstraction from both motive and consequences, belongs not to morality but to taboo.*
>
> H. L. A. Hart, *Law, Liberty, and Morality* (1963)

When it comes to the forbidden we have to distinguish between the authoritarians and the experimentalists, between the essentialists and the pragmatists. The pragmatists – the experimentalists – say, "I, or someone else, have tried this – have done this forbidden thing – and it had, by our standards, catastrophic consequences. We mustn't let anyone we care about do it again." The authoritarians – the essentialists – say, "This is evil. It certainly mustn't be tried, and preferably shouldn't be thought about or discussed. It is what our worst punishments are designed to abolish." Bela Grunberger (1979) was an experimentalist when he wrote that the reason the father should prohibit his son sleeping with his mother was that, if the son did sleep with his mother, he would be unable to satisfy himself or her, and so would be humiliated. In this version of Oedipus the father is not a castrator, but the guardian of the child's future potency. God was being an essentialist in the Old Testament when he told the Jews, "You shall have no other gods before me" (Exodus, 20.1.17), that they shouldn't worship idols, "for I, the Lord your God am a jealous God, visiting the iniquity of the fathers on the children to the third and the fourth generation." Either way, the forbidden is the foreclosure of certain ways of thinking about the future. The forbidden refers to a future that mustn't happen. Once we know what is forbidden, it clears the way for the unforbidden: all those things that the authorities encourage us to enjoy, or fob us off with.

The rules free us to experiment, but an absolute rule – a rule deemed to be beyond conversation, beyond negotiation, as the forbidden is – pre-empts the possibility of improvisation. It is, as they say, defining, though we can never quite know what the forbidden is forbidding us, as Adam and Eve, our first parents, among others, discovered. Once we break the Fundamentall Law we are in uncharted territory. To forbid something is an omniscient act. And that fact has daunting moral implications. Those who lay down and enforce the Fundamentall Laws claim to know what they are and to know what the consequences are of breaking them. In this sense Fundamentall Laws are prophetic; their makers know the future.

And yet, we are all too aware as analysts of people's capacities to render the unforbidden forbidden, either to render it inaccessible and/or to make the unforbidden supposedly more exciting. Psychoanalysis has shown us the defensive potential in upping the rhetorical stakes: we can all too easily say to ourselves, "This is not dangerous, exciting, intriguing. This is *forbidden*!" When the Kleinian analyst Money-Kyrle (1971) wrote that the aim of analysis was to prove the irrelevance of the inhibition, he was alluding to this. In psychoanalysis we work out how it has been worked out by the patient that these are the pleasures he is able and willing to seek, but not those. For the moment, though, I just want to acknowledge how keen we can be to transform the unforbidden into the forbidden in the service of a self-limiting self-protection. I want to attend to how the idea of the forbidden is recruited to manage the unforbidden, as though the unforbidden has its anxieties too. Psychoanalytic treatment, we should remember, is an unforbidden pleasure, or a forbidden pleasure that we want to make sufficiently unforbidden to be useful and useable, pleasurable and interesting, in however unpredictable a way.

When the red lights were removed – and this is one of at least two familiar kinds of modern story – the assumed catastrophe did not occur. In fact, as luck or as something else would have it, it was even better than before. There were fewer accidents, the flow improved, there was less rage, more common sense. The other familiar modern story is that the red lights are removed and futures are created that are beyond our worst imaginings; this is what tragedies are there to tell us about. But after Monderman's experiment, Scott writes, "Small towns in the Netherlands put up one sign boasting that they were 'Free of Traffic Signs,' and a conference discussing the new philosophy proclaimed 'Unsafe is safe'" (Scott, 2012, p. 83).

We know something of what it is like to drop the idea that there is such a thing as forbidden knowledge. And we do and mostly don't really know what it would be like to ban the incest taboo (imagine a society in which children in families, backed up by their parents, were encouraged to murder their mothers and marry their fathers, and murder their fathers and marry their mothers). And we know now what it is for certain forbidden desires to be no longer forbidden. Indeed, some of our most terrible histories are about the forbidding of desires that clearly need not have been forbidden – supposedly forbidden desires. These are histories that, in retrospect, seem to some of us to be the fundamental histories of our times – both wildly unintelligible in their cruelty, and all too intelligible.

And the best bits of psychoanalysis have been able to tell us something useful about the anxieties that prompt the forbidding of desires, and about why, therefore, we should not always be overly confident as forbidders of desire. If psychoanalysis has nothing new to say about the police, it is going to be of limited value.

Nobody believes that we could, or would even want to, abolish forbidden desires, any more than anyone could imagine a culture without the category of the unacceptable – the forbidden being the unacceptable at its most intractable: "To unlock the innermost secret of morality and culture is to know simply: what to avoid," Philip Rieff (2008, p. 223) wrote in his book *Charisma*. And some of us may believe – and psychoanalysis clearly has a stake in this – that forbidden desires, like everything else, can be re-described in a way that makes them, as I say, less forbidden, or certainly less unthinkable. People come to psychoanalysis because of the monstrousness of their desire, or what they take to be the monstrousness of their desire, and the analyst re-describes where she can. But obviously, there can be no psychoanalysis – just as, presumably, there can be no culture – without the idea of forbidden desire. This is so, even if the history of the making and breaking of rules would suggest – and psychoanalysis has a good story about this – not that rules are made to be broken, but that rules are made to be tested, or can only be made by being tested. No rule is safe, but rules are there supposedly to make us feel safe.

Though in psychoanalysis we should remember, at least in its developmental stories, the forbidden is not apparently what we begin with, or where we begin. The parents, by the time they become parents, have been thoroughly initiated into the forbidden, but the infant has not. So what some psychoanalysts refer to as the pre-Oedipal may be, among many other things, a wish to imagine a time in the individual's life of intense pleasures and sufferings that is not lived under the aegis of the forbidden – a time of the intense feeling before good and evil. The child is born, though, into a world actually governed by the notion of the forbidden; it is the medium in which he grows. And so what is supposedly pre-Oedipal for the baby is, in a sense, not pre-Oedipal at all (Laplanche and Pontalis' (1973) "enigmatic signifiers" are one way of talking about this). In this story there is no life before the forbidden, only a life lived before its full realization. Growing up means growing up into what we call knowledge, or appropriate acknowledgment of the forbidden. The forbidden is what adults need to tell children about, explicitly and implicitly, consciously and unwittingly. And the forbidden is essentially a story about the consequences of certain kinds of desiring: a catastrophic story, a punitive story, a by definition intimidating story about what can happen if certain desires begin to flow. In other words, the forbidden and the tragic are made for each other. If tragedy shows us that forbidden desire is really forbidden, comedy shows us what happens when the unforbidden is forbidden.

I want to suggest in this paper – and I cannot think of a less silly way of putting it – that forbidden desire has been a big problem for psychoanalysis. Of course, I don't mean by this that we should be simply finding ways of abolishing the forbidden as a category, or of making forbidden desires less forbidden. Though, as I've said, the history of forbidding some desires has also been the proverbial nightmare from which we cannot awaken. It is, of course, always a question of what we take desires to be, what we can do with and about them, and which ones we are supposed to prefer and why; why we are supposed to prefer certain desires to others is a question of "who says?"; and what, in short, we have been told, one way and another, about what desiring is, and how we should do it (and this means what we have been told by, one way and another, say, parents, teachers, biologists, and novelists, or whomever else we find to be worth listening to, or have had to listen to). But there is a particular sense in which I think that forbidden desire has been a big problem for psychoanalysis – apart, that is, from all the other ways in which it is by definition *the* big problem for psychoanalysis, and not only for psychoanalysis. And it is linked to Monderman's experiment with the traffic lights as a kind of moral parable.

In his essay "Gay betrayals," Leo Bersani suggests that gay men, out of what he calls their "exemplary confusion," should be, or actually are, offering an "implicit and involuntary message to heterosexuals . . . that we aren't sure of how we want to be social, and that we therefore invite straights to redefine with us the notions of community and sociality" (Bersani, 2009, p. 38). The forbidden is that which sets absolute limits to redefining notions of community and sociality, and in ways that the unforbidden may not. Is it absurd to imagine a new kind of outlaw, an outlaw in search of unforbidden pleasures? Psychoanalysts, like Bersani's gay men and women, could be the people, or the profession, that take for granted that nobody is sure how she or he wants to be social. And the forbidden – the idea of the forbidden, the scenario of forbidden desire – has traditionally been the official way we set limits to how we can want to be social.

One might well have thought beforehand that Monderman – in a way akin to Bersani's description of gay men and woman as uncertain of how they want to be social – was taking a considerable risk with his "red-light removal scheme," despite what he ultimately discovered: forbidding things can stop people both from finding new ways, and recovering old ways, of collaborating. Forbidding things can pre-empt the enjoyment of unforbidden things. What forbidding things is meant to oppose is not always clear. Clearly the sociability created by the red lights is different from the sociability created without them. So what I want to consider in this paper is: what have been the consequences of the forbidden dominating the ways we think about pleasure and sexuality in psychoanalysis? If we take forbidden pleasure as the essence of pleasure – as the real pleasure – what happens to the unforbidden pleasures? Do they really exist – are they derivatives, substitutes, sublimations? And if they do exist, what kind of pleasures are they? Are they all poor relatives of the real thing? Are they merely for the timid, the inhibited, the cowardly, the dull? Perhaps psychoanalysis, in its original privileging of forbidden desire, has been complicit with what D. H. Lawrence called "the modern mind . . . falling . . . [into a] . . . form of degraded taboo-insanity" (1994, p. 627). That is, perhaps psychoanalysis has been subject to the insanity generated, in Lawrence's view, by the whole notion of taboo. It may thus be worth wondering again what unforbidden pleasures, of which there are so many, amount to in the story – in the experience – of a life?

Clearly, if we believe, for example, that real pleasure, profound pleasure, passionate pleasure is forbidden or derives from the forbidden, then courage is what we need and risk is what we will celebrate (and idealize). We will need to be as brave as possible in not betraying our desire. Indeed, to promote unforbidden pleasures is to imagine a world in which we don't have to take courage (or cowardice) very seriously. There certainly seems to be an old-fashioned story about heroism lurking somewhere in our commitment to the forbidden – a story in which the bold, the risk taking, the transgressive are by definition having a better time. Is psychoanalysis, then, a kind of military training – perhaps a training in a kind of terrorism – helping people become more the heroes and heroines of their own desire? If one of my greatest pleasures in life is my morning coffee am I, in some sense, a rather pathetic person – too starkly, as people used to say, *bourgeois*? If being as kind as possible gives me the life I want, am I some kind of weakling, merely part of what Nietzsche called a "slave religion"?

If I prefer friendship to sexual relationships or sexual encounters, am I just inhibited? Are the seekers of unforbidden pleasures – who are also of course the seekers of forbidden pleasures, indeed, who can't help but be that also – too bland (i.e., terrified) for real consideration, other than the consideration of analyzing them out of it?

In short, what, from a psychoanalytic point of view, is the unforbidden? Where do unforbidden pleasures stand in psychoanalytic stories about a good life? Are unforbidden pleasures sad substitutes for the forbidden ones? What has the monism of forbidden pleasure – the siren song, the abiding claim on the Freudian subject of the forbidden – stopped us from thinking about pleasure?

The political philosopher John Gray describes what he calls Isaiah Berlin's "agonistic liberalism" as a "liberalism of conflict among inherently rivalrous goods" (Gray, 2014, p. 44). This is a liberalism in which it is assumed that, because there is never only one good that we seek, there will always be conflict, and where there is no conflict there has been tyranny. By persuading us that forbidden and unforbidden pleasures are not inherently rivalrous goods – that we should be suspicious of our desire for the unforbidden pleasures – psychoanalysis may have oversimplified us. It may have given us an impoverished picture of our pleasure seeking and of ourselves as pleasure seekers. Psychoanalysis, it seems, has repressed the unforbidden, refused to elaborate it, wanted to not take it too seriously, or simply interpreted it as a refuge from, or a disguised watered-down version of, the real, horrifyingly exciting thing: forbidden desire.

It is possible that privileging forbidden pleasures grossly narrows the pleasures people can take in each other, overdetermines and confines their moral thinking about what they want to do to and with each other, and so has prevented psychoanalysis from helping people to develop new styles of relating – what Foucault called "new relational modes" (Bersani, 2000). It is possible that the forbidden has been overly forbidding – that there is nothing more conservative, in both senses, than a commitment to certain versions of the forbidden. What would our lives be like, and what would our practice as psychoanalysts be like, if we took forbidden pleasures and unforbidden pleasures as inherently rivalrous goods? That is, what if we didn't take it for granted that forbidden pleasure was the real pleasure, or the only real pleasure? What if we thought of people seeking a multiplicity of pleasures, without a pre-assumed hierarchy of pleasures? And none of this, it should be said, necessitates relegating the erotic. It is, after all, worth remembering, in the psychoanalytic way, that many of the pleasures of childhood are unforbidden.

We can, in other words, do a number of different things with the categories of the forbidden and the unforbidden, as we can with any of the familiar binaries that we have learned not to be too impressed by. Forbidding is censorship at its most hyperbolic. And it has forbidden our thinking about the unforbidden: "Sun destroys the interest of what's happening in the shade" (Larkin, 1964). We are familiar, now, with the more celebrated, more researched, more historicized story about what ideas about sanity have done to ideas about madness, or indeed, about the rational and the irrational as having been mutually defining, or about how heterosexuality has formed and deformed homosexuality, and vice versa.

It should be no less integral to psychoanalysis to track the effects of privileging, if not always preferring, the forbidden pleasures to the unforbidden ones. It can always, after all, be two-way traffic. The parts of ourselves that desire forbidden pleasures might have a lot to learn from the parts of ourselves that desire the unforbidden. The seekers of unforbidden pleasures may know something about pleasure that has never occurred to the transgressives: about the pleasures, for example, of not being single-minded; or about what the pleasures that don't require courage might be able to tell us about the pleasures that do; about what the pleasures of fellow feeling, say, or of friendship, might have to do with erotic relations, and their inevitable violence; or about the difference between intimidation and pleasure; or the difference between mastery and what the alternatives to mastery might be. There is the intelligence of knowing what one can bear and enjoy, and the intelligence of knowing what one thinks one should be able to bear and enjoy.

It is my impression, and it is only that, that even though analysts are not supposed to encourage their patients to talk about anything specifically, they encourage their patients to talk rather more about their forbidden pleasures than their unforbidden ones. Or that unforbidden pleasures are taken to be a clue about the other kind: that analysts tend to listen out for trauma, and for forbidden desire – and, indeed, for the trauma of forbidden desire. When everybody knows the currency is the forbidden, what else are we going to be able to hear and to say? If, as Isaiah Berlin wrote, "the necessity of choosing between absolute claims is an inescapable characteristic of the human condition" (Berlin, 1969, p. 169), then it is worth wondering what would happen – what psychoanalysis would sound like – if it took the pursuit of unforbidden pleasures as one of a person's absolute claims, or as one of the absolute claims everyone has to deal with.

There is, we can say, that which we are unable or unwilling to talk about because it is forbidden (censored, to use Freud's word); and there is that which resists or is recalcitrant to articulation – what Seamus Heaney called "pre-reflective lived experience," as we might call the presymbolic or protosymbolic experience of the younger child. But between these two dramatic and poignant forms of self-protection and inevitable opacity there is something both more accessible and less patent: that which we wouldn't bother to elaborate. It might seem too trivial, too bland, too everyday and ordinary to make anything of.

Neither forbidden, nor apparently obscure, what of all those unforbidden pleasures that are more or less taken for granted? By the same token enjoyed as unconsidered trifles, relatively conflict-free, we need not assume them to be merely sublimated forms of forbidden pleasures. There are the pleasures we mostly don't have, and can't easily talk about; and there are the unforbidden pleasures which, almost by definition, we either don't bother to talk much about, or talk about all too fluently; without apparent shame, or guilt or much embarrassment. Indeed, we all too easily think of the unforbidden pleasures as the sociable ones. It has been one of the mixed blessings of British psychoanalysis – part of its interest, and for some people part of its resistance to Freud – to have spoken up for these unforbidden pleasures. To have wanted to make the unforbidden pleasures as interesting, as intriguing, as formative as the forbidden pleasures. And in Marion Milner's (1934) work, even to make the erotic of a piece with the unforbidden.

Part 3

> NATIONAL: 1. Publick; general; not private; not particular . . .
>
> 2. Bigoted to one's own country.
>
> Samuel Johnson, *A Dictionary of the English Language* (1755)

"One of the central puzzles of English history," the American historian Ethan Shagan writes, is "how England came to represent reason, civility and moderation to a world it slowly conquered" (2011, p. 10). As we know, Freud, who was himself, interestingly, an anglophile, didn't want psychoanalysis to be thought of as a Jewish science. And, of course, when it came to England in the early years of the twentieth century – that is, before Melanie Klein, the Freuds, and other European émigrés arrived – it was not a predominantly Jewish profession. And none of the prominent members of what later emerged after the Second World War as the Middle or Independent Group – most notably, Winnicott, Rycroft, Milner, Khan, Laing, Klauber, Lomas – were Jews. England was, in other words, both congenial and very foreign to Freud's psychoanalysis, as Freud's psychoanalysis was to the English.

That is to say, psychoanalysis arrived in an England that had come to represent "reason, civility and moderation" (Shagan, 2011) to a world that it had quite recently, slowly conquered. It was the England of Darwin and Darwinism. Freud was committed to Darwinian biology, but Darwin himself in his English way was a paragon of reason, civility, and moderation while his ideas slowly conquered the world. And England was also a country, as many people have pointed out, with a literary tradition preoccupied by childhood. In retrospect it is not surprising that psychoanalysis would find a home there; and not surprising that psychoanalysis would be changed in the process, most notably through the pioneering of child analysis by Klein, Anna Freud, Winnicott, and Bowlby.

By the end of the Second World War, the British analysts (as they were now referred to) had learned a lot about early development from children evacuated during the war, and from their mothers who had had to go out and do war work while their husbands were away. But the Middle or Independent Group – unlike the warring Kleinians and Freudians in the British Society – would come to represent, for better and for worse, something akin to reason, civility, and moderation to the psychoanalytic world. If in psychoanalysis only the exaggerations are true, in this version of British psychoanalysis, exaggeration – the metaphysical, the non-empirical, the enthusiastic – was suspect (Winnicott was a pediatrician, Bowlby was interested in ethology). As is well known, none of them took up Freud's idea of the death instinct, and all of them took the observed so-called mother–infant dyad as seriously as, and sometimes more seriously than, they took sexuality. In England, at least, they were not going to sacrifice reason, civility, and moderation to sexuality.

And all of these Middle Group analysts, in what were called their developmental object-relations theories, were implicitly critical of the conquering of the world that was colonization, and more recently fascism;

implicitly because none of them were overtly political. But their developmental theories were a critique of imperialism; the psychoanalytic child they described was a born imperialist who needed to become a democrat. They wanted relationship, not exploitative forms of gratification; they wanted the co-operative, not the predatory in human relations. So they were all, as it were, radically anti-imperialist in their accounts of mothering and adult sexuality, and, indeed, in their accounts of the role of the analyst. The child's adapting to what cannot be adapted to without distortion and deformation was their theme (slightly less guarded was Masud Khan's implicit critique of colonialism in his theory of perversions).

It would be too crude, but partly true I think, to say that it was the potential imperialism of sexuality – and the wish to see satisfaction as collaborative and mutual – that informed their theory and practice; and that could make mothers and babies, paradoxically, their preferred objects of psychoanalytic desire. This made their writing seem at once Freudian and profoundly anti-Freudian, and often somewhat anti-Kleinian, as the Kleinians were the new imperialists, colonizing the minds of their patients. But it is possible to see now that what they were doing was trying to make links to, or even to make compatible, Freud's theories about sexuality and the forbidden – the Oedipal and pre-Oedipal predicament of the Freudian child – with the unforbidden pleasures of infancy and childhood; to join the language of British romanticism to the language of Freudian psychoanalysis – a language that, as Freud acknowledged, was originally based on Darwinian biology.

When you put together the profoundly innocent child of a Protestant British romanticism with the infantile sexuality of the Freudian child you get the Middle or Independent Group in British psychoanalysis. The child of Wordsworth and Coleridge and Blake is notably and naturally kind, sympathetic, and full of fellow feeling. He has a virtually instinctive capacity and need to forget himself, to absorb himself in things (and people) other than himself. Given the chance, he loses himself in nature, in books, in games. He or she is by nature both solitary and sociable and so hates – as the novels of Dickens, Eliot, and D. H. Lawrence make poignantly clear – tyranny, submission, and injustice. This child is not without vigorous, even daemonic, antisocial energies – the energy that was for Blake "eternal delight," and the energy that Wordsworth knew to be violently destructive. But what is pointedly recognized about this romantic child is, as I say, his natural kindness, and his desire to forget himself, to lose himself, to become absorbed. He has an openness to the world that growing up endangers, and that endangers him in the contemporary economic and political reality of the late eighteenth and early nineteenth century. It is the adults who do the terrible, forbidden things. In growing up, natural innocence is replaced by unoriginal sin.

But it is the intensity of these unforbidden pleasures of childhood that the romantics and the novelists promote; and that are taken up, wittingly and unwittingly, in the Freudian work of Winnicott, but more particularly in the work of Marion Milner (1934). What Winnicott started off with in his idea of play – that crucially for him was an essential capacity undisrupted by instinctual desire – Marion Milner elaborated in terms of the child's capacity for absorption, and all that that entailed. In Milner's work – and we should remember that she was supervised by Melanie Klein and analyzed by Winnicott – the forbidden and unforbidden pleasures of childhood are seen to be inter-animating, inextricable, and never mutually exclusive. Indeed, for Milner pathology involved the splitting of the forbidden and the unforbidden. For Milner, as a psychoanalyst, there is something before transgression, before the forbidden; something indeed unforbidden that partly makes the forbidden possible; or is the precondition for the experience of forbidden desire.

Part 4

Concluding her 1956 paper "Psychoanalysis and art," Milner puts her cards on the table. "The central idea of my paper," she writes,

> is that the unconscious mind by the very fact of its not clinging to the distinction between self and other, seer and seen, can do things that the conscious logical mind cannot do. By being more sensitive to the samenesses rather than the differences between things, by being passionately concerned with finding "the familiar in the unfamiliar" (which, by the way, Wordsworth says is the whole of the poets business) it . . . brings back blood to the spirit, passion to intuition. It provides the source for all renewal and rebirth, when old symbols have gone stale. It is, in fact, what Blake calls each man's poetic genius.
>
> (Milner, 1956, p. 14–15)

We might balk now at the anachronism of some of the language, or even of the central idea, even though, in Freud's mythology, it is the work of

Eros that Milner is describing. But I want to use Milner's conclusion here as an emblem of what I am talking about. From this account we could say: the forbidden is the apotheosis, the final formulation of the supposedly not-me, of the wished-for not-me. It draws an uncrossable line; it separates me from what I want, but should not want. But the unconscious mind, in Milner's almost old-fashioned picture, is "more sensitive to the samenesses than to the differences"; doesn't "cling to the distinction between self and other"; has a passion for finding in Wordsworth's words – and it is not incidental that Blake and Wordsworth are invoked here – "the familiar in the unfamiliar"; and that could mean, in this context, finding the unforbidden in the forbidden. Milner's version of the unconscious mind is not, it should be noted, primarily seeking forbidden (incestuous) pleasure. It is seeking unforbidden reunions – the pleasures of sameness, not the pleasures of transgression. This is Milner's theme. These are the formative experiences for her; not the horrifying, exciting urgencies of incestuous desire, but what she calls, quoting Berenson, "the aesthetic moment." It is what she calls the "central idea" that emerges in her great paper of 1955, "The role of illusion in symbol formation":

> The basic identifications which make it possible to find new objects, to find the familiar in the unfamiliar, require an ability to tolerate a temporary loss of sense of self, a temporary giving up of the discriminating ego which stands apart and tries to see things objectively and rationally without emotional colouring. It perhaps requires a state of mind which has been described by Berenson as "the aesthetic moment." "In visual art," [Berenson writes] the aesthetic moment is that fleeting instant, so brief as to be almost timeless, when the spectator is at one with the work of art he is looking at. . . ."
>
> (Milner, 1987, p. 97)

Milner goes on to suggest, in the Winnicottian way, that the patient in analysis, like the child in the family, needs what she calls "the factor of a capacity in the environment":

> It is the capacity of the environment to foster this growth, by providing conditions in which a recurrent partial return to the feeling of being one is possible; and I suggest that the environment does this by the recurrent providing of a framed space and time and a pliable medium,

> so that, on occasions, it will not be necessary for self-preservation's sake to distinguish clearly between inner and outer, self and not self.
>
> (Milner, 1955, p. 101)

This "feeling of being one," this "giving up of the discriminating ego" need not be forbidden, but it could be. It could be described as transgressive, but it need not be; just as such states could be described as omnipotent or as denial of envy or dependence, or aggression, or indeed, of separateness.

Clearly schools of analysis can be distinguished by how much these states are encouraged or tolerated, and in what ways these states are understood. But in these states – which Milner is careful to describe as fleeting, momentary, "partial" returns to the feeling of being one – a rule is not being broken, an experience is being risked: the experience of what happens when vigilant self-holding is relinquished so that one becomes of a piece with the world. One makes the world one's own by forgetting oneself. Sameness is not merely recuperative for Milner, it is the way we recover the future; it makes it possible to, in her words, "find new objects." Finding new objects, in other words, in this story, does not involve a so-called resolution of the Oedipus complex. It involves broaching the unforbidden pleasures, not the forbidden ones. The forbidden keeps us different from ourselves; the unforbidden keeps us the same as ourselves. We may need at least both.

One of the unforbidden pleasures of childhood for Blake and Wordsworth was the child's capacity to be absorbed. It is the loss of that capacity that Milner believes people come to analysis for. Of course she knew about people's real trouble with forbidden desire, but this was her more singular contribution to psychoanalysis. In 1934, in *A Life of One's Own* she wrote of her need for "a method for discovering one's true likes and dislikes. For finding and setting up a standard of values that is truly one's own and not a borrowed mass-produced ideal" (p. 14). What Hobbes called Fundamentall Laws – that which is absolutely forbidden – is perhaps the exemplary or ultimate borrowed mass-produced ideal ("the innermost secret of morality and culture is to know simply: what to avoid"). The forbidden informs us of what our true likes and dislikes must be. Could it follow from this that the unforbidden does not? Or that, as Milner intimates, we have done it all the wrong way round? We have used the forbidden pleasures to tell us what the unforbidden pleasures are, rather than allowing the unforbidden pleasures to be a way of discovering one's true likes and dislikes. Milner's quest, one could say, is for what Seamus Heaney called, "a less binary and altogether less binding vocabulary" (1995).

This paper is wondering whether the unforbidden pleasures have something more to tell us, or at least something else to tell us about pleasure than do the forbidden ones. Were this to be true, a lot of things that we have taken very seriously would seem less serious. The tyranny of the forbidden is not that it forbids, but that it tells us what we want – to do the forbidden thing. The unforbidden gives no orders.

Note

1 A version of this chapter has been published in Phillips, A. (2015). *Unforbidden Pleasures.* New York: Farrar, Straus and Giroux.

References

Berlin, I. (1969). *Four Essays on Liberty.* London: Oxford University Press, p. 169.

Bersani, L. (2000). *Sex and Sexuality.* Chicago, IL: University of Chicago Press.

Bersani, L. (2009). Gay betrayals (Chapter 3). In *Is the Rectum a Grave*? Chicago, IL: University of Chicago Press.

Blake, W. (1988). *The Complete Poetry and Prose of William Blake.* New York: Doubleday.

Boston Change Process Study Group. (2005). The "something more" than interpretation revisited: sloppiness and co-creativity in the psychoanalytic encounter. *Journal of the American Psychoanalytic Association, 53,* 693–729.

Boston Change Process Study Group. (2007). The foundational level of psychodynamic meaning: implicit process in relation to conflict, defense, and the dynamic unconscious. *International Journal of Psychoanalysis, 88,* 843–860.

Deleuze, G. and Guattari, F. (1972). *Anti-Oedipus: Capitalism and Schizophrenia.* New York: Viking Press, p. 33.

Freud, S. (1976). *The Interpretation of Dreams,* 3rd ed. Trans. James Strachey. *The Standard Edition of the Complete Psychological Works of Sigmund Freud,* vol. 4. London: Hogarth Press, 2001.

Gray, J. (2014). *Isaiah Berlin.* Princeton, NJ: Princeton University Press, p. 44.

Grunberger, B. (1979). *Narcissism: Psychoanalytic Essays.* New York: International Universities Press.

Hart, H. L. A. (1963). *Law, Liberty, and Moraligy.* Stanford, CA: Stanford University Press.

Heaney, S. (1995). *Nobel Lecture: Crediting Poetry.* Available online at: http://www.nobel prize.org/nobel_prizes/literature/laureates/1995/heaney-lecture.html (accessed June 23, 2016).

Hobbes, T. and Pogson Smith, W. G. (1909). *Hobbes's Leviathan: reprinted from the edition of 1651.* London: Clarendon Press, p. 334.

Johnson, S. (1755). *A Dictionary of the English Language.* London: Consortium.

Laplanche, J. and Pontalis, J.-B. (1973). *The Language of Psycho-Analysis*. New York: W. W. Norton.

Larkin, P. (1964). The Whitsun weddings. From *Collected Poems*. In A. Burnett (ed.) *The Complete Poems*. New York: Farrar, Straus and Giroux.

Lawrence, D. H. (1994). *The Complete Poems of D.H. Lawrence.* Ware, Hertfordshire: Wordsworth Editions.

Milner, M. (1934, 2011). *A Life of One's Own.* London: Routledge.

Milner, M. (1955). The role of illusion in symbol formation. Reprinted from Klein, M., Heimann, P., and Money-Kyrle, R. *New Directions in Psychoanalysis.* London: Tavistock, pp. 82–108.

Milner, M. (1956). Psychoanalysis and art. In S. Gosso (ed.) *Psychoanalysis and Art: Kleinian Perspectives.* London: Karnac (2004).

Milner, M. (1987). *The Suppressed Madness of Sane Men: Forty-Four Years of Exploring Psychoanalysis.* London: Tavistock.

Money-Kyrle, R. (1971). The aim of psychoanalysis. *International Journal of Psycho-analysis, 52*(1), 103–106.

Rieff, P. (2008). *Charisma.* New York: Random House (First Vintage Books Edition).

Scott, J. C. (2012). *Two Cheers for Anarchism: Six Easy Pieces on Autonomy, Dignity, and Meaningful Work and Play*. Princeton, NJ: Princeton University Press, pp. 81, 83.

Shagan, E. (2011). *The Rule of Moderation: Violence, Religion and the Politics of Restraint in Early Modern England.* London: Cambridge University Press.

Sterne, L (1999). *Tristram Shandy*. Ware, Hertfordshire: Wordsworth Editions.

Chapter 2

Far from the tree[1]

Andrew Solomon

This is from *Time Magazine* in 1966, when I was three years old:

> Even in purely nonreligious terms, homosexuality represents a misuse of sexual faculty . . . a pathetic second-rate substitute for reality . . . deserving no encouragement, no glamorization, no rationalization, no fake status as minority martyrdom, no sophistry about simple differences in taste – and, no pretense that it is anything but a pernicious sickness.

In June 2015, the President of the United States came out in favor of gay marriage. I set out in my most recent book, *Far From the Tree: Parents, Children, and the Search for Identity* (Solomon, 2012), to understand how we got from there to here – how an illness became an identity.

When I was seven, my mother, my brother, and I went to Indian Walk Shoes, and as we were leaving, the salesman asked what color balloons we'd like. My brother wanted a red balloon. I wanted a pink one. My mother countered that I didn't want a pink balloon, and reminded me that my favorite color was blue. I said I really wanted the pink, but under her glare, I took the blue one. The fact that my favorite color now is blue but I am still gay is evidence of both my mother's influence and its limits. She once said, "When you were little, you didn't like to do what other kids liked to do, and I encouraged you to be yourself." She added, only half-ironically, "I sometimes think I let things go too far." I have sometimes thought she didn't let them go far enough. But her encouragement of my individuality, although doubtless ambivalent, has shaped my life.

When I was little, my mother used to say, "The love you have for your children is like no other feeling in the world, and until you have children, you don't know what it's like." I took those words as the greatest compliment in the world. But when I was an adolescent, I thought that as a gay person, I probably couldn't have a family, and so her words made me anxious. After I came out of the closet, those words made me furious. I said, "I'm gay. I'm not going to have children. And I want you to stop saying that."

In 1993, I was asked by my editors at the *New York Times Magazine* to write a piece about deaf culture. I had thought of deafness entirely as an illness, but now I went out into the Deaf world. I went to Deaf clubs, I saw performances of Deaf theater and poetry. I even went to the Miss Deaf America Contest in Nashville, Tennessee, where people complained about that slurry Southern signing. As I plunged deeper and deeper into the Deaf world, I became convinced that Deafness was a culture organized around the shared use of sign language. It wasn't my culture, and I didn't particularly want to join it. But I appreciated that, for the people who were members of it, it felt as valuable as Latino culture or gay culture or Jewish culture do to their constituents. Most Deaf children are born to hearing parents, who often try to cure them; Deaf people often discover community only in adolescence. The pattern seemed to echo the experience of gay people, who are mostly born to straight parents and often find gay identity only in adolescence or thereafter.

Then a friend of a friend of mine had a daughter who was a dwarf. She suddenly found herself confronting questions that now began to seem familiar. Should she tell her daughter that she was just like everyone else, but shorter? Or should she try to construct some kind of dwarf identity and get involved in the Little People of America?

Here it was again. A family that perceived itself to be normal, with a child who seemed to be extraordinary. So I hatched the idea that there are really two kinds of identity. There are *vertical identities* that are passed down generationally from parent to child. Those are characteristics such as ethnicity, nationality, language, often religion. While some of them can be difficult, there is no attempt to cure them. It can be argued that it is harder in the United States, the Obama presidency notwithstanding, to be a person of color. And yet, we have nobody who is trying to ensure that the next generation of children born to African Americans and Asians come out with creamy skin and yellow hair.

Then there are *horizontal identities* that are learned from a peer group. These are identities that are alien within the family of origin. Parents have almost always tried to cure those horizontal identities. People who have these conditions are frequently very angry because they feel as though their parents don't love them, when what actually has happened is that their parents don't accept them. Love is ideally present throughout the relationship between a parent and a child. But acceptance is something that takes time. It always takes time. And in order for a condition to emerge as an identity, three levels of acceptance need to be in place: self-acceptance, family acceptance, and social acceptance. Each of these enables and depends on the others.

When Clinton Brown was born, he was diagnosed with diastrophic dwarfism, a very disabling condition. His parents were told that he would never walk or talk or think. The doctors suggested that they leave him at the hospital so that he could die there quietly. But his mother, Cheryl, said she was going to take her son home. And even though she didn't have tremendous educational or financial advantages, she found the best doctor in the country for dealing with diastrophic dwarfism. In the course of Clinton's childhood, he had 30 major surgical procedures, as a result of which he now can walk. While he was in the hospital, he had tutors to help him with his schoolwork, and because there was nothing else to do, he worked very hard. He ended up achieving at a level that had never before been contemplated by any member of his family. He went to college, where he lived on campus and drove a specially fitted car that accommodated his unusual body. Cheryl said,

> I was terrified about his drinking and driving. I went past a bar and I saw his car parked there – it's very easy to recognize with all those fittings. I didn't think I could march in there like I wanted, but I left him three messages and sat home by the phone waiting for him to call. Then I thought, okay, if you'd told me when he was born, that my worry would be that he'd go out driving after drinking with his college buddies, I'd have been overjoyed.

I asked her, "What do you think you did that helped him to emerge as this charming, accomplished, wonderful person?" And she said: "What did I do? I loved him, that's all. Clinton just always had that light in him. And we were lucky enough to be the first to see it there."

In 1968, the *Atlantic Monthly*, a voice of liberal America, printed an article by the ethicist Joseph Fletcher that argued there was

> no reason to feel guilty about putting a Down syndrome baby away, whether it's "put away" in the sense of hidden in a sanatorium or in

> a more responsible lethal sense. It is sad, yes. Dreadful. But it carries no guilt. True guilt arises only from an offense against a person, and a Down's is not a person.
>
> (Bard and Fletcher, 1968)

A lot of ink has been given to our progress on gay rights; the fact that national attitudes have shifted is in the headlines every day. But we forget how we used to see people who had other differences, how inhuman we could imagine a human being to be.

One of the families I interviewed, Tom and Karen Robards, were taken aback when, as young and successful New Yorkers, their first child, David, was diagnosed with Down syndrome. The educational opportunities for him were not what they should be, and so with a few other parents, they created a small facility with two classrooms to educate kids with Down syndrome. Over the years, that initiative grew into the Cooke Center, where thousands upon thousands of children with intellectual disabilities have now been taught. In the time since that *Atlantic Monthly* story ran, the life expectancy for people with Down syndrome has tripled. People with Down syndrome are actors or writers; some are able to live fully independently in adulthood.

The Robardses had a lot to do with that shift. And I said, "Do you regret it? Do you wish your child didn't have Down syndrome? Do you wish you'd never heard of it?" And Tom said,

> If I could have David [be] who he is but not have Down syndrome? I would do it in a minute. I would do because I think for David, it's hard being in the world with Down syndrome, and I'd like to give him a happier, easier life. But the diversity of human beings makes the world a better place, and if everyone with Down syndrome were cured, it would be a real loss. The personal wish and the social wish are in opposition. The question is whether we collectively learn more than we hurt.

Karen shook her head.

> I'm with Tom. If I could cure David, I would, for David. But I think that we've grown so much as a result of having to deal with this. We've had so much purpose. I'd never have believed 23 years ago when he

> was born that I could come to such a point, but I have. For David, I'd cure it in an instant; but for us, I wouldn't exchange these experiences for anything. They've made us who we are, and who we are is so much better than who we would have been otherwise.

We live at a point when social acceptance for these and many other conditions is on the up and up. And yet we also live at the moment when our ability to eliminate those conditions has reached unimagined heights. Most deaf infants born in the United States will receive cochlear implants, which are surgically placed in the brain and connected to a receiver, allowing them to acquire a facsimile of hearing. A compound that has been tested in mice, BMN-111, blocks the action of the achondroplasia gene. Achondroplasia is the most common form of dwarfism, and mice with the achondroplasia gene who have been given BMN-111 grow to full size. Testing in humans has already begun. Blood tests now in development would pick up Down syndrome earlier in pregnancies than ever before, making it easier to terminate those pregnancies.

I believe in both social and medical progress. But I think it's a tragedy when one of them doesn't see the other. When social and medical progress clash as they have in these conditions, I sometimes think it's like those moments in grand opera when the hero realizes he loves the heroine at the exact moment that she lies expiring on the divan.

The most frequent question of parenthood is what to validate in our children, and what to ameliorate. Jim Sinclair, a prominent autism activist, said,

> When parents say, "I wish my child did not have autism," what they're really saying is, "I wish the autistic child I have did not exist, and I had a different (non-autistic) child instead." Read that again. This is what we hear when you mourn over our existence. This is what we hear when you pray for a cure. This is what we know, when you tell us of your fondest hopes and dreams for us: that your greatest wish is that one day we will cease to be, and strangers you can love will move in behind our faces.

It's a very extreme point of view, but it points to the reality that people engage with the life they have. And they don't want to be cured or changed or eliminated. They want to be whoever it is that they are.

One of the families I interviewed for this project was the family of Dylan Klebold, who was one of the perpetrators of the Columbine massacre. The first weekend I spent with them, I recorded more than 20 hours of conversation. On Sunday night, when we were all exhausted, sitting in the kitchen, I said, "If Dylan were here now, do you have a sense of what you'd want to ask him?" Tom said, "I'd ask him what the hell he was thinking and what the hell he thought he was doing!" Sue looked down at the floor for a minute before saying quietly, "I would ask him to forgive me, for being his mother and never knowing what was going on inside his head." When I had dinner with her a couple of years later, she said,

> When it first happened, I used to wish that I had never had children, that I had never married. If Tom and I hadn't crossed paths at Ohio State, Dylan wouldn't have existed and this terrible thing wouldn't have happened. But over time, I've come to feel that, for myself, I am glad I had kids and glad I had the kids I did, because the love for them – even at the price of this pain – has been the single greatest joy of my life. When I say that, I am speaking of my own pain, and not of the pain of other people. But I accept my own pain; life is full of suffering, and this is mine. I know it would have been better for the world if Dylan had never been born. But I believe it would not have been better for me.

I was struck by how very attached all these parents were to children who manifested shocking challenges. I wondered how they had all found so much meaning in parenting under apparently antithetical circumstances. And then I thought that all of us who have children cherish the children we have, with their inherent flaws. If some glorious angel suddenly descended through my living-room ceiling and offered to take away the children I have and give me other, better children – more polite, nicer, smarter – I would cling to the children I have and pray away that atrocious spectacle. As one mother said when she interred the ashes of her severely disabled child, "Let me bury here the rage I feel to have been twice robbed: once of the child I wanted, and once of the son I loved."

In the same way that we test flame-retardant pajamas in an inferno to ensure they won't catch fire when our child reaches across the stove, so these stories of families negotiating extreme differences reflect on the universal experience of parenting. I have yet to meet any parent who hasn't occasionally looked at his or her child and wondered, "Where did you come from?"

Each of the ten kinds of difference I researched is siloed – isolated from one another. There are only so many families dealing with schizophrenia, only so many families of children who are transgender, only so many families of prodigies. But if one recognizes that all these families are negotiating *difference* and posits that all such experiences are parallel, then it turns out that this a nearly universal phenomenon. Difference is ubiquitous; we have no thing more in common than our variance from the norm. Ironically, it turns out that our differences unite us.

I decided to have children while I was working on this project. Many people said, "But how could you decide to become a father in the midst of writing a book about everything that can go wrong?" And I said, "It's not a book about everything that can go wrong. It's a book about how much love there can be even when everything appears to be going wrong."

My husband is the biological father of two children with some lesbian friends in Minneapolis. I had a close friend from college who'd gone through a divorce and wanted to have children; she and I have a daughter, and mother and daughter live in Texas. And my husband and I have a son who lives with us all the time, of whom I am the biological father, and for whom our surrogate was Laura, the lesbian mother of John's two biological children. The shorthand is that we are five parents of four children in three states.

There are people who think that the existence of my family somehow undermines or weakens or damages their family. But I don't accept subtractive models of love – only additive ones. I believe that in the same way that we need species diversity to ensure a healthy planet, so we need this diversity of affection and family to strengthen the ecosphere of kindness.

The day after our son was born, the pediatrician came into the hospital room and said that he wasn't extending his legs appropriately. She said that might mean that he had brain damage. Insofar as he was extending them, he was doing so asymmetrically, which she thought could reflect a tumor. He had a very large head, which might indicate hydrocephalus. As she told me all of these things, I felt the very center of my being pouring out on to the floor. Though I had been working for years on a book about how much meaning people had found in the experience of parenting disabled children, I didn't want to join their number. Like all parents since the dawn of time, I wanted to protect my child from illness. And I wanted also to protect myself. Yet I knew from the work I had done that if our son had any of the things for which we were about to start testing, those conditions would ultimately be his identity, and if they were his identity, they would become my identity.

We took him to get a CAT scan; we gave over our day-old child for an arterial blood draw. At the end of five hours, the pediatrician said that his brain was completely clear and that he was by then extending his legs correctly. When I asked her what had been going on in the morning, she said she thought he had probably had a cramp.

I knew that day that my mother was right. The love you have for your children is unlike any other feeling in the world, and until you have children, you don't know what it feels like. Children had ensnared me the moment I connected fatherhood with loss, but I am not sure I would have noticed that if I hadn't been immersed in this research. Encountering so much strange love, I fell into its bewitching patterns, and saw how splendor can illuminate even the most abject vulnerabilities. I had witnessed and learned the terrifying joy of unbearable responsibility, recognized how it conquers everything else. Sometimes, I had thought the heroic parents in this book were fools, enslaving themselves to a life's journey with their alien children, trying to breed identity out of misery. I was startled to learn that my research had built me a plank, and that I was ready to join them on their ship.

Note

1 This chapter first appeared as an article in the 2014 edition of *The Parents League Review*. ©2014. The Parents League of New York (212) 737–7385 www.parentsleague.org.

References

Bard, B. & Fletcher, J. (1968). The right to die. *The Atlantic Monthly*, 3, 59–64. Available online at: http://www.riverbendds.org/index.htm?page=fletcher.html.

Solomon, A. (2012). *Far From the Tree: Parents, Children, and the Search for Identity*. New York: Simon and Schuster.

Time (1966). The homosexual in America. January 21. Available online at: http://content.time.com/time/magazine/article/0,9171,835069,00.html.

Part II

The traumatic field

Psychoanalytic growth and the growth of psychoanalysis

Chapter 3

Reflections on the concept of "a traumatic field"

Philip M. Bromberg

As I started to write this paper, I reread the blurb that introduced our panel and was struck in a new way by the question with which it ends: "Is psychoanalysis, in theory and practice, a traumatic *field*?" As I read it this time, the first thing I felt was "Wow! It sounds like the beginning of a ghost story!" I could even imagine the sentence being, "Is the psychoanalytic field really a haunted house?" A moment later I realized I had already written that sentence, somewhat playfully, as the title of an article I called "One need not be a house to be haunted" (Bromberg, 2003) – for which I owe Emily Dickinson a debt of gratitude. Playfulness, however, is not a state of mind for which Dickinson is typically known. In her poetry and, it is said, in her own internal world, *trauma* is what takes center stage. For Emily Dickinson, trauma was not a concept but an ongoing state of *affective hauntedness*, and she chillingly communicates it as such in the following excerpt from her Poem 670 (1863/1960, p. 333):

> One need not be a Chamber – to be Haunted –
> One need not be a House –
>
> Far safer, through an Abbey gallop,
> Than unarmed, one's self encounter –
> In lonesome Place –
>
> Ourself behind ourself, concealed –
> Should startle most –
> Assassin hid in our Apartment
> Be Horror's least.

Dickinson is not presenting the experience of trauma itself. Trauma has no mental representation as an experiential memory (see Laub & Auerhahn, 1993). What she is describing is the *legacy* of trauma – hauntedness – the price paid for mental survival. It is this affective legacy that accompanies survival, and it is this legacy – underwritten by a dissociative mental structure that vigilantly serves as a smoke detector – that a patient brings to the psychoanalytic relationship. Hauntedness is part – sometimes a central part – of who the person *is*, not simply a symptom from which she needs relief. The aloneness of the "lonesome place," as Dickinson calls it, is what the healing aspect of the analytic relationship most addresses – the aloneness of the patient's self-cure that has created a dissociated shadow of affective hauntedness to be dealt with alone. This shadow is perpetuated interminably by certainty that around every corner, waiting to be encountered, is a "not-me" that is ready to annihilate "me" if one is unarmed – a dreaded assault by either one's own *"not-me" otherness* or by the terrifying otherness that will spring from the *un*-sprung depths of a person the patient has innocently trusted.

For now, I am going to be focusing on the *clinical* meaning of the word "field," but as I continue, the implications of *field* in its more inclusive meaning will, I hope, become equally clear. I will draw on Dickinson's phrase "lonesome place" as an opportunity to enter this topic by sharing two things that I believe are highly relevant to the question of whether psychoanalysis is inherently a *traumatic* field.

The first is that *developmental trauma* is inescapable. It contributes to shaping adult personality in *everyone*, and it is independent of whether someone qualifies for inclusion in the disorganized/disoriented category of attachment in the Adult Attachment Inventory (Main & Solomon, 1986, 1990; Main & Hesse, 1990). It shapes adult personality to varying degrees in *every* category of attachment, including "secure."

Second, the psychoanalytic relationship is never that of a non-traumatized self (a therapist), treating a traumatized other (a patient). Every therapist, as well as every patient, enacts his or her own unprocessed developmental trauma.

That said, I want to now share something that I believe to be even more foundational: that *the analytic relationship is a personal relationship with negotiable professional aspects – not a professional relationship with negotiable personal aspects.*

I am hoping that, in talking about Dickinson's phrase "lonesome place," I will start to clarify why my view that the analytic relationship is *intrinsically* a personal relationship is so foundational. Most fundamentally, things not otherwise possible become possible in a relationship that is experienced as intrinsically personal rather than one which ambivalently "smuggles in" personal moments. A patient is able to increasingly experience her internal world as less a "lonesome place" when the analyst is truly open to feeling the lonesomeness as a *shared state* (see Schore, 2003; Bromberg, 2011). The lonesomeness cannot be shared by verbal communication alone. By recognizing and accepting that what we call an "analytic" relationship is a *personal* relationship, the analyst becomes most open to shared *affective* experience, and this includes the relative "edginess" of aspects of the relationship that he cannot anticipate. Whether or not a particular school of analytic thought endorses the phrase "personal relationship," by my lights what is therapeutic about psychoanalysis is *based* on it being just that. It is its personal nature that enables the analytic relationship to nourish what I believe to be the deepest source of both therapeutic healing and therapeutic growth – "*the negotiation of otherness*."

In other words, it is *because* the analytic relationship is personal that the process I call "the negotiation of otherness" holds the potential for the most enduring analytic growth – but also holds, *simultaneously*, a potential for misusing what is otherwise its most basic therapeutic asset. Why so? During enactments, self-states of both people are at certain times going to collide messily. *Messily*! Not the first time I've used that word when writing about enactments. I'm very pleased to report that the day after I finished writing my final draft of this paper, an "op-ed" piece by Kathleen Vohs appeared in the Sunday *New York Times* review section (September 15, 2013) titled "It's not a mess, it's creativity." So, now that my messy creativity has been "sort of" endorsed by the *New York Times*, I'm going to develop my broader point in that same spirit: it has to do with a *subcategory* of enactments that I hold to be in a class by itself – enactments that involve "not-me" self-states created through developmental trauma that shaped a patient's *early attachment pattern* with a significant "other," leading that attachment pattern to interact affectively with aspects of the analyst's own "not-me" self-experience. An analyst who finds himself in the middle of this particular "field" will typically agree with my use of the adjective "messy."

Attachment-organized enactments are inherently messy because early attachment patterns are *established* procedurally and thereby must be *enacted* procedurally because there was no mentally representable cognitive context to begin with. The messiness is more built-in than usual because attachment-organized enactments are tied to the foundation of one's core sense of self, and *thereby* expose a patient to the greatest threat of self-destabilization in the face of being challenged by the unanticipated experience of increased *otherness* in the analyst, especially if the otherness is mainly affective and the analyst is seemingly unaware of having become more personally distant. This affective threat to the safety provided by a patient's core identity pulls the analyst into something that is challenging to both of them, and it is within this shared dissociative cocoon that the greatest potential for healing and growth exists – or so I would argue.

Enactments are challenging, and if you choose to work with them analytically, the choice carries a *responsibility* that must be honored as intrinsic. The responsibility is to communicate your dedication to your patient's affective safety as well as your dedication to the affective *risk* that comes with self-growth. "Safety" is not something that can be *delivered*, but genuine dedication to your patient's affective safety can and must be communicated as inherent in everything that takes place.

Before I talk about what this looks like relationally, let me first tell you that it is impossible for the analyst to do it "right." Why? Because of the impossible duality of the analytic task – a duality that requires the analyst to be living with a patient within the enactment and simultaneously be living in the "real-world" here-and-now – without losing either reality *unreflectively* – for too long. The key word is "unreflectively." The analyst's responsibility is to be as quickly attuned *as possible* to his own dissociative processes so as to recognize when he may have lost and needs to restore – his connection to the *duality* of his task. It is his dedication to it that needs to be restored, regardless of whether it is possible to do it "right." Losing one or the other aspect comes with the territory because such is the nature of paradox. But, as strange as it sounds, not being able to do it right is part of why enactments have such amazing therapeutic potential.

It is also why working with enactments invariably has an edginess, and why there can be times when an analyst is unable to contain the edginess because it stops feeling "edgy" and starts to feel sufficiently dysregulating to sometimes approach self-destabilization.

I want to quote something written by the Boston psychoanalyst and researcher Gerald Stechler. I want to quote it not only because it is such a profound insight about this same point, but also because I feel that his insight comes to a halt right at the edge of something so important that I want to speak to where I believe it can lead. Stechler (2003) first points out that "the possibility of the emergence of new states and organizations that arise during times of dysregulation has become one of the hallmark principles of contemporary theories of self-organizing systems" (p. 716), and that "in therapy, the work often consists of a renegotiation of old patterns, facilitating the creation of new organizations and new states" (p. 718). He then develops the implications of this as follows:

> Whether that new state is a richer, more complex, and more appropriate foundation for further development, or is the less advantageous choice in the sense of narrowing through toxic adaptation, may depend on whether the partner in this self-organizing system biases it in one direction or the other. The more toxic adaptation can stem from an interactional partner who reacts as if the destabilization were toxic. That is, if the therapist's (or parent's) primary aim is to reduce his own destabilization and its accompanying anxiety as if it were toxic and intolerable, the partner's aim and choice will be biased in the same direction. *If the therapist can stay connected with his own and with the patient's destabilization and can bias his own subsequent state choice toward openness and affective authenticity, then the patient's will be similarly biased. On the other hand, if the patient feels the freezing or the pretense of the therapist at critical moments, the work of the therapy cannot proceed well.*
>
> (p. 723, italics mine)

His insight is that a part of the therapist's task is to stay connected with his own and with the patient's dysregulation, and that when he loses this capacity unreflectively, the work of the therapy does not proceed well. Stechler's phrase, however, was "*cannot* proceed well," implying that the therapist's failure to remain connected is the source of the problem. Because Stechler was emphasizing only the potential *danger*, he doesn't develop his insight any further: that the failure to stay connected is not an actual "failure" because the nature of dissociative processes makes it *impossible* to stay connected. As the saying goes, "You can't sit on two pots with one behind," and it is inevitable that the connection to one or the other of the dual elements of the task will oscillate as part of the process. It is in fact this inevitability that allows psychoanalysis to succeed as psychotherapy. The actual danger is that the connection may fail to be *restored*, and by "restored" I mean within the interpersonal/relational context as opposed to an "as-if" restoration. "As-if," because when the therapist is trying to go it alone within the confines of his own mind, he is trying to speak *as if* he were related. Stechler accurately describes this stance as "freezing," but in his calling it "pretense" I would here disagree. I don't think that dissociation is ever "pretense." Something highly authentic and real is taking place – but dissociatively.

When the analyst's dissociated need to restabilize himself leads him to escape into a self-contained hiding place, then his patient, who is sharing the dissociative cocoon, will experience him as needing protection from *her*, a phenomenon that is most often a core aspect of an *attachment-related* enactment. If the analyst's "freezing" makes him *unable* to mobilize his self-reflectiveness, then the duality of his task can be *truly* lost – not because he waited too long to restore it, but because his dissociative solution to his fear did not require duality. He became dissociatively trapped within *one* of the dual realities – and, at least temporarily, he is freed from the "not-me" grip of shame and affect dysregulation.

Shame, unlike guilt, is the affect signifying that who we *are* has no legitimacy in a human context. For a patient, its dissociated presence is most frequently a sign that certain of her "not-me" self-states have become active while reliving developmental trauma, and have not been sufficiently acknowledged by the analyst. Her "yearning" for such acknowledgment is accompanied by the shame-ridden illegitimacy of the self that is experiencing the yearning. I am using the word "yearning" rather than "wanting," because "wanting" is a conscious cognition, and "yearning," especially during an enactment, is affective and procedural. At such a moment, a patient is shamefully hungering for recognition of her pain in the here and now – shamefully, because the person from whom she needs recognition of her pain is, once again, the person least likely to offer it because at that moment he is also the person most contributing to it, however inadvertently.

The very nature of such enactments creates an *interpersonal* shame dynamic that is destabilizing to each person because it is linked to the emergence of a "not-me" part of self. For the therapist, the shame is most strongly connected to trying to provide something growth-enhancing and "good" to someone he cares about, while simultaneously experiencing his very effort as causing additional pain to his patient. What is most important, and simultaneously most difficult for the analyst, is to watch for signs of dissociated shame *both* in himself and in his patient – shame that is being evoked by the therapeutic process itself in ways that the analyst is, at least for the moment, unaware of cognitively.

While writing the paper, it was at this point I said to myself:

> Hmm! Stechler focuses only on what happens when the analyst *withdraws* affectively. He dissociates from being affectively connected with his patient and as soon as the analyst does that he becomes full of – full of words and thoughts which he delivers not in a relational context, but through their now unlinked patient/therapist roles. He has become a handmaiden to the enacted 'professional' role of *understanding* – understanding what is going on in the patient without experiencing himself as part of it.

This is when I had an insight of my own. I asked myself what it might look like if the analyst's dissociated fear of increasing his own destabilization leads *not* to enshrining himself protectively within an "as-if" professionalism, but instead, to unreflectively surrendering it (hopefully temporarily) and telling himself that *only their personal affective connection is valid.* In other words, instead of becoming a prisoner of unshared impersonal cognition, he becomes a "prisoner" of shared personal affect as a place to escape from his own fear. The duality of the task is simply surrendered in a different way – that of dissociating his shared connection to the *here-and-now* reality of their commitment to the joint task that includes his professional role as *part* of it.

Every analyst *already* knows what this feels like to one degree or another, at least with a few patients – and has more than likely seen it in action when working as a supervisor. Typically, what shakes an analyst the most and has the greatest potential to lead to fear of runaway dysregulation is when a patient seems to be falling apart in front of his eyes and everything he tries seems to be making it worse. It is my experience that this is most often embedded in the enactment of an attachment-related developmental trauma, and that its intensity quite frequently signals the presence of *annihilation dread.* In this regard, what takes place enactively almost always includes some manifestation of the patient's escalating dread of attachment rupture, the experience of irreparability, and loss of selfhood.

Wouldn't it make sense, I said to myself, that some therapists find it a more natural form of restabilization to protect themselves *not* by hiding within a self-made fortress of thoughts and words, but by giving themselves completely over to the *affective reality* of the enactment? For a change, the part of me I was asking didn't argue with me. So I kept going – and here's what I now want to offer as something to meditate on: the possibility that the *emotional closeness* of the enactment can become for some analysts an *affective* hiding place – not a place to escape from affect, but a place to escape by hiding *within* it – a sanctuary that, *because* it feels good and feels right, might serve to keep the couple (and himself) from the dread of "breaking apart." Unlike Stechler's scenario, it is the "professional" reality of the analyst's dual task that would tend to suffer dissociation.

This scenario, despite its potential to become edgier than the one Stechler so brilliantly portrays, happens with *regularity* during enactments, and paradoxically is the source of the most powerful synthesis of therapeutic healing and therapeutic growth. *Most* powerful because it is here that the work is most *open* to the dissociative processes in both partners and thus to the co-created pathway leading to healing: *the joint experience of the affective shadow* of early attachment trauma in an interpersonal/relational context that can both access it and process it – experientially, procedurally, and cognitively.

Its edginess lies in the openness of both people to *accepting* how real it is, and that part of what is real is the love that is felt between them – the foundation of what I call "the nearness of you." It can feel scary when you stop needing to always call it "transference," but when it is accepted as love, it leads to a shared solidarity that values the "work" (including its messiness and edginess), not only the love. My experience with patients, supervisees, and in speaking to colleagues, has been that even with attachment trauma (perhaps *especially* with attachment trauma), the personal quality of this solidarity is no small part of what is healing. There is a special sense of strength in hanging in together that restores not only trust in human-relatedness but pride in the expanded self that risked allowing it, even though the processing of the enactment includes having to accept shame as part of being human, having to accept loss of what is not possible, and having to experience deep grief that has been for so long avoided.

It is when the analyst's dissociated need for self-protection cannot be held as a *lived* part of the enactment that the analyst runs the risk of abandoning the duality of his task, and by so doing, runs the even greater risk of abandoning the shared evolution of this *personal* relationship—sometimes with consequences that make us justifiably wonder whether psychoanalysis is indeed a "traumatic" field.

References

Bromberg, P. M. (2003). One need not be a house to be haunted. *Psychoanalytic Dialogues*, 13: 689–709. Expanded version in *Awakening the Dreamer: Clinical Journeys*. Mahwah, NJ: The Analytic Press, 2006, pp. 153–173.

Bromberg, P. M. (2011). *The Shadow of the Tsunami: and the Growth of the Relational Mind*. New York: Routledge.

Dickinson, E. (1863). Poem 670. In *The Complete Poems of Emily Dickinson*, ed. T. H. Johnson. Boston: Little, Brown, 1960.

Laub, D. & Auerhahn, N. C. (1993). Knowing and not knowing massive psychic trauma. Forms of traumatic memory. *International Journal of Psycho-Analysis*, 74: 287–302.

Main, M. & Hesse, E. (1990). Parents' unresolved traumatic experiences are related to infant disorganized attachment status: is frightened/frightening parental behavior the linking mechanism? In *Attachment in the Preschool Years: Theory, Research, and Intervention*, ed. M. T. Greenberg, D. Cicchetti, & E. M. Cummings. Chicago, IL: University of Chicago Press, pp. 161–182.

Main, M. & Solomon, J. (1986). Discovery of an insecure-disorganized/disoriented attachment pattern: procedures, findings and implications for the classification of behavior. In *Affective Development in Infancy*, ed. T. B. Brazelton & M. Yogman. Norwood, NJ: Ablex, pp. 95–124.

Main, M. & Solomon, J. (1990). Procedures for identifying infants as disorganized/disoriented during the Ainsworth strange situation. In *Attachment in the Preschool Years: Theory, Research, and Intervention*, ed. M. T. Greenberg, D. Cicchetti, & E. M. Cummings. Chicago, IL: University of Chicago Press, pp. 121–160.

Schore, A. N. (2003). *Affect Dysregulation and Disorders of the Self*. New York: Norton.

Stechler, G. (2003). Affect: the heart of the matter. *Psychoanalytic Dialogues*, http://i1203.photobucket.com/albums/bb390/creemcheeze/Sherlock/awkward.gif 13: 711–726.

Vohs, K. D. (2013). It's not a mess, it's creativity. *The New York Times*, September 15 (Sunday Review Section), p. SR 12.

Chapter 4

Dissociative enactment and interpellation

Donnel B. Stern

As I thought about the question of whether psychoanalysis might itself be considered a symptom of trauma, I found myself drawn to the role of linked pairs of terms in Western thought, and especially to the thinking of Jacques Derrida, one of the most influential twentieth-century philosophers, who devised and described what has become widely known as the deconstruction of meaning. I am going to try to combine the sweep of Derrida's ideas with the contribution of another French philosopher, Louis Althusser; I am then going to connect these ideas about ideology with ideas about dissociation and enactment; and eventually, I am going to arrive at a thought about the practice of psychoanalysis.

I am not thoroughly grounded in Derrida's work, but I know enough about it to understand that it is a variety of the kind of dialectic analysis that I have been thinking and writing about for many years. In a deconstructive analysis, meaning is shaped not only by what it is, but also by what it is not. This principle applies to any writer's work, and for that matter, to all other art or scholarship; in fact, although deconstruction is most commonly applied to verbal language, the principles of deconstruction apply to any human experience that is given symbolic form – not only language, but dance, painting, and so on. For example, we might think of our experience of bodies this way. We might ask about the ways that belonging to our particular time and place lead us, without awareness, to emphasize certain perceptions and meanings of our bodies, and just as unconsciously to deemphasize others. To which bodily experiences do we grant special significance, and what other such experiences do we tend to keep in shadow?

The structural linguist Saussure long ago put forward the idea that the units of language are defined by means of what he was the first to call "binary oppositions." One cannot understand either term in a binary opposition without also understanding the other, and the relation between the two. Think of "good" and "bad." Some decades later, Derrida added to this account in an important way, arguing that certain highly significant binary oppositions are organized hierarchically and violently, so that one of the two terms dominates and governs the other. I'll offer an example of this phenomenon in just a moment.

In an article in the popular press, written as a kind of intellectual obituary for Derrida and published just a few days after the philosopher's death, the scholar Mark C. Taylor (2004) concisely describes Derrida's principal idea:

> The guiding insight of deconstruction is that every structure – be it literary, psychological, social, economic, political or religious – that organizes our experience is constituted and maintained through acts of exclusion. In the process of creating something, something else inevitably gets left out.

Through Derrida and others, we have become familiar over the last several decades with the harm binary oppositions lead to when our minds are created in their images. A classic example is race in the United States. In the white/black binary opposition, no longer consciously acceptable but nevertheless unconsciously influential on us all, blackness is not only "other" to whiteness, but also defined in a way that devalues blackness. Whiteness is not necessarily actively idealized, but it doesn't need to be, because it is drained of "bad" qualities, which tend to be assigned to blackness, leaving whiteness to occupy the position of standard, uncontroversial decency, without much edge or definition – in a word, normality. Thus white people don't often characterize their own whiteness. They don't need to. It's like physical health: health is what is expectable, and so we understand disease as a deviation from it. Whiteness, especially for white people – although also for people of color under some circumstances – is the "normal" standard from which blackness deviates. Blackness, on the other hand, tends to be characterized in more detail, and often more negatively, and so both white people and black people are inclined to be much more aware of meanings for blackness than for whiteness. We have become familiar over the last decades with similar analyses for many other identity categories defined by binary oppositions: male/female, young/old, straight/gay, and so on. It is not accidental that all these examples have moral or political implications, because, as I've already said, for Derrida binary oppositions always involve power differentials. One term always dominates the other.

As I thought more about these connections, and although I recognized that Derrida was not thinking about trauma when he described the domination of one term in a binary opposition by the other, the conceptual links between deconstruction, psychic trauma, and dissociation fairly leaped out at me. Let me explain.

Consider what happens when trauma leads to dissociation: the outcome is the separation, or sequestration, of states of being from one another. Each exists in isolation from the other; and yet each part of the experience is the missing part of the other, and so each state is the reason that the other is meaningful.[1] I am the familiar "me" only as long as I can keep my dissociated experience – that is, "not-me" – at bay. And "not-me" only continues to exist as long as "me" cannot allow it to become part of itself. We might even say that it is the exclusion of not-me that creates the boundaries of what feels like me. That is why it is so hard for the self to change. To allow not-me to become part of the self is to be a different me.

One could say, using poststructuralist language, that dissociation results in "either/or" experience – me or not-me – and that the challenge in psychoanalytic treatment is to create "both/and" experience. In fact, although I can't explore this more fully here, this point has been made for decades by relational psychoanalytic writers. Jessica Benjamin (e.g., 1990), in particular, describes the shift to intersubjectivity from the "doer-done-to" dynamics of reversible complementarity. Her work is a meditation on the movement from "either-or" to "both-and."

What I want to suggest is that dissociated states of being, the outcome of trauma – me and not-me – constitute a kind of binary opposition. We see this in dissociative enactments, in which the other person in the interaction is treated as if s/he were manifesting one's own dissociated state. The interaction is commonly structured as something like this: "*I'm* not bad (or narcissistic, hateful, envious, contemptible, and so on). No, *you're* bad." One has access only to a portion of experience, the part that's tolerable; the remainder is assigned to the other, and the two parts must be kept separate. It is a case of either/or: one can occupy *this* state of being or *that* one, but the both/and alternative, which would be to occupy the two states simultaneously, is not feasible until, if things go well, the treatment makes it possible. And notice, just as in the case of the binary oppositions I have already mentioned, that the pole of the dissociative enactment that one characterizes negatively – that is, the experience and conduct of the other – is defined in more detail than the pole that one characterizes positively – the part of the experience attributed to, and experienced as, oneself. In a dissociative enactment, in other words, just as "black" is characterized by those who are white more completely than is "white," in an enactment of my dissociated experience, *you* are characterized more completely than *I* am. *You* are very often some very particular kind of bad (sadistic, or unreasonable, or impossible); but *I* am simply what you are not – good or reasonable in some fairly generic way.

All right: all this may be interesting to think about, but why does it matter to link dissociation/enactment theory and deconstruction? Here we reach the points I most want to make. For Derrida, binary oppositions and their implications for theorizing come about through a social process that we might characterize as more or less impersonal – impersonal, that is, in the sense that the process affects all of us, not just those of us from certain backgrounds or who have suffered certain traumatic experiences. In the United States we are all implicated, to go back to my example, in the continuing existence and reproduction of the identities of "black" and "white," identities that participate in shaping our minds.

Binary oppositions, in other words, tend to be expressions of ideology, the kinds of influences that a large collection of Marxist (e.g., Gramsci) and postmodern (e.g., Foucault) theorists have taught us have the effect, when we acknowledge them (as we all do, like it or not), of constituting our subjectivities. Ideology constitutes us by a process that Louis Althusser (2000/1969), adopting a term and an idea already in circulation at the time he wrote, labeled "interpellation." In Althusser's famous example, when the policeman "hails" us, shouting, "Hey, you!", in the very act of turning around to acknowledge the hail we are shaped into subjects in society's image. In their work on the relation between interpellation and recognition, Guralnick and Simeon (2010) describe the outcome of the policeman's hail this way: "We immediately morph into *self-as-criminal*, thereby revealing where the force of the State and our identity as individuals meet" (p. 407). Our subjectivity congeals in such a moment: we are now *a person who can be hailed in that way by a policeman*; we are subject to that authority; we feel guilty of something. This kind of influence is well-nigh unavoidable.

In interpellation we have the structure of the binary opposition: the two poles, and the dominance of one by the other, all instantiated in a way we might call automatic – or better for our psychoanalytic purposes, unconscious. In the process of interpellation there is no conscious intervention on the part of any of the individuals involved. The process is not individually motivated; the subjection of the individual is a social matter.

When we are treated as black or white, we are "hailed," in a sense; and when we acknowledge that treatment, which we do frequently without giving the matter conscious thought, we are in that very moment constituted as participants in the world of black and white, but without the opportunity to consider whether this is what we want, or even approve of. That is what ideology does. Binary oppositions, it seems, are built into the very process by which subjectivity is constituted.

We usually think of dissociative enactments in clinical psychoanalysis and psychotherapy quite differently than that. For one thing, we think of these enactments as personal exchanges, not impersonal ones. But consider what dissociative enactment and interpellation have in common. In both, one person treats another in a way that assigns a certain shape to both subjectivities: in Althusser's hail, I am a policeman and you are subject to my authority; in a dissociative enactment, I am a reasonable person and you are not. Often enough, in a dissociative enactment, precisely because the attempt of the other to control the interaction is unconscious to both parties, the one accused, like the person hailed by the policeman, is affected without knowing it. Unthinkingly, the accused one takes on the attribution – by which I *don't* mean that the one who is accused of being unreasonable (for example) necessarily accepts that she *is* unreasonable. Actually, the unthought part of the interaction is most often simply that the one who is accused takes part in it in a natural, reciprocal way. What comes naturally, for instance, might be the feeling that *I'm* not unreasonable – no, *you're* unreasonable for accusing me in this crazy way. The effect of the dissociative accusation on the one who is accused, that is, often comes about even if the accused one *disputes* the attribution, because denying influence doesn't necessarily dispel it. In fact, denial, especially if it is defensive in nature, is as much a participation in the enactment as blind acceptance of the attribution would be. Denial can even make the influence less visible and therefore more insidious. In psychotherapy, when the patient unconsciously pressures the analyst to assume an uncomfortable role, the shaping effect on the analyst's experience can come about even if the analyst responds with no more than the quiet defensiveness that we would all agree is probably unavoidable when one person floats an accusation against another.

And so we might say that the analyst is "hailed" by the patient in the transference (and sometimes, of course, the patient is hailed by the analyst in the same way), and presto! – there is the countertransference! We might even go so far as to say that in a dissociative enactment one party is *interpellated* by the other. That is similarity number one between interpellation and dissociative enactment: a transformation of subjectivity takes place as the result of the unconsciously motivated treatment of one person by the other.

Now, similarity number two, about which I will be briefer: both interpellation and dissociative enactment result in the establishment of either/or binaries: I am being reasonable; you are not. Complexity vanishes. Similarity number three: in both the case of binary oppositions and dissociative enactments, either/or phenomena are defined by the domination of one term by the other. Derrida makes this point explicitly about the binaries he describes. Dissociative enactments, too, tend to be adversarial, because these interactions are created by the attempt of one person to foist an unconsciously refused and unformulated part of his or her subjectivity on to another.[2]

Where does this leave us? We are brought full circle, back to the question of whether clinical psychoanalysis itself might sometimes be a symptom of trauma. Through our interaction with patients, this view would have it, we sometimes participate in interpellations that call aspects of identity into being – in ourselves and the other; and in this way, outside our awarenesses, these events, the dissociative outcomes of trauma, shape the subjectivities we adopt with particular patients.

I may perhaps be offering a new way to express this point, but the thought itself is hardly new. We've long taken it for granted, after all, that countertransference comes about without our awareness. That's the *point* of countertransference. I'm merely adding that who we are with each of our patients, those states of our being that are called into existence from outside our ken, may come about in a way that bears a similarity to interpellation: there exists a continuity, in other words, between the process of dissociative enactment and the process of interpellation.

Let me finish my remarks by asking about the upshot of this relation of dissociation and interpellation for the aims of our clinical work. I think about this question by first reminding myself what we psychoanalysts seek to accomplish: we try to bring into clinical relatedness what has been excluded from it, and thereby broaden and deepen the field between patient and analyst so that it evolves more freely than it could before. Our work with enactments – which are, after all, rigidities in relatedness, what the Barangers (2009) call "bastions" or "bulwarks" in the field – is primary in this respect. Our work with enactments is where new relational freedom (Stern, 2013) comes from. We try to grasp what eludes us, remembering that the unconscious is two things at once: yes, that which is unknown to us – absences that may even be impossible to symbolize; but also that which is a matter of blind belief, i.e., that which is so present that it's absent: we don't see it or feel it or think it. Unconsciousness of either sort is the absence of curiosity – which means that to be unconscious is not only not to know, but even more importantly, not even to know that we don't know. The roles taken by analyst and patient in a dissociative enactment are frequently so thoroughly taken for granted that, like racism, the meaning or significance of the enactment, of the interpellation, however deeply felt and intensely expressed it may be, remains stubbornly invisible to those living it out. Under these circumstances, the best we can do to avoid being indefinitely mired in the aftermath of trauma – the trauma of the patient, the trauma of the analyst, and all that other trauma suffered by earlier generations and sedimented in our theories and practices – is to embrace uncertainty at every opportunity. We need to recognize in our own rigidity an opportunity for the creation of a new freedom. We often need to wait and watch, accepting that we are not transparent to our own scrutiny, and that we therefore may very well be deeply and unwittingly involved in just the problems in relatedness that we think we are learning to know. It is often the case that, to paraphrase John Lennon, psychoanalysis is what happens while you're busy making other plans.

Derrida agreed with all this. He believed that wisdom, in the words of Mark Taylor (2004), whom I quoted earlier, is "knowing what we don't know so that we can keep the future open." We need to respect the tenacity and insidiousness of ideology. In psychoanalysis, that means not only that we must attend to all those same unconscious effects of identity, such as race, that also take place routinely in the other parts of our lives; we must also maintain a respect for the tenacity and insidiousness of enactment in the clinical situation, while simultaneously tuning ourselves to the pitch of freedom. That's easier said than done, as I have tried to say. It's a hard-won and fragile vision, and every time we locate it in the clinical process, we lose it; it disappears, so that we're constantly in the process of refinding and recreating it. But as hard-won as this vision may be, it is a sound basis for moral and political life – for all human relatedness, for that matter, which is always at risk of collapsing into the kind of interpellative interaction that transmits trauma. It's certainly a sound basis for psychoanalysis.

Notes

1 A colleague pointed out to me that readers who are not familiar with relational dissociation/enactment theory may wonder why the use of the concept of dissociation adds anything to the more familiar idea of splitting. For a discussion of these issues, see Stern (2004, 2010).

2 In my conception, all the subjectivity that exists outside the range of consciousness, including the part of subjectivity that is dissociated, is unformulated. By "unformulated experience" I mean to refer to *potential* conscious experience, not fully formed content hidden in the mind or distorted in a way that makes it unrecognizable. Unformulated experience is a vaguely organized, primitive, global, non-ideational, affective state. For an explication of this way of conceptualizing unconscious process and dissociation, see Stern (1997, 2010).

References

Althusser, L. (2000). Ideology and state apparatus. In S. Zizek (Ed.), *Mapping Ideology* (pp. 100–140). New York: Verso. (Original work published 1969.)

Baranger, M. & Baranger, W. (2009). *The Work of Confluence: Listening and Interpreting in the Psychoanalytic Field.* London: Karnac Books.

Benjamin, J. (1990). Recognition and destruction: an outline of intersubjectivity. In S. A. Mitchell & L. Aron (Eds.), *Relational Psychoanalysis: The Emergence of a Tradition.* Hillsdale, NJ: The Analytic Press, 1999, pp. 183–200.

Guralnick, O. & Simeon, D. (2010). Depersonalization: standing in the spaces between interpellation and recognition. *Psychoanalytic Dialogues*, 20: 400–416.

Stern, D. B. (1997). *Unformulated Experience: From Dissociation to Imagination in Psychoanalysis.* Hillsdale, NJ: The Analytic Press.

Stern, D. B. (2004). The eye sees itself: dissociation, enactment, and the achievement of conflict. *Contemporary Psychoanalysis*, 40: 197–237.

Stern, D. B. (2010). *Partners in Thought: Working with Unformulated Experience, Dissociation, and Enactment.* New York: Routledge.

Stern, D. B. (2013). Relational freedom and therapeutic action. *Journal of the American Psychoanalytic Association*, 61: 227–255.

Taylor, M. C. (2004). What Derrida really meant. *New York Times*, October 14.

Chapter 5

The traumatic field

Psychoanalysis as trauma translated

Don Troise

a ghost always has the architecture of a storm

Cole Swensen[1]

My mother died suddenly just before I turned three. Ten years later my father died. In between, my brother developed an addiction to drugs that would later kill him at 44. He was a psychoanalyst. These events marked me like none other. They crushed me, of course. But they also gave me intention, a way forward. I can't conceive of the person I'd be if these things hadn't happened to me, but it's unlikely that I'd be a psychoanalyst. I don't think my brother would have been one either.

Why do we come to this field? What compels us to immerse ourselves in work that is steeped in sorrow and suffering, work that's frequently strange and sad and lonely? We hear things that most other people will never hear. Why do we want to?

Psychoanalysis is a kind of forgery. Originally, it wanted no past other than the patient's past, no influence beyond that which patients contended with. In the incipient iterations of psychoanalysis, the story being told was thought to be exclusively the patient's, and it therefore precluded aspects of the analyst's own story. Thus, the analyst was expected to be, in a sense, outside of time. Unencumbered by his history, he was beyond its influence. Without a past, and, most particularly, without a traumatic past, he was free to discern and to analyze. He was free to devise meaning rather than remember it. To this day, and despite the great paradigm shifts that have occurred in the field over the last 30 years or so, psychoanalysis still seems reluctant to recognize itself as a narrative practice forged from a haunted past, a notional account of personhood that has arguably been convened in the service of explaining, and enduring, trauma.[2]

A good *deal* of psychoanalysis is about deciding: deciding where to start; deciding what we want, what we can live with and what we can't; deciding what to value. It is decisions, those made for us, and those *we* make, that advance or arrest us. Decisions are consequent to experience; they are accommodations. Something happens, and we decide what it means and what to do about it. In this way, every action is a *re*action, a response to circumstance – a rejoinder; the future departs from and with the past. We may wonder why something has happened, but it seems more important, more gainful, to wonder why we've reacted as we have. Why this response and not another? Why did my brother choose psychoanalysis? Why did I? Why does anyone?

Among the first questions children ask is: How did I get here? And when someone new arrives at our offices, we ask something similar: What brings you here? Our patients might ask the same of us. How would we answer? We would, of course, rather not. And we have reason not to. The reason – the decision – to not answer this or any such question is ostensibly bound to a theory, an idea about why we shouldn't or, at the least, about why it might be best not to. If it's an idea that is culturally or professionally sanctioned, it becomes a sort of creed, and there's the risk that we may stop wondering how our theories can apply to us. We may forget that our theories are basically stories and are, to a great degree, expressions of our personal historical experience. They are *our* stories. The decision to be a psychoanalyst and, following this, the decision to be a certain *kind* of psychoanalyst, to subscribe to or draft a *theory* of psychoanalysis, has more to do with our lived experience than we're usually comfortable admitting.

Theory is regularly written and performed in the shadow of the past. It describes experience as much as it imagines it. Much of psychoanalytic doctrine and its alterations over time can be viewed as a translation and a transformation of the traumatic past. To a great degree, theoreticians have contributed to our psychoanalytic lore by contextualizing and structuralizing that which has influenced them, by *explaining* themselves, and what has harmed them, *to* themselves in the guise of explaining others. At its core, psychoanalytic theory, at once a variation and an explication of that which haunts us, is experience rendered, abstracted, and universalized.

But for some, in order for theory to be convincing, it can neither be personal, an emanation of lived experience, nor hallucinated. It must be objectively, demonstrably true. It must be verifiable. There will always be those who prefer that there be nothing gossamer about theory and those who believe that theory is, essentially, sheer. Whatever we judge objective truth to be, and however we attempt to measure it, the insistence of some on veridicality has gotten psychoanalysis into a lot of trouble lately. We are routinely in the position of having to describe the ghosts we're seeing. The more we try to convince others that our theories are true, not ideas but observations, or, at the least, ideas *based* on observations, the crazier we seem and the more we're marginalized by the prose sciences. Apparently, our ghosts don't haunt everyone (Troise, 2016).

So, there's a relationship between biography and theory. As such, there is no reason to think that psychoanalytic theorists don't elaborate from aspects of their personal history. Like most theory, psychoanalysis is a kind of speculation – speculation informed by observation, imagination, and experience, but speculation nonetheless. In my view, psychoanalysis runs aground when it purports to be a science that operates outside the realm of the analyst's lived experience and his feelings about this experience. It is, instead, a history-bound, scientized conversation, which addresses conditions of possibilities and constraints. It follows that, as the past provides the template for what binds us and/or enables our freedom, we must – in our work and in our thinking about our work – spend a lot of time there: in our own past, in our patients' pasts, and in that past which we share. And if we know anything about the past, we know that it's never really past. It is always with us *immediately*. How does our relationship to the past inform our theories? Are our theories less valuable because they partly derive from our particular experience? Or does it depend on what that experience is (Troise, 2013)?

Broadly speaking, there are two categorical responses to trauma that theory engages: affiliation and dissociation. The kind of response that proceeds from affiliation allows that all experience is connected and derivative; the past has happened and is, in one form or another, with us still. Responses that proceed from dissociation posit experience as essentially disconnected and therefore prospectively imaginable; the past has *not* happened and so we can imagine it and a future free of its influence. In this context, imagination is a benign, and somewhat paradoxical, variant of dissociation, an allusive, innovative response to trauma rather than a delusive, constricted one. Affiliation permits one kind of understanding – experience is per proximity knowable – and allusive dissociation engenders another – experience is imaginable; it can be thought up. Among other things, to find meaning is to *not* imagine it, and *to* imagine is to not find meaning, i.e., to not explain. Just as there is no possibility for the elaboration of meaning without affiliation, some degree of dissociation is essential to the elaboration of imagination. How have these responses to trauma influenced the course of psychoanalysis?

Like all of us, the architects of psychoanalysis were time-bound. They lived in a moment, a period, an age. They are today, as we will be for future generations, reminders of the past and of what was conceivable then. Freud conceived of psychoanalysis. Working into and from himself, he thought it up. His dream, so to speak, became ours. Much of what informed Freud's imagination has been transferred to us and so has informed our imaginations but without the context. Freud spun his dreams *out* of time and *into* theories. His dreams (like all dreams) were extrapolations from material, contextual reality. Knowing what we do of Freud's early history, we can surmise – surmise is often the most we can do – that his dream of psychoanalysis was compelled to some degree by trauma.

Freud's early life was marked by isolation, loss, and disruption. His first home was in a town where there were very few other Jewish families and where there were regular reminders of the persecution of Jews and of their minority status. Soon after Freud was born, his mother gave birth to a second child. She named this son after her beloved younger brother who had only recently died, at 20, of tuberculosis. Within six months or so after his birth, the child died. Freud was not yet two. Having just lost her brother and her son in quick succession, Freud's mother was likely depressed, if not devastated. Freud's early care in this period was entrusted to a Czech Catholic nursemaid who was subsequently arrested and imprisoned for petty theft. Freud was two and a half, and he never saw her again. Up until Freud was ten, his mother was regularly pregnant, delivering seven children at home. Just before he turned four, his father's business collapsed and the family was forced to move, leaving behind an extended family that had provided some security for Freud during the tumult of his early years.

In his biography of Freud, from which this account is drawn, Louis Breger (2000) maintains that the traumatic experiences of Freud's first four years effectively "vanished from his awareness" (p. 17), that they were dissociated. To a notable degree, Freud turned away from the ostracization, failures, and grave losses that characterized his early life and replaced them with heroic identifications and fantasies of greatness. These early, defensive identifications set the stage for the boy warrior to murder his father and win his mother's affectionate, indeed lustful, attention. In a letter to Wilhelm Fleiss, Freud wrote:

> A single idea of general value dawned on me. I have found, in my own case too, the phenomena of being in love with my mother and jealous of my father, and I now consider it a universal event in early childhood.
>
> (Masson, 1985, p. 272; also quoted in Breger, 2000, p. 126)

This is a striking remark, not least because "it is the conflict, fear and guilt about *this situation* that became Freud's principal explanation for the symptoms of adult neuroses, both his own and those of his patients" (pp. 2–3). Freud's "idea," born of his dissociation, was thus exalted to orthodoxy.

Before commenting further on the significance of Freud's transformation of his trauma, it's worthwhile considering for a moment the other great traumatized architect of psychoanalysis: Harry Stack Sullivan. Sullivan was the only son of a poor, uncommunicative, Irish Catholic farmer and an extremely unhappy mother who felt she had married beneath her. Prior to Sullivan's birth, she lost two sons in infancy. Soon after his birth, she apparently suffered some kind of depressive collapse and disappeared from the family for several months. Sullivan grew up in a rural area of New York State that was hostile toward Irish Catholics. He was the only Irish-Catholic student in his town's one room school. He had few friends and, by all accounts, was exceedingly lonely. Sullivan's best friend, an older boy who accompanied him to school on a regular basis, clearly influenced his later description of isophilic love, or chumship, as a crucial developmental epoch. This relationship, whether sexually achieved or not, was evidently a sexualized one for Sullivan and presaged his adult homosexuality. Sullivan's homosexuality was likely the most important of his experiences of difference, and it may have played some part in a suspected schizophrenic break he sustained in early adulthood (Troise, 2012). Taken together, these circumstances constitute a veritable catalogue of alienating experiences, of traumas even. Sullivan thus came to regard historical, cultural, and social factors as crucial to the foundation of personality. His entire interpersonal psychology evolves from this awareness. Sullivan's great sympathy for those on the margins of society, and his capacity to help them to the degree that he did, derived from his own traumatic losses and from his experience of marginalization. If Freud's discoveries were rooted in dissociation, Sullivan's developed from affiliation.

I don't intend this as a criticism of Freud. Rather, I'm interested in the two different responses to trauma and what they can teach us about the action of psychoanalysis and the discipline itself. Both responses, in addition to having influenced the advancement of theory, were *personally* useful. In their different ways, they probably helped Freud and Sullivan transform their traumas. We may well wonder what might have happened to them if they hadn't found a way to narrativize their experience, to translate their traumas into psychological epistemologies. Consequent to his dissociation, Freud universalized his incipient heterosexuality as "the Oedipal complex," while Sullivan reified, from his homosexuality, "chumship" as a developmental epoch. These ideas, these theories, are explanations from both men's experiences, whether formulated or not. It does not diminish either man's achievement to say so. Because each was able to translate from his trauma, to imagine that his experience, real *or* fantasied, was not his alone, they could transmute it. This capacity represents both the growth *and* the action of psychoanalysis. As both a field of inquiry and its method, psychoanalysis is trauma translated.

It's worth remembering here that, in addition to being a *response* to trauma, psychoanalysis began as a *method* for treating it. Neurotic symptomology was first considered to be a consequence of sexualized trauma that was not socially acknowledged as such. Freud's first patients were principally women who were believed to have been sexually abused, or "seduced," in childhood, by their adult caretakers. Freud's eventual abandonment of the seduction theory for one that privileged intrapsychic experience, and particularly fantasies, was fateful. Where once a patient's memory or perception was thought to be true, or to point toward some crucial, actual occurrence, it was now more likely to be understood as an interpretable wish or fantasy.

The shift in emphasis from explanations for adult neuroses based on material experience to those based on psychic experience had profound consequences for the development of psychoanalytic theory, of course, but also for the evolution of technique. In a sense, interpreting replaced listening. The analyst's function was no longer to hear, but to imagine. It is a great irony of psychoanalysis that its method came to represent an iteration of the very kind of traumatic experiences, the effects of which it was meant to cure. Any version of experience that the patient offered, including her experience of the analyst, was now likely seen as a transference distortion, a sort of lie. Insofar as patients were once again in the position of having aspects of their experience denied, skepticism was methodized and became an essential component of psychoanalytic technique, if not its nucleus. Doubt thus superseded, and often supplanted, trust. An attitude of irresolution, a degree of which *is* essential to the analytic endeavor, predominated to the point that practical, material considerations were often disregarded. Psychoanalysis, which perhaps initially overvalued materiality, now skewed in the direction of discounting it. The field that began as a response to trauma and redress for its victims became, for a time, traumatizing itself.

There is reason to believe that the founders and early practitioners of psychoanalysis were led to this position, at least in part, from a need to dissociate their own traumas. It has been argued (Breger, 2000) that Freud in particular dissociated his significant early losses and disruptions and in the process conceived of psychoanalysis. In a sense, he needed to disavow trauma to *find* psychoanalysis. This is, effectively, what happened when he abandoned the seduction theory, a historically based understanding of neuroses, in favor of intrapsychic explanations for the same. Conversely, it would seem that Sullivan, despite dissociative tendencies of his own, nonetheless elaborated the basic principles of his interpersonal psychology from the recognition that his suffering – an acute, abiding loneliness – was affiliative, i.e., closely bound to experiences of alienation and marginalization that certain others had as well. He explained "difficulties in living" not on the permutations of fantasy, but on lived experience as mediated by a range of historical, cultural, and social factors. Both men theorized their traumas from categorically opposing positions: Freud from dissociation, and Sullivan from affiliation. These posts create a spectrum along which most other psychoanalytic theories can be located.

It wasn't until the advent and ascendance of intersubjective and relational perspectives, rooted as they are in a variety of experiences of marginalization and in the great social change movements of the twentieth century that were a response to these experiences, that psychoanalytic theory and practice were significantly altered and some balance between appreciations of both the patient's and the analyst's experience *and* imagination was achieved. Without the need to disavow material *or* psychic reality, and the mutual expressions of each, we are better positioned now to know our patients and ourselves and to find our future. All of our psychoanalytic theories today register somewhere on the continuum between those elaborated from dissociation and those elaborated from affiliation. Taken together, as languages that carry and describe trauma, they delimit psychoanalysis.

What Freud and Sullivan were able to accomplish in order to contend with the traumatic aspects of their histories is that which all of us seek through psychoanalysis – transliteration, the transcription of self-experience into that which may connect us or restore our connection to others. Where trauma is concerned, this capacity to narrativize experience must be accompanied by the belief that our experience, no matter how bad or seemingly unspeakable, is not singular, is not ours alone.

Knowing that our experience, our story, is correspondent in some materially proximate way to someone else's story is crucial to recovering from trauma, but imagination, too, helps loosen trauma's hold on us. We must imagine ourselves in order to utilize, or to brook, the impact of circumstance. As much as we're marked by material reality, we are shaped by wishes, by dreams. Where a life is concerned, what happened matters, but it's never the whole story. Facts may bear some relation to the truth, but they cannot, they must not, substitute for imagination.

Experience is where imagination starts. How we organize and reconvene experience, how we imagine ourselves consequent to it, is the toil of memory and how we become the persons we are – how we have stories to begin with. Freud and Sullivan were able to tell us a story about development from *their* stories, from *their* development. It may not matter whether our stories are true or not – in a sense, stories are never exactly true – nor may it matter whether they stem from wishes or from memories, from dissociated experience or from that which has been recognized and formulated. What matters most is whether or not these stories are good stories, stories that help us to know ourselves and others more deeply, stories that we can live with. Experiencing and observing ourselves in all complexes of memories *and* wishes, and living to reinvent ourselves through narrative, is the wellspring and the *action* of psychoanalysis.

In our stories we are, always, characters and authors both. This recognition is akin to Sullivan's description of the analyst as a participant observer, one who both acts and is acted upon, who notices and is noticed. It admits the role of influence and its bidirectionality in our development and in our work as psychoanalysts. It's a central task of living to recognize the varieties of influence upon us and then to account for them. Theory, of course, is one kind of accounting. It follows an awareness – conscious or unconscious, cognitive or sensory – of experience. Paradoxically, influence prompts theory and theory explains influence. Influence is an expression of some experience in material reality, and theory is an imaginative elaboration of and from that experience. It's not enough to amble in the precincts of the mind when the world routinely has its way with us, just as it's not enough to forswear imagination and fantasy for veridicality. Material and psychic reality necessarily converge in theory.

It's one of the great myths of our theory that the analyst can stand apart from his own participation. Participation and absorption are essential concomitants of influence and necessary adjuncts to perception. We can't perceive others without the willingness and the capacity to be absorbed by them. The fantasy that we can and should be past embeddedness, past immersive absorption, and that we can accomplish some stringent neutrality, disavows our vulnerability to influence. Many in our field still believe that conceptual clarity can only be achieved outside the realm of participation – that it's pure mentation. But we don't know ourselves, or others, through mentation alone. We learn things, and we learn them by formulating experience and by *experimentation*. Experimentation, the attempt to do something new or to see what will happen, entails our participation. Such involvement is often unwitting and beyond our awareness. And it changes us. In psychoanalysis, the wish to stand outside of our participation, or to disavow it altogether, is the wish to renounce influence and vulnerability *methodized* as a psychoanalytic ideal (Troise, 2014). It can be argued that this wish is itself a response to trauma.

Because trauma has played and plays such a significant role in our thinking about therapeutic action *and* in therapeutic action itself, the analytic field, as both a dynamic, potential space and as a profession, is a field wherein the analyst is a medium to repair its participant selves. Thus, in the analytic field, the analyst does not provide experience, he is experience. In terms of dynamic relevance, the form of an analytic exchange – how we are with our patients determined by our experience and how we see things – gives shape to the field and to its content (Troise, 2013). This is to say that our influences *and* our experiences are responsible not only for how we think about our work, for the theories we imagine or espouse, but *also* for how the field itself is forged and for how it develops. In the analytic field, patients and analysts reconvene important aspects of their histories and, as they do this, the field expands and coalesces into some variation of experiences that they have both lived before. As the form of a psychoanalytic exchange is determined by every lived and fantasied experience that both participants bring to it, it's very likely that some dimension of trauma is often, if not usually, a significant part of this interchange. In this way, the analytic field may be regarded, in practice *and* in theory, as a traumatic field.

In the face of trauma, we hope for fantasy. What is wounding about experience, what may corrupt our reason and hurt us past what seems bearable, is that which imagination cannot modify and transfigure. All psychoanalytic theories are essentially poetics, experience transmogrified into aesthetic expression. They are, perforce, imaginative constructs, mutative, and so crucial, counterfeits. Whatever we know, we know because of what we have experienced *and* what we have imagined, what we have forged. We cannot say which is more important, which better describes what it is to be sensate and alive. Imagination and experience are correspondent practices. Each needs the other to begin. If our experience has been specifically traumatic, marked by some immutable sorrow or terror, we must hope for an act of imagination to free us from the constraints of memory. But if we cannot remember, if we are, in a sense, *too* imaginative, delusive rather than allusive, then of course we are destined to repeat that which we cannot know until at last we can know it again. And then we must forget again. Psychoanalysis represents both of these responses to trauma. It is a haunted rendition of remembering and forgetting, a house apart from and a part of what we can see. If there are ghosts storming against its invisible walls, how can we say that we are not among them?

***

Psychoanalysis starts with a question – well, two questions really. One is: What happened? And the other is: How shall I live? We need to know the truth about what happened, insofar as it's possible, and then we need to translate what we've learned, to make it credible or *in*credible, so that we can live differently than we have been. This is especially true where trauma is concerned. How we accommodate or deny the force of influence and its impact upon us is how we find our way to theory, to the stories we live by. The history of psychoanalysis has its roots in trauma. Its architects, Freud and Sullivan chief among them, transformed their suffering into theory, though from very different standpoints. If things go well, we help our patients, especially those who have known trauma, do the same. We do this in a dynamic field that is shaped by our separate but intersecting histories. We hope that when our patients leave us, they will have their *own* story, their *own* theory.

When I was a boy and my mother disappeared, I asked where she went. I was told she was shopping. So I developed a theory: I reasoned that if she were shopping, she'd be back. After a while, when she didn't return, I abandoned *this* theory, and for a time I forgot all about her. But not really. Today, if I'm honest, I think there are ways in which I'm still waiting for her – not to return, but to tell me that she's gone. That's the theory now.

Notes

1 Cole Swensen, *Gravesend*, © 2012 by the Regents of the University of California. Published by the University of California Press. Reprinted with their kind permission.

2 Parts of this chapter are published in a volume edited by A. Harris, M. Kalb, and S. Klebanoff, entitled *Ghosts in the Consulting Room: Echoes of Trauma in Psychoanalysis* (Routledge, 2016). Reprinted by permission of Taylor & Francis, LLC.

References

Breger, L. (2000). *Freud: Darkness in the Midst of Vision*. New York: John Wiley.

Masson, J. M. (ed.) (1985). *The Complete Letters of Sigmund Freud to Wilhelm Fliess, 1887–1904*. Cambridge: The Belknap Press of Harvard University Press.

Troise, D. (2012). Inventing Sullivan: a review of *Sullivan Revisited: Life and Work. Contemporary Psychoanalysis*, 48, 590–596.

Troise, D. (2013). Field of vision: radical uncertainty and the analyst's conduct: commentary on paper by Donnel B. Stern. *Psychoanalytic Dialogues*, 23, 517–525.

Troise, D. (2014). Men under influence: a review of *Thirteen Ways of Looking at a Man: Psychoanalysis and Masculinity. Contemporary Psychoanalysis*, 50, 274–280.

Troise, D. (2016). A crucial counterfeit. In A. Harris, M. Kalb, & S. Klebanoff (Eds.), *Ghosts in the Consulting Room: Echoes of Trauma in Psychoanalysis*. London: Routledge.

Chapter 6

Trauma and psychoanalysis

Hierarchies of suffering

Jack Drescher

In reflecting on the question, "What has the effect of trauma been on the development of psychoanalysis?" I found myself thinking about the post-war period during which émigré Jewish analysts spoke and wrote disparagingly of "homosexuals." A scholar who has contributed important work on this subject is Kenneth Lewes (1988). In his book, *The Psychoanalytic Theory of Male Homosexuality*, he documents a post-war period in language that faintly echoed the moralizing, anti-Semitic diatribes of the Nazis:

> It is a striking fact of our history that both the conviction that homosexual object choice was necessarily psychopathological and the extremity of negative characterizations of homosexual general functioning became prominent in the years following World War II . . . I suggest that the historical trauma of the war was one cause of this shift in opinion . . . It is remarkable how many times in the postwar period homosexuals were compared to Nazis [and] this period [saw the use of a] chilling phrase, *a solution to the problem of homosexuality.*
>
> (p. 232, italics in original)

More recently, Emily Kuriloff conducted interviews with analysts who survived the Holocaust (2014). She theorized about the impact of the Shoah on psychoanalysis: not just those analysts who were personally caught up in it, but its impact on psychoanalytic theories and organizations around the world. I was one of several analysts Kuriloff interviewed because she wanted to include children of Holocaust survivors. In her interview, she asked me how my "sensibility as a thinker, writer, and clinician" has been affected by the Holocaust. It was an interesting question, as in the decades prior to being invited to participate in her project, I had mostly written about gender and sexuality (Drescher, 1998, 2007, 2010), but I had never written about the Holocaust. I knew, however, even before I became an analyst, that I had been deeply affected by my Polish Jewish parents' experiences and how they transmitted those experiences to my two brothers and me. Further, my life partner's parents were survivors of the Armenian genocide. Obviously it is not a coincidence when children of survivors find each other.

Yet I was somewhat reluctant to go down this route. I have difficulties with reductionist formulations that I (or anyone) would make a series of professional and personal choices based entirely on unconscious factors associated with parental trauma. It's a little bit like being told you are an alcoholic or that you are depressed because you have a genetic disease. Whether you do or not, this type of paradigm can sometimes come across as downplaying the role of free will and personal agency in making life choices.

On the other hand, I also sensed that part of my reluctance to engage with Kuriloff's questions stemmed from a desire to dissociate from the painful feelings that such an inquiry would entail. Given that much of my clinical and academic work emphasizes the value of psychic integration over dissociation, uncomfortable as that may sometimes be, I decided to answer her. Some of those thoughts and feelings are what follow.[1]

My parents were both born in Poland. My father, who died in 2003 at the age of 91, lost his parents, two sisters, and innumerable relatives to the concentration camps. My mother, who passed away in 2016 at the age of 91, was only 14 when Poland was invaded in 1939. Her nuclear family survived intact as they, like my father, fled the German invaders of Poland by moving to the Soviet-occupied side of the 1939 invasion. All of my mother's extended family who could not leave and stayed behind perished.

After going east, my parents spent the war years in the Soviet Union, which is how they survived.[2] Shortly after Polish refugees arrived at the Russian-occupied side of Poland, in what is now the Ukraine, my parents were offered citizenship. They – and many like them – refused because they were told that Soviet citizens could never leave the country. Those who refused citizenship were then regarded as enemy aliens and deported to Siberian work camps. Before they met each other, both my parents spent 14 months in those camps.

In 1941, Germany invaded Russia, which then switched sides and joined the Allies. Poles were no longer considered enemies of the state but citizens of an allied nation. Since they could not be sent back to German-occupied Poland, many were relocated to Soviet Central Asia. My parents ended up in Bukhara in Uzbekistan, where they were introduced and eventually married.

In 1946, my parents were repatriated to Poland but, as many returning Jews who feared for their lives did, they left rather quickly, staying only six weeks. They made their way from Poland – by bribing their way across several illegal border crossings – to Austria, where they surrendered themselves as refugees to the western allies and were sent to a displaced persons camp in Ulm, Germany. My older brother and several cousins were born in that displaced persons camp in 1947. Thanks to my father's cousin, who came to the U.S. before the war, my parents and brother were given permission to enter the U.S. in 1949. They arrived on October 12, Columbus Day, and as it was a holiday, were not allowed to disembark until October 13. I was born in 1951 and my younger brother in 1953. My parents became naturalized U.S. citizens in 1954.

I have a recurrent visual memory of being seven or eight years old with the entire family seated in front of the television watching a Channel 13 documentary about the Holocaust. My parents said, "Sit, watch, and learn," or something along those lines. In my mind's eye, I can still see an image of splayed naked, dead bodies piled up inside a gas chamber or outside a crematorium. However what I "see" could not have happened as I now remember it because I see the images, which in reality were black and white, as yellowed – like old photographs or newspaper clippings.

Obviously, transmitting lessons about catastrophic historical events can be traumatizing to young children. I contrast this "screen memory" with my experience in the mid-1990s of visiting Washington DC's Holocaust Museum with my parents and my younger brother's family. His twin boys, not yet 12 years old, were not allowed into the main museum. I distinctly remember a light bulb going off in my head: *age-appropriate learning!* Not a concept with which my parents or their cohort were familiar when I was growing up. As an adult, I came to understand that they tried to protect us by teaching us about the dangers they had faced as Jews. As an analyst, I came to understand some of the possibly hostile, aggressive, and envious meanings of these actions as well.

As a psychiatric resident in the early 1980s, I met fellow trainees who identified as, and went to support groups for, "children of survivors." However, I was wary of taking on the formal identity of "child of Holocaust survivors." In retrospect, it felt too much like embracing a victim's identity. One lesson I had taken away from the Passover *hagaddah* and seven years of *talmud torah* (Hebrew school) was *how* the Israelites had to transcend victim status. Moses said, "Let my people go." He *demanded* they be freed from slavery. Then, after a period of recidivism, a lapse in faith that led to the creation and worship of a golden calf, he and his people were forced to wander in the desert for 40 years. Another lesson I learned: no one who had grown up with the mindset of a slave would live to enter the Promised Land.

My family history undoubtedly shaped some of my present-day attitudes about taking on a victim role. Early in my career, I came up with a term, which I've only written about once in passing (Drescher, 2000), that I call *hierarchies of suffering.* In our family the hierarchy of suffering went something like this: given what my parents had endured, how could any problem we children faced *ever* compare with that? My exasperated mother's favorite line when she felt angry and overwhelmed by three energetic boys? "What Hitler and Stalin didn't finish, you kids are going to finish!" This was not exactly the kind of thing one usually hears in response to a note from the teacher saying she wants to meet and discuss your school performance with your parents.

In other words, like many who have experienced life-threatening trauma, my parents found it difficult to react proportionately to mundane childhood problems. You have a problem with a teacher? "Teachers are *always* right, so better not to have problems with them at all because it's probably your fault." The underlying message: better to work any problem out yourself than bring it to your parents. Mundane problems, what Interpersonalist analysts think of as *problems in living,* could be infused with levels of anxiety of catastrophic proportions associated with *problems of survival.* In order to keep parental anxieties at bay, as children we had to make no waves, go to school, get good grades, do as we were told, become good Jews, grow up to be successful professionals (God willing a doctor), marry Jewish girls (ideally girls who had Polish Jewish parents as well), be fruitful and multiply, and replenish the world with new Jews to replace those who had been lost in the Holocaust and for whom we children, *Srul*, *Yankel* and *Moishe*, were all named. At least I managed to get the "be a doctor" part down correctly.

Hierarchies of suffering did not just organize parent–child relationships in our family. There were other permutations. When I was an adolescent, my mother told me, in what I today remember as an embarrassed whisper, that she and my father were "not really survivors." "Real survivors" was a term intended for those who had been in concentration camps. My parents had no arm tattoos, one of the most visible scars of *true* Holocaust survivors. They were just "escapees." Internment in Siberian forced-labor camps, relocation to Bukhara, the loss of nuclear and extended family, all their possessions, and their native homeland – none of those entailed as much hierarchical suffering as being in a concentration camp.

Then, even among the "real survivors," hierarchies of suffering emerged along diverse lines: how horrific were the events leading up to one's internment; the reputation of a particular concentration camp; how many family members and relatives were lost; which relatives were lost: parents, spouses, or children – or everybody; how much time was spent in the camp, and the like. And symbolically placed at the apex of the hierarchy, even above survivors who suffered most, were the six million who were lost. These hierarchies of suffering were a group adaptation, creating a new sense of order in which every European Jew, regardless of what he or she had endured, had a place.

I have used the hierarchy-of-suffering concept in my clinical work, both with couples and with individuals. For example, each member of a couple usually enters treatment with a litany of complaints. Each seeks to occupy some *moral high ground* that equates and elevates one's own injuries at the hands of a spouse or partner to a higher plane of suffering.

I tell couples who cannot get past this starting position that their differences remind me of the Israeli–Palestinian conflict. There, both sides intermittently seek to occupy the moral high ground by insisting *as a precondition for negotiations* that their own history of suffering be acknowledged as the greater of the two. Occasionally, both sides in the Middle East are able to move past this deadlocking posture of "who has suffered the most" and talk to each other. Then some incident reactivates the need to claim the moral high ground ("I was injured; you need to condemn the injuring party before I will go forward"). Sadly, whatever other purposes such posturing may serve, it is difficult, if not impossible, to negotiate a lasting agreement with a spouse or partner (or a hostile neighbor) from the position of the moral high ground.

In the remainder of this paper, I turn to the question, "Is psychoanalysis, in theory and in practice, a traumatic field?" The answer is yes. Specifically, Kuriloff (2014) takes up the issue of how the field and its practitioners were traumatized by the Shoah. Further, the analytic setup itself could reasonably be contextualized as "a traumatic field." Our patients come in because they are in pain and we invite them to dig up painful memories. Presumably, we draw upon our own painful memories to assist us in empathizing with patients.

Yet part of me responds to the question of whether psychoanalysis is a traumatic field by wanting to know, why ask the question at all? Here I'm reminded of the analytic version of an old Jewish joke, "Why does a psychoanalyst answer a question with a question?" The response is, "Why shouldn't a psychoanalyst answer a question with a question?" So other questions come to mind in response to this question. Does asking about one's trauma arise from a desire to claim some moral high ground in some as-yet unformulated hierarchy of suffering? If so, to whom and to what might psychoanalysis be compared?

For example, is psychoanalysis more traumatized than fields where one comes into contact with physical and mental trauma on a daily basis: police, firefighters, emergency medical services workers, oncologists, and emergency room physicians? Could the effects of trauma, which in individuals may provoke severe dissociation, provide any insights about the fragmentation of psychoanalysis into "part-fields," as Paul Stepansky (2009) characterizes the differing schools with diverse starting assumptions about what constitutes analytic inquiry and treatment?

Are the field's practitioners feeling traumatized by attacks from managed care companies? Is the present cultural tendency toward quick fixes for complicated problems demoralizing enough to provoke traumatic responses? Is there a pill to fix what ails psychoanalysis? Is it wrong to wish for that? Is this question about trauma motivated by the current crisis in which psychoanalysis finds itself? In other words, has psychoanalysis been traumatized by its descent from its once lofty professional stature of the mid-twentieth century?

Frankly, many historians, both inside and outside psychoanalysis, would accord us a rather low position in any professional hierarchy of suffering. This is because it is the most innocent who populate the apex and, as any student of analytic history knows (Eisold, 2003), many of the field's injuries are self-inflicted. Psychoanalysis has hurt itself by promoting theoretical dogma over rigorous testing; by rewarding adherence to dogma over skepticism; by adopting rigid seniority systems that stifled innovation by younger colleagues; by an unwillingness to integrate data from non-analytic sources that contradicted analytic claims; by overpromising therapeutic efficacy; and by fragmenting into "schools" that willfully practiced in isolation from, or in opposition with, each other as long as they had enough candidates and patients to do so.

Yet repeatedly lamenting our field's present state of suffering will not help regain the social and professional stature psychoanalysis once held. What might? Psychoanalysis needs to abandon the victim stance. If we were treating a patient, we would start by empathizing with her losses but then eventually point out her need to reconsider the repetitive way of doing things and the need to try different kinds of actions. In this case it means psychoanalysis has to give up any claims of occupying a moral high ground. Instead, it would be more helpful to admit errors, to acknowledge past shortcomings, and to identify and correct the ways in which psychoanalysis contributed to its own decline.

Such corrections would involve greater integration of contemporary psychoanalysts with other disciplines, particularly hard and social sciences where academic rigor carries greater weight in scientific journals than poetic writing. For a field so engaged with the use of language, it is not particularly clarifying to have multiple meanings for terms like transference and countertransference. Analytic schools need to work collaboratively and identify the essence of what is good and useful about analytic work – regardless of school or theoretical position – and then demonstrate those merits to skeptics.

It would also help if analysts learned to explain to the public what they can and cannot do using language that most people can understand. Just as competent physicians can translate complex medical jargon into terms patients can comprehend, psychoanalysts might benefit from learning to do the same.

And, for the record, the public is uninterested in questions that repeatedly preoccupy analytic journals, such as, "Are there one, two, or three people in the room?" or "Are we a science or a hermeneutic discipline?" or "How many times a week constitutes a real analysis?"

By doing something different, by taking responsibility for presenting what we do to the world we actually live in, rather than the world we would like to live in, psychoanalysis might have a chance of bringing an end to its own suffering.

Notes

1 In retrospect, my decision was correct. Although I considered applying for Polish citizenship in 2003 after my father's death, I only made one inquiry at New York City's Polish consulate and then let the matter drop. However, after a detailed response to Kuriloff's queries in 2010, I actively embarked upon the citizenship process. This involved getting a lawyer in Warsaw, consulting with my mother for more details of their refugee odyssey, and obtaining and translating numerous documents from U.S., Polish, and international agencies. After seven months of activity, I was granted Polish (and European Union citizenship) in May 2011 and a Polish passport a few months later.

2 A 2007 documentary, *Saved by Deportation*, chronicles the experiences of Polish Jews saved by Stalin's deportations. According to the film's website (http://www.savedbydeportation.com/), "In 1940, a year before the Nazis started deporting Jews to death camps, Joseph Stalin ordered the deportation of approximately 200,000 Polish Jews from Russian-occupied Eastern Poland to forced labor settlements in the Soviet interior. The deportees constituted the overwhelming majority of Polish Jews who escaped the Nazi Holocaust."

References

Drescher, J. (1998). *Psychoanalytic Therapy and the Gay Man.* New York: Routledge.

Drescher, J. (2000). Cornucopia: responses to Rosario, Cohler, Orange, Roughton and Shelby's discussions of *Psychoanalytic Therapy and the Gay Man. Gender & Psychoanalysis,* 5(3): 291–319.

Drescher, J. (2007). From bisexuality to intersexuality: rethinking gender categories. *Contemporary Psychoanalysis,* 43(2): 204–228.

Drescher, J. (2010). Queer diagnoses: parallels and contrasts in the history of homosexuality, gender variance, and the *Diagnostic and Statistical Manual* (DSM). *Archives of Sexual Behavior,* 39: 427–460.

Eisold, K. (2003). The profession of psychoanalysis: past failures and future possibilities. *Contemporary Psychoanalysis,* 39: 557–582.

Kuriloff, E. A. (2014). *Contemporary Psychoanalysis and the Legacy of the Third Reich: History, Memory, Tradition.* New York: Routledge.

Lewes, K. (1988). *The Psychoanalytic Theory of Male Homosexuality.* New York: Simon and Schuster.

Stepansky, P. E. (2009). *Psychoanalysis at the Margins.* New York: Other Press.

Part III

Utters from the gutters

Political loyalties and the clash of deeply held values in the consulting room

Chapter 7

Political identity and countertransference

Steven Tublin

In the brief essay that follows, I will address a class of transferential and countertransferential experience that receives little attention in the Relational psychoanalytic literature. I am referring to the emotional reactions one experiences when engaging a person whose political identity and values clash with one's own. I will highlight the unique difficulties that such transferential matrices create and will argue that the technical stances adopted to address such conflicts are not likely to resolve these difficulties in treatment.[1]

A clash of political identity – what, for simplicity's sake, I will call "political transference" – is unlike other transference/countertransference matrices. First, to state the obvious, political identity is unlike other identity categories in that it is intrinsically and inescapably adversarial. Being a Democrat or a Republican is therefore not like being a Sagittarius or a Philadelphian. Neither is it fully like "deeper" categories such as male/female or gay/straight, which, though depicting opposite ends of a constructed binary, need not imply hostile opposition. In the American two-party system, being a Democrat or Republican entails, *by definition,* being opposed to the other party – as political figures, as people, and as moral actors in the cultural domain. The two parties exist to engage each other in a battle for power, for a vision of a just society, and for group prominence. And, the more deeply identified one is with one political group, the sharper one's antipathy toward the other party and its members.

Second, I think it is important to recognize that politics, at least for those who hold positions on these matters, is a more fundamental, inner-dwelling component of self-definition than the domain of ideas and opinions which can be altered with relatively little disruption to a person's sense of self. Political identity is a meaning-giving, morally driven sense of one's place in the world, one that influences not only one's fundamental values and how one sees things, but where and how one lives, who one associates with, how one dresses, what one spends money on, and how one feels about oneself. In a word, one doesn't vote Democrat or Republican so much as one *is* a Democrat or Republican.

And last, the partisan experiences his or her politics with remarkably little friction. However prone to ambivalence a person might be in all other areas of life, politics seems to be felt with utter certainty. One never hears, for instance, "I'm a Democrat, but I hate myself for it." Political identity imposes a clear moral order upon the world, and the partisan knows who the good guys are and what are the proper principles. Political identification thus provides the person with a sense of belonging and an assurance of moral soundness. To say that I am a Democrat means that I am a member of the blue team; they are *my* people. I consider their values to be morally proper, their policies the ones that lead to a more just world, and the members of that group to be better human beings.

The world is thus simplified and the partisan finds he's always on the right side. This is then reinforced in conversation with like-minded group members who share talk of the greed, mendacity, and cognitive limitations of the other guys. Indeed, politics is the only area of contemporary life that I can think of where a kind of conscious splitting is utterly normative. For the partisan, there is little room for doubt, as equivocation carries the whiff of betrayal and risks questions of character. Indeed, venomous disparagement – really *hating* the opposition – connotes a righteous commitment to the just cause.

Committed activists carry this mode of adversarial certainty several degrees further, but the general picture described above could be applied to many citizens who consider themselves politically aligned. This would include most educated, well-informed citizens, a group that would encompass the vast majority of psychoanalytic clinicians and a great many patients. As such, both participants in each analytic dyad often enter the consulting room ready to view the other as either on their team and therefore morally sound and versed in the realities of the world, or on the other team, whose view of the world invites a measure of suspicion or negative judgment. Therefore when analyst's and patient's politics diverge, a morally inflected relational matrix will often emerge that creates an unusual challenge for both parties.

We have become accustomed to working with an array of countertransferential experiences – some intense, some puzzling, some disorganizing – the emergence of which, while unsettling, provides the analyst with information about the patient that is then ideally interwoven into the treatment. Analysts struggle daily with the complex task of remaining open to such experiences while at the same time trying to stand apart from them in order to reflect upon their origins and meaning.

However, political countertransference is often experienced and handled differently. The Relational analyst, working with an assertive, conservative patient, as he talks about his enmity toward Muslims, the corrosive effect of government entitlement programs, or his opposition to same-sex marriage and the rest of the "homosexual agenda," can certainly grow annoyed, infuriated, even disgusted. The registration of a passing hostility toward such a patient is itself unremarkable.

More notable, however, is that there seems to be little inclination with political countertransference for the analyst to thoroughly interrogate his own subjectivity. The analyst in my above example may wonder why the patient is speaking in a way likely to provoke his disdain, or what his own negative feelings might say about the patient's inner world. But, the notion that these feelings and attitudes might be shaped as much by the analyst's history, biases, and particular moral principles – that they are as subjective and relative as any other experience – has not, to my knowledge, been considered.

Rather, the Relational analyst facing the conservative's worldview and values is often thought to be reacting the way any reasonable, decent human being would respond in the face of an objectively noxious stimulus. The analyst might silently wonder, "What experiences led this person to such objectionable positions?" Or, in more explicitly partisan terms, "What led this person to become an awful Republican?" But, what I have not heard asked in this context is: why do Republicans *seem* so awful? And relatedly, how did it happen that Relational clinicians are all Democrats, progressives, or neo-Marxists?

To those on the left, the answer to the first question seems sadly obvious. During the most recent legislative session, the Republican majority in the House of Representatives attempted to cut the budget for food stamps. Left-leaning citizens generally hear this and ask, "What kind of person wants to starve poor children?" The Republican party wants to balance the government's multi-trillion dollar deficit by cutting Social Security and Medicare benefits. Again, the left would ask, "What kind of person wants to impoverish old people and reduce their medical care?" Republicans (albeit with some increasingly prominent exceptions) seem far more willing than Democrats to employ the ferocious power of the American military throughout the world and seem less concerned with the death and destruction that ensue. To most on the left, this seems incomprehensibly callous. These policies and the people who promote them seem awful because, to those on the left, they simply *are* awful.

The nearly universal leftward tilt among Relational clinicians logically follows. We are all liberals or progressives because we're smart, educated, and compassionate people (or so we like to believe). Many readers, genuinely puzzled, might well ask, "What else would we be?" To the left-leaning partisan, conservatives and Republicans seem to be morally repellent people; in the United States, it simply makes no sense for informed, decent people to be anything other than Democrats or liberals. That conservatives harbor very similar feelings – that *they* are right and good and smart, that the left is populated by the selfish, the ill-informed, the arrogant, and the hypocritical – provokes only fury and confusion on the left.

Of course, some experience this political disjunction far less viscerally. Some Relational analysts live their politics with greater distance. So, while their values may largely align with their more assertive peers, they can put aside at least some political disagreements and retain their stance of general acceptance toward their right-leaning patients.

However, it's hard to know how many accomplish this task, or how they manage it, because no one to my knowledge has written about the issue of political divergence. Rather, the modest literature addressing the issue of politics in the analytic consulting room seems to assume a leftward tilt in the politics of both the analyst and the patient (e.g., Botticelli, 2004; Samuels, 1993, 2004). So seamlessly does this work present the meeting of two left-leaning people that, in reading it, one gets the impression that there are no right-leaning Relational analysts (which is probably not true) and no right-leaning patients (which is obviously not true).

But, absent a thorough sample of politically introspective accounts, it is hard to know how analysts deal with the conflict of values that I am addressing. From anecdotal evidence drawn from conversations with colleagues and students, as well as many intriguingly unguarded posts on online colloquia (where the medium seems to cultivate a fantasy of unanimity and safety which then fosters an unusual candor), my impression is that the approach most commonly employed is to work with the right-leaning patient as best one can while trying to avoid the tension of mutual political antipathy.

Not surprisingly, those who try this approach report that it's quite difficult. I've heard a number of people describe it in pained and awkward terms, as the silent, if unwelcome, disdain felt toward the patient generates a certain cynicism and a feeling of hopelessness about the treatment. Some analysts describe nevertheless persevering in such circumstances, hoping the treatment will cultivate a greater capacity for empathy in the patient and then somehow a natural evolution to the more "humane" politics of the Democratic party. Beyond the bleak cast imparted to a treatment conducted in this manner, it is worth noting that this approach effectively treats right-leaning politics as intrinsically pathological, a premise arguably true in more extreme cases but one meriting a more nuanced conceptualization in a thorough understanding of political identity.

A less common solution to this problem is to make it a matter of professional policy never to work with Republicans. There is a simple elegance to this stance and certainly all clinicians ought to retain the right not to see a patient they'd prefer not to see. Though, if widely employed, this policy would yield a situation in which Relational psychoanalysis and psychotherapy become treatments offered only by progressives to other progressives.

One occasionally encounters a third approach, in which the analyst, hoping to bring the potentially destructive tension out of the shadows, speaks openly about his political inclinations and the depth of disagreement that exists between him and his patient. One can imagine how this approach might offer the potential to integrate these divergences into the dyadic engagement. But this position too carries considerable risk if presented in a hierarchical or judgmental manner. If, for instance, the analyst proceeds in an evangelical spirit where the analyst endeavors to "teach" the patient the proper politics (e.g., Walls, 2006), one should anticipate suboptimal results. Discussing politics openly but *without* judgment or a wish to influence can be very, very difficult – imagine, for a moment, trying to maintain non-critical curiosity while listening to a patient rail about "libs'" infringement on second amendment rights immediately following the Newtown massacre – but if this issue is to be engaged at all I think this is the only way it can be done.[2]

That is because, in order to navigate this dilemma, the analyst must be prepared to do something that may feel impossible. In order to fully engage a Republican in treatment, not in the truncated way that treads carefully around his political worldview and identity, the analyst must be prepared to reflect upon his own most basic political assumptions and be ready, not just to learn a thing or two, but to reflect upon his defining values. In a word, the analyst must consider negotiating his non-negotiables (Pizer, 1998), the values he would otherwise never think to question.

There is now, within Relational psychoanalysis, a growing literature employing political theory and constructs to understand patients' suffering, therapeutic change, and technique. This literature is uniformly and unapologetically left in its perspective (cf. Dimen, 2004; Guralnik and Simeon, 2010; Harris, 2012; Layton, 2009; Walls, 2006). Therefore, to get a perspective that looks at political divergence in a non-partisan manner, it is necessary to consult psychological sources outside the domain of psychoanalysis.[3] Here I will be relying primarily on the extensive research of the social psychologist Jonathan Haidt and his colleagues, who have studied the moral underpinnings of various political positions. Haidt (2013) has analyzed several large samples in the United States as well as a variety of demographic groups in India and Brazil. And he has found that moral intuitions rest on five distinct foundations (as he calls them): care/harm, fairness/cheating, loyalty/betrayal, authority/subversion, and sanctity/degradation.

All five have at least some resonance with most people, but there are enormous cultural differences, differentiated both by class and geographical region, in the prominence accorded the various foundations in the formation of moral judgment. The end result of this differentiation – and here I am collapsing a library full of social science theory and data – is that around the world and even here in our own country, people rely on widely divergent moral principles to arrive at the values that underlie their politics. Each of these principles is defensible in evolutionary terms and equal in the hold that it has on the psyche of the individual. As a result, we live among people whose morals and politics we find utterly repugnant. And they feel exactly the same way about us.

In particular, Haidt and his colleagues (Graham et al., 2009, 2011; Haidt and Graham, 2007, 2009) found that the politics of the left rely primarily upon two moral foundations: those of care/harm and fairness/cheating. This is why policies diminishing the welfare state are anathema to the left for whom reducing the social safety net beneath the poor and old seems both cruel and unfair and therefore immoral.

But Haidt found that the moral intuitions of people on the right rest on a wider base of principles. As with the left, they do incorporate an ethic of care in their moral intuitions, though they weight it less strongly. And the right also values fairness but, interestingly, they define it differently. Fairness on the left is measured in terms of equality. No one should get too much or too little. The presence in a society of abject poverty juxtaposed with opulent wealth is viewed as evidence of injustice in social policy. However, fairness on the right is measured via what Haidt (2013, p. 169) calls "proportionality." You get what you earn, not more. Inequality is not, in and of itself, immoral.

But the most marked differences come from the right's greater reliance upon the remaining three moral foundations (Haidt and Graham, 2007). Sanctity, for instance, figures prominently in social conservatives' condemnation of many behaviors involving sex or the body in general. One hears the phrases "sanctity of life" and "sanctity of marriage" in debates about social issues. And homosexuality is deplored in religious terms that borrow from the lexicon of purity or decadence. Sanctity as a source of moral judgment barely registers on the left.[4]

There is also, on the right, a far greater reverence for tradition and a wish to protect social institutions such as conventional marriage. Such institutions are viewed with suspicion among the left as instruments for the maintenance of oppressive power relations (thereby violating their ethic of fairness). But among the right they are revered for their ordering of society and the cultural wisdom they are thought to embody.

As it happens, the moral foundations of leftist politics overlap perfectly with the guiding premises of Relational psychoanalysis. Both rest primarily upon empathy, care, and the notion of fairness as defined by equality. Moreover, Relational psychoanalysis retains a subversive, anti-authoritarianism. This theme has been present in psychoanalysis perhaps since Freud and later came front and center in the writing of theorists like Erich Fromm (1941, 1947). That element has been further emphasized in recent Relational work bearing the strong influence of critical and post-structural theory (e.g., Botticelli, 2004; Cushman, 1995, 2009; Dimen, 2004; Harris, 2009, 2012; Layton, 2006, 2009, 2014; Rozmarin, 2010, 2011). This recent work views conformity and adaptation with suspicion and aims to fortify patients in the struggle with what are viewed as oppressive trends (e.g., heteronormativity and rampant consumerism) that exist within broader society. Moreover, like much of progressive politics and more than other psychoanalytic groups, Relational psychoanalysis, in its moderation of the analyst's role as expert and its emphases on reciprocal influence and mutual inquiry (Hoffman, 1983, 1996), rejects the traditionalism and reverence for authority that so influence the moral intuitions of the right.

As a result, one can expect that, when treating right-leaning patients, the left-leaning Relational analyst will encounter a worldview premised on at least some moral intuitions that seem not moral at all. And because these are deep value judgments, the ensuing countertransference will often lodge in the analyst's psyche in ways that easier differences, easier Othernesses (Haidt et al., 2003), will not. For this reason, I believe therapeutic management of such situations requires much deeper consideration than has been dedicated to date.

In sum, political identity presents a unique countertransferential dilemma in that awareness of it provides no avenue towards its resolution. The visceral hold of political identity, its inherently adversarial orientation, its associated moral certitude, and the evolutionary utility of the group belongingness that accompanies it, create a substantial obstacle to the general acceptance of the other that we regard as a necessary condition for transformative analytic work. In order to perform this work, the analyst must imagine himself having different basic moral principles, in effect not valuing the premises that make him decent and humane in his own eyes. Moreover, in broadening the scope of potential moral intuitions, the analyst risks being shunned within his own community, because psychoanalysis, like everything else, is embedded in world riven by political difference. And in politics, you're either one of us, or you're one of them (Berreby, 2006).

Notes

1 Almost all Relational analysts identify politically left (a situation I address later in this chapter). For that reason, in discussing treatments where the participants' politics diverge, I portray an analyst who identifies somewhere on the left and a patient somewhere right. There are, to be sure, a small number of right-leaning Relational analysts, and I apologize to them as this paper will seem not to address their work experience.

2 Once explicit, it may become apparent to either member of the dyad that the political or moral differences are too stark to overcome and that the extended meeting of *these* two minds is not in the patient's best interest.

3 The field of psychology, like most of the academy today (e.g., Gross, 2013), leans decidedly left (Duarte et al., 2015; Redding, 2001). That skew, while marked, is less pronounced than is observed in Relational psychoanalysis.

4 One does encounter some reliance upon notions of purity and sanctity in the environmental movement and in other narrower concerns regarding food supply.

References

Berreby, D. (2006). *Us and Them: Understanding your Tribal Mind.* New York: Little, Brown.

Botticelli, S. (2004). The politics of relational psychoanalysis. *Psychoanalytic Dialogues,* 14: 635–651.

Cushman, P. (1995). *Constructing the Self, Constructing America: A Cultural History of Psychotherapy.* Reading, MA: Addison-Wesley.

Cushman, P. (2009). Empathy – what one hand giveth, the other taketh away: commentary on paper by Lynn Layton. *Psychoanalytic Dialogues,* 19: 121–137.

Dimen, M. (2004). The return of the dissociated: discussion. *Psychoanalytic Dialogues,* 14: 859–865.

Duarte, J., Crawford, J., Stern, C., Haidt, J., Jussim, L., and Tetlock, P. (2015). Political diversity will improve social psychological science. *Behavioral and Brain Sciences,* 38: 1–13.

Fromm, E. (1941). *Escape From Freedom.* New York: Avon Books.

Fromm, E. (1947). *Man for Himself: An Inquiry into the Psychology of Ethics.* New York: Holt, Rinehart, and Winston.

Graham, J., Haidt, J., and Nosek, B. (2009). Liberals and conservatives rely on different sets of moral values. *Journal of Personality and Social Psychology,* 96: 1029–1046.

Graham, J., Nosek, B., Haidt, J., Iyer, R., Koleva, S., and Ditto, P. (2011). Mapping the moral domain. *Journal of Personality and Social Psychology,* 101: 366–385.

Gross, N. (2013). *Why Are Professors Liberal and Why Do Conservatives Care?* Cambridge, MA: Harvard University Press.

Guralnik, O., and Simeon, D. (2010). Depersonalization: standing in the spaces between recognition and interpellation. *Psychoanalytic Dialogues,* 20: 400–416.

Haidt, J. (2013). *The Righteous Mind: Why Good People Are Divided by Politics and Religion.* New York: Pantheon Books.

Haidt, J., and Graham, J. (2007). When morality opposes justice: conservatives have moral intuitions that liberals may not recognize. *Social Justice Research,* 20: 98–116.

Haidt, J., and Graham, J. (2009). Planet of the Durkheimians, where community, authority, and sacredness are foundations of morality. In J. Jost, A. C. Kay, and H. Thorisdottir (Eds.), *Social and Psychological Bases of Ideology and System Justification.* New York: Oxford University Press, pp. 371–401.

Haidt, J., Rosenberg, E., and Hom, H. (2003). Differentiating diversities: moral diversity is not like other kinds. *Journal of Applied Social Psychology,* 33: 1–36.

Harris, A. (2009). You must remember this. *Psychoanalytic Dialogues,* 19: 2–21.

Harris, A. (2012). The house of difference, or white silence. *Studies in Gender and Sexuality,* 13: 197–216.

Hoffman, I. (1983). The patient as interpreter of the analyst's experience. *Contemporary Psychoanalysis,* 19: 389–422.

Hoffman, I. (1996). The intimate and ironic authority of the psychoanalyst's presence. *Psychoanalytic Quarterly,* 65: 102–136.

Layton, L. (2006). Racial identities, racial enactments, and normative unconscious processes. *Psychoanalytic Quarterly,* 75: 237–269.

Layton, L. (2009). Who's responsible? Our mutual implication in each other's suffering. *Psychoanalytic Dialogues,* 19: 105–120.

Layton, L. (2014). Grandiosity, neoliberalism, and neoconservatism. *Psychoanalytic Inquiry,* 34: 463–474.

Pizer, S. (1998). *Building Bridges: The Negotiation of Paradox in Psychoanalysis*. Hillsdale, NJ: The Analytic Press.

Redding, R. (2001). Sociopolitical diversity in psychology. *American Psychologist*, 56(3): 205–215.

Rozmarin, E. (2010). Better identity politics. *Psychoanalytic Dialogues*, 20: 181–190.

Rozmarin, E. (2011). To be is to betray: on the place of collective history and freedom in psychoanalysis. *Psychoanalytic Dialogues*, 21: 320–345.

Samuels, A. (Ed.) (1993). *The Political Psyche*. London: Routledge.

Samuels, A. (2004). Politics on the couch? Psychotherapy and society – some possibilities and some limitations. *Psychoanalytic Dialogues*, 14: 817–834.

Walls, G. (2006). The normative unconscious and the political contexts of change in psychotherapy. In L. Layton, N. C. Hollander, and S. Gutwill (Eds.), *Psychoanalysis, Class and Politics*. New York, NY: Routledge, pp. 118–128.

Chapter 8

The persistence of the past

Legacies of homophobia in a gay male therapy dyad[1]

Steven Botticelli

In our current moment of legalized same-sex marriage and other advances for gay rights, gay people would seem to have much to celebrate. Yet not all feel like celebrating. Some of us would like to look away from the damage done to us by homophobia as we look forward to the lives we may be able to lead in a more equitable, less hostile society. Yet others find the damage hard to forget. This paper is about a clash of subjectivities between a gay male therapist and his gay male patient, one trying to look toward a better future, the other determined not to forget the past.

From the beginning of our work together, it was clear that Gary lived in the grip of a redemptive fantasy. The signs of this were not subtle. "I want to be rescued," he told me. Gary's childhood had been unhappy: he'd grown up with an alcoholic father; witnessed his father screaming at and threatening his mother; he had been homophobically taunted by neighborhood kids and some years (not all) by kids at school; and he had, crucially, gone unmentalized by each of his parents. Gary's was an unhappy childhood, but not manifestly much worse than that of many other gay men I've known or worked with in therapy who have managed to make emotionally sustaining and satisfying lives for themselves. By contrast with such men, Gary lived his life in accordance with a benighted vision of gay life that most contemporary gay men have made every effort to escape. Painfully lonely but finding so much to distrust and dislike about other people, especially other gay men, Gary spent most of his time by himself in his apartment. Attractive enough that he sometimes was approached by other men on the rare occasions he put himself in their company, Gary nevertheless restricted his sex life to assignations with hustlers. He lived his life in a mode of regret for missed opportunities and choices not made, never seeming to notice (despite my repeatedly calling it to his attention) how this preoccupation kept him from becoming aware of the possibilities of the present.

In all of this Gary was the example *par excellence* of what queer theorist Heather Love (2007) has called "feeling backward." In her book *Feeling Backward: Loss and the Politics of Queer History*, Love cautions us against turning our backs on our "backward" feelings – shame, sadness, loneliness, regret, despair (and this is just part of her list) – all the emotional "stuff" of our personal and collective gay pasts. With epigrams like "Still Hurting" and "The Art of Losing," she means to bring into focus those aspects of our histories and current lives that we may wish to put behind us as we try to look ahead to a bright gay future. Nevertheless, in a turn of thought that is familiar to us as psychoanalysts, Love argues that the effort to maintain an "affirmative political vision" (2007, p. 105) will be haunted by the specter of our unhappy gay past to the extent that this past cannot be openly acknowledged, and even felt. "[I]t is the damaging aspects of the past that tend to stay with us" (p. 1). We are inevitably and specifically shaped by the ways we've been damaged. As Love astutely notes, the major tropes of gay liberation, pride and visibility are precisely the mirror images of the shame and secrecy that were the experience of the closet. Such seeming transformations are inevitably fragile: "Shame lives on in pride, and pride can easily turn back into shame" (p. 28). She questions the "culture of redemption" (Bersani, 1990) by which the history of antigay violence and stigmatization gets pressed into service to justify an insistence on progress and visions of an ever-improving gay future. Such insistence, she argues, "makes it harder to see the persistence of the past in the present" (p. 19).

As far as Gary was concerned, his current life had been fully determined by the injuries and insults of his childhood, which he revisited with me in all its sad, shame-ridden detail. How different it might be if he had been raised by different parents, in a different world and time, he mused. One day he saw my son and Noah (known to him by sight as my suitemate, not – consciously at least – as my husband) walking together outside the office. Noticing how carefully Noah seemed to be listening to our son as he spoke, Gary reflected bitterly on the lack of such attention he had received as a boy from his own parents.

How ashamed he felt about being gay. How often in telling me about a sexual image or fantasy would he next tell me about the disgusted reaction he imagined a heterosexual person would have to that image or fantasy. Often he was able to recognize the disgust as his own. "The idea of two old men as lovers – it's just gross," he told me one day. He was so immersed in living his shame, we never got to explore it. I knew what his shame felt like. I could empathize with him in these moments – to a point. I had had my own shame-filled childhood and adolescence, but lived now in a different relation to it than he. I remembered what it felt like to feel the way he did about men being physically and sexually intimate with each other, and listening to Gary, I'd feel relieved I didn't feel that way any more. In my own life I had worked hard to get past the feelings he described. As I came to recognize my distancing and relief as a countertransference block, I tried to notice the moments in my listening when I would shift away from his perspective to a place of some remove, wondering whether it would make a difference if I could stay closer to him through his shame-ridden reveries. Sometimes I felt angry at having to make the effort. It was 2005 (2006, 2007 . . .) for Christ's sake, things were different now; why couldn't he get with the program, go with the flow, make the best of the new possibilities that had opened up for us – as I had? Why couldn't he be more like me?

I had not always received Gary's feelings with exasperation. In the first years of our work, I had sometimes been brought to tears as Gary told me about an experience that evoked for me the memory of some adolescent mortification of my own. I had felt quite a bit for and with him in the pain of his childhood and had not questioned his wish for me to rescue him, working implicitly in accord with Anna Ornstein's (1995) precept that patients' "curative fantasies – no matter how infantile – [need to be] accepted as a legitimate insistence on experiences that they consider to be essential for the completion of their self-development" (p. 115). Over time, however, perhaps influenced by the birth of my son and my new acquaintance with my own redemptive wishes, I became impatient. I could watch my son growing and changing every day; Gary, on the other hand, seemed to stay the same. Furthermore, no one – nothing – was going to make it up to us, I was learning. One had to mourn one's losses and get on with life.

Especially concerning to me was the way in which Gary's very agency was countermanded by his curative fantasy, as its fulfillment was contingent precisely on his not acting on his own behalf. It seemed that if he could be passive enough, make himself abject enough in my eyes, not step out into the world in any of the ways he frequently imagined but never acted on, then I would be moved to step in and rescue him. For several years, Gary's fantasy took the form of the romantic, sexual relationship we would have, to be initiated by me at some point in the future, for which this time in therapy was serving as a prelude, a kind of extended courtship. The therapy had come alive as Gary spun out highly elaborated fantasies about us. These fantasies had provided a context for us to examine Gary's wishes and fears of closeness with another man, even as other avenues of exploration seemed foreclosed by his preoccupation with the question, "When are we going to do it?" I enjoyed Gary's fantasies, as they created a forum for our mutual engagement. What's more, sexually speaking, Gary often had my number. But his fantasies also made me anxious, as Gary seemed to talk about getting together sexually as something we might actually do. Apparently my initiating a relationship outside the therapy was the means by which I was supposed to rescue him.

As I came to realize that what I had taken as an arena for play – our mutual creation of our life together as lovers – was for him a matter of deadly seriousness, I had gradually to disabuse him of its real-life possibility. My introduction of reality led to rupture and his feeling betrayed, from which it took us some time to recover. We continued in a sobered, lower key, his life now appearing all the more involuted without the spark our flirtation had lent it, the desolation of his life and his passive relation to it all the more stark. He continued to seek little human contact outside our relationship, as if by such seeking he would reveal to me his agency and thereby forfeit the prize he was holding out for, the savior who would finally recognize his helpless, abject state and step in to make everything all right, make up to him all he had suffered.

This understanding helped me tolerate the lack of movement in the therapy, even as it suggested Gary and I were locked in a permanent impasse. I wasn't sure how any of this was going to change, and neither were the supervisors I consulted to help me think about my work with Gary. In the meantime, perhaps engaging in the kind of self-deception to which Slavin and Kriegman (1998) remind us we therapists are susceptible, I consoled myself with the thought that Gary's life would surely be worse without me. I never seriously considered referring him elsewhere; what would be different with the next person? In this I may have been influenced by Gary's odd acceptance of his lonely, abject state, his complaints resembling the plaints of the melancholic: I'll bear this unhappiness, as long as

I can loudly berate you for it. I like Heather Love's take on this circumstance, expressed in her nonpsychoanalytic language: "Backwardness can be deeply gratifying to the backward" (2007, p. 146).

Still, it was hard not to feel like a failure in my work with Gary, a feeling made worse by the fact that I wasn't the only one who could see it. I felt ashamed as I imagined what a bad therapist I must seem in the eyes of Gary's psychiatrist, who could observe how spectacularly unhelpful I had been to Gary after years of working with him. I cringed in listening to Gary tell me of his bitterly complaining to this person of my inefficacy, of my failure to encourage him enough. For his part the psychiatrist (with whom I conferred occasionally by phone to discuss Gary's treatment) had long since started recommending to Gary cognitive behavioral therapy groups and other forms of therapy he might pursue.

It seemed that if I couldn't get Gary to join me as an apparently happy, well-adjusted twenty-first-century gay man, he'd make me share in his own sense of shame, loss, and failure. In part this was my punishment for having spurned his love, for refusing to rescue him. His wish for redemption – which he both insisted on, on his own terms, and refused, under any of the terms on which it might have in some senses been possible – consigned us both to disappointment and frustration. But in making his life a memorial to seemingly irreparable damage, Gary succeeded in forcing me to feel again the shame and failure of my own childhood and young adult life, made me confront my idea of having "moved on" as a turning away from something I could never fully separate myself from. Gary, to me: "You *must* remember this" (Harris, 2009, p. 17). Assuming the mirror image of the structure of homophobia itself, my repudiation of Gary's homophobia showed me just how much my and others' apparent acceptance of my own homosexuality was necessarily a partial and fragile achievement. As someone who had grown up in and continued to live in a homophobic society, I could never fully escape a sense of exclusion, difference, and shame, even if I might sometimes be able to disguise or displace it – as I had with Gary. Beneath the trappings of my normalcy – my career, marriage, and child – Gary and I had more in common than I wanted to think.

Heather Love (2007) writes movingly that sometimes we need to live with injury, without fixing it. To a therapist's ear, her quiet acceptance of this circumstance jangles, clanking against our therapeutic ambitions, our will to repair, our wishes for our patients' (and our own) progress.

Yet with some people it may be all we can do, all we're allowed to do, to be a witness to injury. As I discovered, the process of witnessing (however limited, however failed) may engage us with a patient in deep and unwanted ways that implicate our own histories, even if it does not always move toward what would conventionally be regarded as a therapeutically satisfying outcome. I present my work with Gary as a testament to the complex and deeply personal purposes to which our patients may put us, purposes undreamt of in the mind of the "evidence-based" treatment researcher. It is testament, too, to the way in which our own unhealed wounds may curtail our empathic responsiveness to our patients.

Note

1 A different version of this case was presented as part of a book chapter under the title Perspectives on gay fatherhood: emotional legacies and clinical reverberations, by N. Glassman and S. Botticelli (2014) in S. Kuchuck (Ed.), *Clinical Implications of the Psychoanalyst's Life Experience: When the Personal Becomes Professional*. New York: Routledge.

References

Bersani, L. (1990). *The Culture of Redemption*. Cambridge, MA: Harvard University Press.

Harris, A. (2009). "You must remember this." *Psychoanalytic Dialogues,* 19: 2–21.

Love, H. (2007). *Feeling Backward: Loss and the Politics of Queer History*. Cambridge, MA: Harvard University Press.

Ornstein, A. (1995). The fate of the curative fantasy in the psychoanalytic treatment process. *Contemporary Psychoanalysis,* 31: 113–123.

Slavin, M., and Kriegman, D. (1998). Why the analyst needs to change: toward a theory of conflict, negotiation, and mutual influence in the therapeutic process. *Psychoanalytic Dialogues,* 8(2): 247–284.

Chapter 9

Ruffians, mavericks, bullies, and traders

Kenneth Eisold

I was a shy, bookish kid. Growing up in New York, I did not play on the streets. At school, sometimes, I became the focus of rougher boys who sensed my fears and taunted me. Occasionally they threatened to beat me up after class, away from the protection of teachers, and on a few occasions they did.

Those painful memories were activated some years ago, when I was approached by several oil traders who were losing money. They did not threaten me, of course, as they wanted my help. But they powerfully reminded me of those bullies. They definitely did not belong to the social groups I had joined as an adult and with whom I had come to feel comfortable. They tended to be impulsive, aggressive, obsessed with sports, and such fast-paced activities as jet skiing or driving all-terrain vehicles. Many of them drank a lot, did drugs, and frequented "titty bars," as they called them. Their favored vacation spots were Las Vegas and Miami. They had season tickets to the Knicks or Rangers, while I went to the Metropolitan Opera. On the floor of the Mercantile Exchange, they would frequently brawl and play crude practical jokes on one another. Generally speaking, they were not highly educated. They got a start in commodities trading through a relative or friend or because someone gave them a chance to work as a clerk or a runner. Higher education was not an asset in this business. What counted was talent. If you had ability as a trader you could make money – often a lot of money.

Though they represented the world I had tried to avoid throughout my boyhood, they treated me with respect, believing I could help them, though I was in the beginning not at all sure I could. I started out tensely wondering if we could even understand each other. Describing their trades, they spoke a kind of jargon that completely bewildered me. Not only did I not understand their business, I couldn't understand their language. What was a "spread"? a "20 Dec"? a "closing"?

As you might suspect, there were other significant differences. Many of them relied on intuitive reasoning to make their trades. It seemed as if they could see the numbers and grasp trading opportunities before they could explain them to others or even to themselves. In another context, many of them might be thought to suffer from attention deficit disorders. That is, their minds moved so quickly, they could not reflect on their own experience. It was as if they needed to focus on objects that moved as fast as their minds in order not to be distracted or bored.

In addition to being restless and easily distracted, they tended to be right wing. Working directly in money markets, they valued free markets and respected those who understood how they worked, as well as those who took risks, as they did all the time. They were deeply suspicious of attempts to control or regulate market forces, and they were contemptuous of those charged with oversight. They also had a strong and virtually visceral hatred of taxes, more than most, and a suspicion of welfare programs. As money was very tangible for them, it was as if the IRS was putting its hands in their pockets, taking out cash they had worked hard to win.

I have described this work before (Eisold, 2008), and it's not my intention here to discuss it in any detail. Suffice it to say, I was able to be helpful to them because I focused on their ability to think. I came to see that many of these men lost huge sums of money, often very quickly, because they were distracted in their trading, and I helped them to become more aware of what was distracting them.

Over time, I witnessed a profound change in the markets themselves. When these men first came to me, they traded in circular "pits," where the traders could see and hear each other. Gradually it shifted from this "open cry" system to electronic computers. The physical jockeying and shouting, the scribbled orders and trading scripts, key features of the pits, were replaced by computer screens and electronic records. Traders now could trade from any place. And because trading now was global, someplace in the world a market was open 24 hours a day. The pits continued to be available, but gradually they emptied as activity transferred to the electronic platforms. The noise was gone, but so was much of the subliminal information the traders had picked up from trading together, along with the opportunities for whispered conversations and private deals.

For some this was a godsend. Not only could they think more clearly, they were free of the pressure of the group, the collective effort to track the market. In addition, new traders entered the markets, mathematically sophisticated, capable of developing complex computer programs to guide their moves. Intuition became less essential.

As I said earlier, I had written about these traders before. What had interested me then was trying to describe the value I brought to their work, especially given the fact that I was so much in the dark about how they actually did what they did. I also tried to help them adjust to the change in the markets by listening carefully to the new opportunities that came their way as the old ways of trading faded.

For many, though, who had relied on the group process to guide their thinking, the switch to computerized trading was a disaster. Their "skills" did not transfer to this new trading format, and they floundered. Some gave up trading, others joined groups where they could supplement their own intuitions about the market with those of their colleagues, and occasionally get tips.

Essentially, the raucous community that had grown up around the pits faded away. There was of course much grumbling about this, and resentment towards those "upstairs" who profited most from the change. Those with sophisticated computer programming skills tried to find ways of using those skills, but the old-fashioned intuitions that had served them so well over the years were clearly becoming obsolete.

A few years ago I was describing my work with these traders at a professional meeting, largely of business consultants. As I was coming to the end of my presentation, and discussing the changes in the markets and the decline of this world, I was completely surprised to find myself seized up with emotion. Choked up, I was silenced for several minutes. Obviously, I was more emotionally involved with these men and their dilemmas than I had realized. I had actually come to like a number of them, but I also sympathized with their dilemmas.

My first reflection about that moment was that the alien world that had felt threatening to me as a boy had come to feel familiar. Now, included in their world by them, and identified with them, I felt their loss directly. My tears expressed a grief that reflected theirs. The more I thought about it, however, the more I realized that they had never been as alien as I had originally believed. My fear of the aggression and high spirits, the threats that I felt as a boy, masked what struck me now as a kind of envy. Those boys were free to go after what they wanted, to play roughly and to fight.

They were able to be boisterous and enjoy their impulses, as I had not been.

Working with them and being invited into their world, then, had been doubly gratifying. I felt included and useful, but I had also overcome an inner alienation reflected in my envy. I could be freer myself, and indeed many years of psychoanalysis and professional development had made me more able to accept my own aggression, eroded my envy, helped me to gratify the fantasy of being one of them.

My training, moreover, had helped me to see that behind the bluster of bullies usually lay a form of insecurity. Bullies are motivated to feel stronger by pushing others around because they can see a more powerful self than they actually feel reflected in the eyes of their intimidated victims. As a boy I could not see that, of course. I was completely inside the bullying dynamic, naively investing them with the power I could not feel in myself.

During the years I worked with the traders I had a kind of double consciousness. As they desperately threw good money after bad, trying to reverse their losses, I saw their insecurities. And frequently they could acknowledge them directly. At the same time, my archaic transferences on to them, stemming from by boyhood experiences of intimidation, led me to see them simultaneously as somewhat larger than life. No doubt this was helped along by their flamboyant lifestyles, their expensive vacations and private flights, not to mention the sheer accumulation of wealth for those who had managed to hold on to the money that flowed through their fingers. And they could also be extremely vulnerable. The markets required a kind of spontaneity, which in turn inspired a kind of trust. Their trades were usually as good as their word. This led to a kind of camaraderie, but also occasionally to hurt and anger when they felt misled or betrayed. And they also often had a lot of fun.

But when their world disappeared in the era of digital trading, so did my idealization, my intimidation, my inflation and empowering of them, and my disempowering of myself. The world underwent a radical simplification. The "other" was gone. That, I think, is what lay behind my tears. It was a loss, no doubt, but it was also a relief. And I could let it go.

Reference

Eisold, K. (2008). What makes traders trade? – and how it is changing in the digital age (presented as a paper for the 2008 ISPSO Symposium). Available online at: www.keneisold.com.

Chapter 10

Feminism in the consulting room

Melissa Ritter

My theme may be a bit less heated than that of some of my fellow authors addressing the topic of politics in the consulting room. Since my practice likely self-selects for folks with political views similar to my own, I can count the number of other than Progressive-identified folks with whom I've worked on one hand. Politics do come up, but rarely is there much contention. For me, the first thing that came to mind when asked to think about the topic of politics in the consulting room was feminism and the politics of gender performance. Let me explain.

I was born in 1960, turned ten in 1970, and 20 in 1980. So I was lucky enough to grow up female in what seems to me to be one of the best times with respect to gender roles, expectations, and freedoms. Women born even just ten years earlier had to fight for rights and recognition in ways that I did not. I grew up with *Ms. Magazine*, Gloria Steinem, and a lively women's movement already fully formed in many aspects. Feminism was respected and woven into the culture, at least that of New York City, and specifically the Upper West Side, where I was born and raised. I also went to an all-girls high school that emphasized education and achievement for girls and women. I never felt militant; I felt matter of fact: women were equal to men in all ways. And heterosexual romantic relationships were understood as relationships between two equal partners – things like finding a husband, having a big wedding, assuming a husband's last name, staying home with children never crossed my mind, or ever were, as far as I recall, the topic of conversation among my friends. And our interest in sex was *our* interest in sex, not in providing pleasure for men, or presenting ourselves in some culturally constructed costume deemed "sexy." Of course, this was not true for everyone.

Not at all. But I am speaking here of my specific experience – that of a middle-aged heterosexual Caucasian woman of economic privilege – which informs every clinical exchange.

Within this particular context, there seems to have been a shift, and not for the better, as far as I'm concerned. I am going to speak here, specifically, about young woman now in their 20s, primarily Caucasian heterosexual women, who are tyrannized by gender role expectations in sexual and romantic relationships. Their lesbian and queer sisters, often enough, infuse their femininity with a subversive, transgressive aesthetic and politic. In general, they more easily examine and question the current construction of appropriate, desirable, female performance in romantic relationships. If they opt for a "fem" presentation, it is often done so deliberately, and with sly defiance. (I have not worked with enough young hetero women of color to have a sense of whether my observations apply outside of the narrow group I'm describing.)

On multiple occasions I have found myself just plain shocked as a 20-something straight woman describes her ideas about courtship, partnering, and sex. While I am not proud of this, most of my patients are quite privileged. Not necessarily economically so, but they almost invariably possess access to cultural capital, which includes the expectation of education and professional opportunity. These women all expect to work, at least until they have children, at which point they often anticipate reducing their work hours significantly or leaving the workplace altogether. But the point is that, with respect to their professional lives, the wonderful legacy of feminism is generally woven rather seamlessly into their projected life narrative. That is, they will have a career. However, their relationships with their male romantic partners do not seem to benefit similarly from feminism. For this young cohort, ideas about how women should behave and be treated can be rigid and, to my mind, reactionary: if a man does not pick up the tab, bad thing; having sex "too soon" will mark the relationship as somehow second class, less than; men should initiate, at least most of the time; providing a blow job is an expectation, though reciprocity is not only not expected, it is often viewed as understandably aversive or unnecessary; men need to propose marriage in some elaborate, choreographed way; women will change their last names to that of their spouse. Books like *The Rules* (Fein and Schneider, 2001) carefully detail the imperatives of courtship if one expects to achieve "commitment" in the relationship. Genuineness and spontaneity are to be foresworn in favor of elaborate strategy designed to perform a particular, highly stylized form of desirability. I find all of this deeply disturbing. And, of course, herein lies the difficulty: these are, after all, *my* feelings.

An especially smart and artistically talented patient in her 20s was dating a man with whom she was very much in love, and he with her. They moved in together and she wanted to get married, for reasons not entirely obvious to me. The daughter of a self-identified, outspoken feminist mother, Alice was raised with clearly articulated ideas about female equality in all domains. Yes, she has a very conflicted relationship with her mom, so this informs the specific way in which she has taken in her mother's gender politics,. There is more than a little contempt for her mother's ardent dismissal of all traditional gender convention. But, overall, Alice would also identify as a feminist and is quite capable of holding forth on the topic in a compelling, energetic, and nuanced way. So when she started lamenting her partner's apparent reluctance to propose, I was curious about what was so important to her about getting engaged (and, indeed, that was how she put it, "I want to be engaged"). In my experience, it's difficult to even pose such a question because it is one of those things – those *many* things – that's thought to be self-evident: why, on earth, wouldn't one want to be engaged after living with someone for a year (or some other random interval)? This is the expected, the anticipated, trajectory of a heterosexual relationship, is it not?

Whenever I ask such a question, I begin with an overt acknowledgment that this may seem a surprising, even silly, line of inquiry. But that, even though it may *seem* obvious, each of our reasons for wanting – even wanting that which is expected – is shaped individually, and that it's often worth trying to understand what's up. So I inquired; a slight shadow crossed her face. She had read a blog post I had written on weddings and understood me to be, at least a bit, unconvinced of their importance, or even goodness. She said that being engaged, then married, would make her feel more loved, safer, that she could relax more into the relationship. Internally, I felt squinty-eyed, doubtful, because I don't believe women feel any "safer," that is, more securely loved, when they are engaged or married, but they do feel more regard, more value, within our sociocultural context. And the proposal, the way it's crafted – or not – has come to convey the sincerity and involvement of the male partner. There is, to my mind, a regressive emphasis on the woman's value as measured by the devotion of the man with whom she's partnered. But, given how clearly important all this was to my patient, and my sense that she was all too ready to feel challenged by me, I thought it wise at this point to just nod and listen.

Alice went on to say, somewhat anxiously, as well as with a bit of irritation, that she knew I thought weddings and marriage were silly, but they were important to her. Tricky. Because in many ways she was correct, and this is clearly a value-laden issue so steeped in cultural custom and norms as to render any attempt at objectivity absurd on its face. But there was so much to unknot: indeed, her particular distress did have a transferential cast, and her mom was very much in the room with us; Alice was also, absolutely, reading my reaction with some accuracy and discernment; and neither one of us was more "correct" than the other, the whole matter being entirely subjective. So I said all this to her, leading with the dilemma in which we found ourselves with respect to talking about this topic. She eyed me warily, in no way persuaded that my own agenda would not obliterate her views; that my capacity to focus on her well-being was not compromised.

As the months went on, the topic persisted, though Alice was neither obsessional nor preoccupied. Eventually her partner did propose by way of a modestly elaborate vignette that included a trip to Spain. I was sincerely delighted that she was entirely thrilled by this event. Truly. But, simultaneously, I was eyebrow-arched with disbelief. "Um, a trip to Spain?" I thought, but did not say. What I wanted most to temper in my reaction to her was anything shame inducing. It's so easy for a tone shaded with surprise to be felt as shaming, as critical. I think I was successful in conveying only appreciation for her pleasure. But I had to ask myself what was up that I felt an immediate impulse to deride. Not overwhelming or only that, but it was nonetheless present. Yes, I noted a feeling of indignance about my perception of power disparity inherent in such a ritual display, but also, perhaps, a bit of envy?

There are always so many layers. Along with my disapproval of the gender performances characterizing the engagement scenario, there was a visceral response to the joy Alice was experiencing at having been granted, however fleetingly, access to a romantic narrative that was unfolding precisely as we are currently informed it *should* be. She was the princess, the treasured object, the cherished female in both the larger cultural context, as well as in the more particular interpersonal context of her actual romantic relationship. Belonging and acceptance is compelling and seductive for us all. I was confronted with her youth, her hopefulness, her giddy surprise at being given exactly that for which she had hoped. No, it didn't come in the package I would have selected, but could I completely deny that one aspect of my reaction was that of nose-pressed-to-the-glass longing? It's just true that one's political views are held in the context of our psychological selves, and vice versa. If our various aspects of self are kaleidoscopic (cf., Davies, 1998), ever shifting and re-forming into novel patterns, then the clinical encounter requires examination of each aspect, to the best of our ability. It requires a deliberate, aware, and constant effort to untangle our own interior.

I didn't think it would be useful to Alice to disclose my envy. I believed disclosure would only serve to inhibit our exploration by making her feel frightened and guilty. What *was* useful was my internal acknowledgment, to the degree this was possible, that my own experience, my own political identity was not, is not, immune to cultural colonization. This in no way discounts or erases my position with respect to gender performance in heterosexual romantic relationships, but did enable me to more clearly articulate my position – without derision – for Alice, and to actively explore with her where we both landed in the discussion, and how it informed her experience.

I believe very strongly that when we encounter difference, particularly significant, disturbing difference, between ourselves and our patients, we must carefully examine our inclination – often an inclination to convey disapproval – following the initial internal bristle. Neglecting our personal reactions can so easily lead to shaming the other, a dynamic that pervades interpersonal interaction and serves an ongoing defensive purpose for us all, albeit to varying degrees. This is not to say that there aren't legitimate political differences, but in the consulting room we are organized around the psychological. In order to keep ourselves as open and non-defensive as possible, unrelenting self-examination is mandated: what are the psychological dimensions of *my* reaction? This question is, for me, critical. The next step is explicitly requesting permission from the patient to privilege the psychological dimension, since this is our enterprise, while simultaneously acknowledging that this is a constructed choice, that we could have the discussion differently. I want the decision to be collaborative.

So Alice and I considered our choice candidly: we could have decided to locate ourselves in the purely political, but that this would not have served our therapeutic purpose. It would likely have assumed the contours of debate. This was not the purpose of our meetings, and so we elected to relegate this aspect to the background. In the course of achieving our "agreement" about placing the psychological – the interpersonal and intrapsychic – in the foreground, we did talk about our different ideas about male and female roles in romantic relationships. Alice and I came to know we could differ politically, but still retain our love for one another, which was a critical therapeutic experience for Alice. And, to use a hackneyed expression: we agreed to disagree on some things. But to also sincerely entertain the thoughts of the other.

We have had similarly heated, deeply engaged exchanges about sex and gender performance. The headline here is that Alice struggles with the tyranny of what she terms porn sex, a reference many young women have made in discussion with me. In this domain I cannot locate any envy on my part. I am truly sad and angry at the apparently sanctioned disregard for female sexual pleasure, at least as described by my patients. They, as much as, or sometimes more than, their partners, place the man's pleasure as primary. And this has been true of Alice. Here, I find myself, not infrequently, making little speeches about the importance of female sexual pleasure, of orgasm, of comfort with one's body. Not that most contemporary psychoanalysts would take issue with this position, but I do make it quite explicit, and then the conversation proceeds. I am, hopefully, willing and able to allow the patient to land wherever she is ultimately going to be most comfortable, but it can be a challenge to refrain from conveying the aghast, disapproving reaction I sometimes have.

So Alice and I were able to use our differences to know each other and, most importantly, to know her better. We were able to incorporate the larger world with curiosity and expansiveness. We were able to acknowledge the multiple layers within which all our lives are necessarily embedded. And we continue a lively discussion now that she is married and negotiating questions about gender performance that accompany the terms "husband" and "wife." What *does* it all mean?

I believe this was possible, in part, because the content, while fraught, has represented a politics of choice, that is, no one is being oppressed by the law, as in, for example the issues of marriage equality, or abortion rights. These, for me, would be thornier to negotiate should my patient and I have vastly different views that somehow became relevant to our work. I am not at all certain I would be able to pilot such a conversation with sufficient calm.

From my point of view, the most important part of what I'm discussing is the clinician's capacity to speak as freely, as non-defensively, as possible.

This doesn't always happen for a variety of reasons that, I think, generally fall into one of two categories: the analyst's limitations and the patient's limitations. I refer to "limitations" because I believe, optimally, all should be discussable. But, of course, we can only approximate this ideal. It is never fully realized. However, this does not render the ideal any less worth striving toward.

Another young woman, whom I'll call Nancy, became engaged shortly after we began working together. An educated, professional woman of substantial economic advantage, Nancy comes from a sociocultural background in which the behavior and expectations surrounding marriage and weddings are highly codified. When we began our work together Nancy was already living with her longtime boyfriend, and they became engaged about a year into our relationship. The engagement, like that of my other patient, was achieved by way of a highly choreographed "surprise" organized by Nancy's boyfriend. In this case, details of the wedding itself became matters of controversy about which a considerable amount of session time was devoted. I struggled with this, but opted, to start, with locating the affective meaning in the material as best I could.

My patient was delighted by the engagement, even though it arrived later in the relationship than she might have wished. She was torn about the wedding – was it big enough, was enough money spent, was it OK that her parents were excluded from certain decisions? Her fiancé was involved and enthusiastic, and, for this, she was most appreciative. But his preference was for a smallish, intimate event, and she worried others would judge, assume she was not sufficiently loved by him to be granted the princess-for-a-day status her family and friends anticipated. She insisted all these details didn't really matter to *her*; her concern was how others would perceive the quality of the union. She was similarly concerned about whether or not to change her last name. Her fiancé was adamant about his preference for her to do so, but she was anxious her family would feel betrayed. Unquestionably, there are myriad aspects to all these concerns, many of which can be attended to without reference to the political. And one might argue that this is the prudent way to proceed.

The gender performance issues embedded in these difficulties were not raised or considered at all by my patient. When I inquired about this with respect to her name change, she was quite matter of fact in her dismissal of this as a consideration. I was, on a visceral level, disturbed. It was an almost – or maybe, fully – in-the-body reaction of "What could you be thinking?" In that moment the gulf between us seemed large and dark and unbridgeable. I was, however, able to move back into our shared space and inquire about what I discerned were the various factors of consequence. I did disclose my own bias and its history: that when I was her age it was less common for women to assume their husband's last names after marriage, that the prevailing view was that this suggested a form of "ownership" and submission that women actively rejected. She listened politely with that vaguely far-away look of one whose interest has wandered elsewhere. When I had completed my little presentation, she nodded in polite appreciation and said flatly that none of this was of any concern to her and did not factor into her deliberation at all. In response to my inquiry, she further asserted that my differing perspective did not at all worry her with respect to my ability to help her sort her own issues. This clearly did not seem a discussion she wanted to have.

I was less animated, less relaxed perhaps, with Nancy than with Alice, who I knew to be more open to transference/countertransference discussion, and more interested in the issues of context, the ways in which the larger world influences each of our day-to-day lives and choices. My strain persisted, as I was frustrated in my attempts to develop either personal or political meaning from the content. Again, there was the question of how to parse the political from the psychological. I was unable to make genuine headway on either front, though my comments regarding the possible interpersonal meaning of what was going on during the wedding planning were met with mild interest. Clearly something was transpiring independent of the content, and the steady focus on the execution of a traditional wedding and marriage was, well, annoying to me. Again, I had to look inward and recognize that Nancy's choices in these domains were not my concern, but that the examination of her affective experience was the central project. Very likely, my "irritation" with her sociopolitical choices was, at least in part, a displacement of my overall frustration with our work. I believe I would have had less countertransferential annoyance if I'd felt more welcome in our relationship: here, the political became a container, of sorts, for some of the interpersonal difficulties between us. I consciously reminded myself that the contempt I felt toward Nancy's choices was likely due to feeling of little use to her in our work together. There is no happy end to this story as I never felt comfortable enough to address this directly: my sense of a prickly, defensive, rigidity held me at bay, and Nancy abandoned the treatment abruptly. I felt badly about this, and relieved when she did call later wanting to resume.

This is where I land: it can go better or worse, but, ultimately, it is up to the clinician to tolerate and work with whatever discomfort is evoked by the patient's politics. For me, this includes disclosure of my own position, should it seem useful. Of course, there are limits. As I said earlier, a racist or homophobic patient with such views in awareness and avowed would pose a different challenge, one I cannot imagine learning to tolerate. I assume I would have to refer the patient elsewhere, likely with an explanation. Gratefully, I have not had to confront such a situation. Weddings, consenting sexual behavior, name changes (or not), these all feel uncomfortable, but manageable. My own highly individual, transferentially infused view of the world informs every moment of clinical exchange. For me, as for all of us, the primary challenge is to consistently invite awareness of this into our work, and, often enough, into the actual clinical dialogue.

References

Davies, J. M. (1998). Multiple perspectives on multiplicity. *Psychoanalytic Dialogues*, 8: 195–206.

Fein, E. and Schneider, S. (2001). *The Rules*. New York: Grand Central Publishing.

Part IV

Stuck in the middle with you

Encounters with the analyst's subjectivity

Chapter 11

Commitment fears

Why the analyst avoids analysis[1]

Sarah Schoen

My patient Ben lay down on the couch. He told me that the night before he'd had a dream. This was a first. We were six *months* into a three-times weekly analysis, but we were six *years* into what had been a once-weekly therapy, and I was looking for signs of life.

Six months before, Ben had turned 45, and he'd been taking stock. He'd asked me, had he done what he could in therapy? Was it time to stop? I'd never had high hopes for this treatment, or thought seriously about Ben as an analytic patient. A successful investment banker, Ben had come at the behest of his then girlfriend, one of many who'd suffered his emotional impenetrability and commitment fears. While I'd raised the possibility that he come more often – given that he managed fears about getting involved by keeping one foot in and one foot out of relationships – this, like most of what I said, slid right off him.

Six years later, I easily reassured myself about my good-faith effort. Ben was more aware of his feelings and the ways he walled them off. He'd made some key links to his history. He'd tasted the depth of his fear of interdependent entanglements. He could feel the loss of the son he'd once imagined having. In truth, I found Ben easy to take and easy to leave, and I quickly rationalized the limits of what was possible, given his character armor, our lack of adhesiveness, and our once-a-week structure. Besides, my hours were full. I was feeling flush, maybe even enjoying the freedom of not needing him at all.

As an afterthought – I mean, after we'd picked a date for our last session – I offered a closing analogy to Ben's extra-therapy relationships, wondering aloud if his inclination to end treatment might mean that the question of deeper commitment was in the air. With some warm teasing that I vaguely registered as unusual, I asked Ben if part of him was hoping I'd beg him to stay, to fight for him to take a leap with me.

What I did *not* expect was for this gambit to work – for us to find ourselves, six months later, with Ben on the couch, announcing his first dream:

> I'm maybe three or four, playing outside. No one else is there, but I'm OK on my own. I see a little girl across the street – and I want to play with her. So I start to cross, but a car is coming, and I can't go fast enough. The faster I try to go, the more I'm immobilized – it's like this sticky tar is hardening all around me. I look up, and I see my mother at the window, watching me, but with no expression, as if nothing is happening at all. The car is about to crush me but what's strange is – I'm so calm – like I'm just watching too.

Ben sounded calm as he spoke, too, but it was not the calm stemming from his usual remove. Ben was not talking *about* his dream. He spoke *as* the numb, terrified boy about to be crushed, and as a boy who also believed he was talking to a parent/analyst who could protect him. But, in response, I felt myself to be anything but. Instead, I was thrown into a disorganizing affect storm, not only because the dream foreshadowed what real contact with Ben might require going forward, but because it simultaneously undermined my understanding of the treatment's past, mocking my good-faith effort, exposing me at once as both the figure who'd watched from the sidelines and the figure who was willing to drive away unscathed. As this recognition ominously took root, I thought, "Oh fuck. No wonder I didn't want to do this." Here it was, my unthought known (Bollas, 1987): I had told myself it had been Ben who couldn't commit, who was afraid to really want something from me, and it turned out I was right there with him all along.

What is it that makes us think of one patient as "analytic" and another one not? What is at stake when we do or do not choose to make the case, even to fight, for the deep, extended engagement that a psychoanalysis entails? In what follows, I will explore these questions by highlighting: (1) how, in the absence of "objective" criteria for making this choice, we underestimate the degree to which we evade risks with and limit opportunities for some of our patients; (2) that if we do not successfully make the case for a more frequent, intensive treatment, we may never have enough data to recognize the enactments in which we are already participants; and

(3) that the choice to make the case for analysis is inextricably entwined with the activation of the analyst's personal needs and desires within the specific relational context of each treatment dyad. In raising these points, I am going to assume that, despite a lack of general consensus on the definition of a psychoanalysis, for most practicing analysts, *frequency* matters in providing enough continuity and intensity to kindle analytic alchemy. Further, what's most relevant to the question I'm posing – what makes us think of one patient as analytic and another one not – is how a particular patient may or may not "fit" with our own subjective definitions of analysis, rooted as they are in our personal webs of identifications and aspirations, and inseparable from the conflicts, traumas, and longings informing both our conscious and unconscious participation in the clinical encounter (Slochower, 2011; Tublin, 2002).

Indeed, today's relational analyst, practicing in an era in which claims to objectivity offer little recourse, relies primarily on the notion of "goodness of fit" to guide every facet of clinical judgment, including our views on "analyzability" (Hirsch, 1984, 1997; Stolorow, 1990). With regard to "analyzability," it's difficult to argue with the notion of "fit." Shouldn't we undertake an ambitious treatment only when we can imagine success? Doesn't this allow us the freedom and flexibility to make use of our personal idiosyncrasies? On the other hand, if these proclivities are embedded in part in personally and dyadically derived unconscious processes, should we accept them simply at face value?

The choice to make the case for psychoanalysis, like all clinical choices, will emerge within the specificity of each dyad (Aron, 1999; Greenberg, 1995). Yet this choice, in particular, is one in which the analyst's desire is both required and overburdened. As such, it highlights *both* the mutual influence *and* the asymmetrical structure of the analytic couple (Aron, 1992). Most patients will not come wanting an analysis – just picture the latest *New Yorker* cartoon – and it will fall to the analyst, with her own multiply determined investments, with her wish to express and protect her analytic identity, to make the case – to be willing to put herself on the line.

Yes, we are free to choose those patients with whom we "fit." But if our choices – not just how we think, feel, or fantasize about our patients, but what we do – take place in the countertransference,[2] it follows that we should look closely at *what we do*. And one thing we do is propose psychoanalysis to some patients and not others.[3] In embracing "fit," we are too complacent about those treatments where we don't really try the idea of analysis on for size. Of course we can recommend analysis because of our own preferences. But we are also capable of *not* proposing it, *not* because of a rational assessment of the patient's needs, but rather, *because of how we feel about providing it* (cf., Mitchell, 1991). We settle, and we are responsible for our patients settling too, without sufficient awareness of our own motives and without spelling out for them what may be at stake.

Ben was an expert at disavowing *his* needs. When he was eight, his parents were hit by a drunk driver. His father, mostly uninjured, was driving, and his mother was paralyzed from the neck down. The official story is that it was *the other guy* who was responsible for the collision. But just below Ben's mother's stoicism lay her rage at his father (whom she silently blamed) and her icy withdrawal. When Ben was 15, his father moved across the country for a lucrative professional opportunity, leaving Ben's practical needs attended to by an army of aides. Aside from the toxicity in his parents' relationship and his father's desertion, Ben did not feel that his mother's accident changed much between the two of them. He'd always found her inaccessible. In all the years that she could use her arms, he had not a single memory of being held.

Of course my take-him-or-leave-him indifference toward Ben – an indifference I *experienced* as neutral, not hostile – included multiple, shifting identifications with the figures in Ben's history, ones with whom he too identified: the inaccessible mother, the abandoning father, the hit-and-run driver. And my indifference was also an identification with Ben's way of escaping the pain of recognizing the depths of his unmet needs – his terrors of failing someone counting on *him*. But during our six years of psychotherapy *this* escaped *me*. Had this treatment ended before becoming an analysis, I would have believed it had been "good enough." I would have believed that my participation had been benign, not disengaged. I would have believed that I was appropriately reluctant to impose my agenda, not that I was unwilling either to encounter fully these identifications or to want – much less need – something from Ben. I would have believed I'd "realistically" appraised our mutual limitations, not that I was protecting myself from failure were I to have real ambition for our relationship. And I would have been wrong.

What does it mean when we think of a patient as a potential analysand? It means that we are willing, for reasons about which we will be both conscious *and* unconscious, to get deeply involved, to see a lot of one another, to become embedded in a mutually transformative relationship. In that sense, it is like embarking on any budding love story. And we often do *not* think seriously about a patient as a potential analysand, *not* when we don't think it would be helpful, and *not* because the patient could never commit, but because, as Ogden (1992) has described, *we are afraid of what might happen if they were to actually say yes.* After all, we could get our hearts broken. We could lose ourselves. We could go right out of our minds.

If our influence is inevitable, our subjectivity "irreducible," our awareness incomplete and retrospective (Renik, 1993), and everything we do will be determined and given meaning by the distinct interactive matrix created by each analytic dyad (Greenberg, 1995), then we rely on finding our way into, and out of, enactments as the new mainstay of therapeutic action. But there are some enactments that are elaborated as psychoanalyses progress, and others that prevent them from taking off (e.g., Bass, 2003). And we need *enough contact* with a given patient that there will be opportunities for more of what the analytic couple may be mutually repudiating to emerge. We need, to borrow from Stern (2004), enough contact for things to "chafe."

What "enough contact" is will depend on the patient, and rigid prescriptions for frequency cannot define analytic process. But to those who might dispense with this criterion all together, I would argue that frequency, more than any other feature of the "frame," is responsible for whether a given dyad become involved enough with one another to enter and hold sway over each other's inner worlds. When we see more of a patient, we don't just have more of the same, or intensify what is already there. We enter a relationship of a different ilk. We take up residence in each other's psychic lives. And when we do *that*, some of what may be implicated for the analyst are her most unresolved, most disavowed, and most archaic experiences of self.

How then, could today's analyst not run scared? How could we not, like our potential analysands, both long for opportunities to surrender (cf., Ghent, 1990) and fear disruption to our narcissistic equilibrium, including our preferred analytic ideals (Slochower, 2006, 2011)? This dynamic, like the interactive matrix it's part of, is not something we choose to participate in – it's something, to quote Greenberg (1995), that simply *is.* And while at play with all our patients, it's of particular relevance with patients like Ben. In Botticelli's words, "We need our patients to want things from us" (2012, p. 564). It gives us something to respond to. It lets us believe we matter. And making sure no one could matter was Ben's calling card.

Consider, by way of contrast, Davies' (2004) patient Karen, with whom Davies vividly illustrates the experience of becoming a patient's "bad object" when that requires becoming one's own as well. Her patient, Karen, was difficult because she wanted things, impossible things, from her analyst who had to choose between a connection to her patient and the integrity of her own mind. Davies shows us how some patients will evoke for some analysts what is most unbearable in themselves, while also reminding us that her Karens may not be ours. And the point that I am making here is that sometimes our Karens will look, when they first come to see us, more like Ben. They won't insert themselves into our minds. They won't ask for much. And we, given the option to stay off the hook, won't even notice that we've failed to ask for much in return.

Having been warned during our one-person era about imposing our agendas, our desires, on our patients, we are now, in these two-person times, told that our interest in, vision of, and hopes for our patients are crucial. To reverse Bion's (1970) renowned aphorism – psychoanalysis requires the evocation of memory and desire for both participants.[4] It turns out that our patients need *us* to want something from *them*, and this is never more relevant than when we do, or do not, propose psychoanalysis. This is conceivably the most dramatic way in which we try to want more for our patients than they are able to want for themselves (cf., Ghent, 1995).

But while the analyst practicing in contemporary times is blessed with permission to make use of herself as a personal subject (e.g., Benjamin, 1998; Slavin, 2010), she is cursed by being simultaneously too much at the mercy of her own subjective – here I mean *unwitting* – participation. Further, cultural caricatures of analytic knowledge – like epistemological deconstruction – leave the analyst's assessment of what she can offer too dependent on the pull of the relational matrix (Greenberg, 2001). There is little to hold (cf., Slochower, 1996) the analyst who, with her *potential* Karens, her Bens, finds herself caught in the more destabilizing waves of a relational unconscious (Gerson, 2004).

Celenza tells us that the question, "Why can't we be lovers?" (2010, p. 177) should have its moment in every treatment – is there too much erotic feeling, and the risk of crossing some boundary, or too little, and the absence of erotic vitality (Celenza, 2007, 2010)? To my mind, the question, "Why not psychoanalysis?" has much in common with the question,

"Why can't we be lovers?" It confronts the analyst with the presence or absence of her desire to be intimately connected to, involved with, and affected by a particular patient.

Of course the dangers of boundary violations are real (e.g., Celenza, 2006; Gabbard & Lester, 1995), but there is more than one way to be penetrated (Davies, 1998). And sometimes it is the analyst's protection of her psychic boundaries, rather than her openness, that is the problem. After all, Eros is too complicated to confine its expression to sexual seduction. Our desires to contain and repair, to transform and experience, to know and be known – to become an analyst in the first place – can hardly be untangled from love.[5]

As for Ben, this has remained a disruptive and brutal love, one only underscoring love's complex relationship to the terrors of trust and tenderness, to the disavowed desire for care and mutual recognition. I have asked myself many times what it was that had *already* changed (cf., Stern, 2004) by the time I proposed psychoanalysis and Ben was able to accept. My hunch is that, ironically, my invitation genuinely conveyed my conscious lack of investment – my openness to letting him go – and that perhaps this made space for Ben's desire, and allowed him to choose more safely to move toward me. I would guess, though, with all the benefit of hindsight, that unconsciously, I was much more attached to Ben – that we were much more attached to each other, and much more pained by the prospect of saying goodbye – than either one of us knew.

But what I did know, all too viscerally, was how, in wake of that first dream, Ben crashed into me, filling me repeatedly with the horror of being the icy mother unmoved by her child's need, the desolate child with a frozen mother, the accused father preferring an easy way out, and the unraveled kid left to manage on my own. Yet this map of relational configurations sounds much too orderly to convey what it's been like, or to capture how Ben's map mapped all too well on to mine. I do tend toward omnipotent solutions to the shame and despair borne of my own early failures to create the parents whose arms could really hold me.[6] While I thought, pre-Ben, that I knew this well about myself already, becoming entangled with Ben brought new forms of these demons to life. It's left me perpetually feeling as though I'm driving a car I might steer – or fearing I'd *already* steered – over a cliff; having my insides suddenly invaded by the malevolent tar in Ben's dream; rendering me wholly incapacitated, with no faith in anything about my faculties I'm used to trusting. I've lost sleep, lost myself, and, indeed, lost my mind.

This is what it's meant to be open to Ben – to stew in all of my own, and all of his shame-riddled longings. Attempting survival has meant sustaining some hard blows to my personal analytic ideals – and thus reawakened the conflicts, traumas, and longings that led me to them in the first place. It's meant consultation with a supervisor from another psychoanalytic world. It's meant encountering the threat of spectacular failure, and the repeated differentiation between masochistic self-loathing and real responsibility for my impact. The thought, "Oh fuck. No wonder I didn't want to do this," has crossed my mind again and again in this analysis. But despite these hardships, I have suffered most my earlier years of indifference – the loss of potential that we enacted in real time.

In year five of this analysis, year eleven of our relationship, I now have poignant moments of romantic illusion – a sense of who Ben might become, of what we might mean to each other. They are fleeting, and I'm quick to guard against getting my hopes up. But I try these days to allow my hopes to coexist with my fears. And sometimes, when I anticipate my losses, it's not the familiar dreads of crashing and burning that loom, but an inchoate sense that things might just go well enough that one day Ben could rightfully leave me behind (cf., Loewald, 1979). For the first time, Ben is in love with a woman to whom he feels hopelessly attached. Although terrified, almost drowning in doubt, he's no longer mourning the loss of his imagined son, but tentatively considering having a real child of his own. How could he do this now? Let others rely on him when he is so unsure whether he has what it takes? When he is on the other side of 50, his mortality unavoidable? Maybe it would be wiser to tell himself it's already too late. But he finds, to his surprise, that while the hazards are real, he doesn't want to retreat. Like me – with me – he has changed. He would rather go down trying, no matter the risk to his heart.

Notes

1 A longer version of this chapter was published as: Schoen, S. (2015). Afraid to commit: proposing psychoanalysis and the paradox of the analyst's desire. *Contemporary Psychoanalysis,* 51(4): 649–679. The material is reprinted here by permission of the William Alanson White Institute of Psychiatry, Psychoanalysis and Psychology and the William Alanson White Psychoanalytic Society (www.wawhite.org).

2 See, for example, Aron (1996), Greenberg (2001), Hirsch (2008), Hoffman (1992), Mitchell (1997), Stern (2004).

3 Among its many contributions, a historical critique by Aron and Starr (2013) highlights the degree to which the longstanding binary between psychoanalysis and psychotherapy

has direct clinical consequences, one of which informs the degree to which we are willing to invest in and value those patients with whom we can envision a "psychoanalysis," and may overlook those with whom we don't.

4 See, for example, Benjamin (1998), Botticelli (2012), Bromberg (2009), Davies (1998), Fast (1998), Gentile (2013), Hoffman (2009), J. Slavin (2010), M. Slavin (2006), and Summers (2000) for varied explications of both development and clinical process that highlight this shift.

5 See, for example, Bach (2006), Benjamin (1998), Davies (1998), Ghent (1990), Loewald (1979), Wyre and Welles (1994), and Winnicott (1949), who have all profoundly recognized the intimate, complex relationship between psychoanalytic process and love.

6 See Harris (2009), who locates analysts' contributions to impasse as arising from their vulnerability to omnipotence and their attachment histories, often marked by some form of "ego precocity" (p. 8). Her description of this particular trajectory is one in which I find it easy to locate myself.

References

Aron, L. (1992). Interpretation as expression of the analyst's subjectivity. *Psychoanalytic Dialogues*, 2: 475–507.

Aron, L. (1996). *Meeting of Minds: Mutuality in Psychoanalysis*. Hillsdale, NJ: The Analytic Press.

Aron, L. (1999). Clinical choices and the relational matrix. *Psychoanalytic Dialogues*, 9: 1–29.

Aron, L., & Starr K. (2013). *A Psychotherapy for the People: Toward a Progressive Psychoanalysis.* New York: Routledge.

Bach, S. (2006). *Getting from Here to There: Analytic Love, Analytic Process*. Hillsdale, NJ: The Analytic Press.

Bass, A. (2003). "E" enactments in psychoanalysis: another medium, another message. *Psychoanalytic Dialogues*, 13: 657–675.

Benjamin, J. (1998). *Like Subjects, Love Objects: Essays on Recognition and Sexual Difference.* New Haven, CT: Yale University Press.

Bion, W. R. (1970). *Attention and Interpretation: A Scientific Approach to Insight in Psychoanalysis and Groups.* London: Tavistock.

Bollas, C. (1987). *The Shadow of the Object*. New York: Columbia University Press.

Botticelli, S. (2012). Weak ties, slight claims: the psychotherapy relationship in an era of reduced expectations. *Contemporary Psychoanalysis*, 48: 423–596.

Bromberg, P. M. (2009). Truth, human relatedness, and the analytic process: an interpersonal/relational perspective. *International Journal of Psycho-Analysis*, 90: 347–361.

Celenza, A. (2006). Sexual boundary violations in the office: when is a couch just a couch? *Psychoanalytic Dialogues*, 16: 113–128.

Celenza, A. (2007). Analytic love and power: responsiveness and responsibility. *Psychoanalytic Inquiry*, 27: 287–301.

Celenza, A. (2010). The guilty pleasure of erotic countertransference: searching for radical true. *Studies in Gender and Sexuality*, 11: 175–183.

Davies, J. M. (1998). Thoughts on the nature of desires: the ambiguous, the transitional, and the poetic: reply to commentaries. *Psychoanalytic Dialogues*, 8: 805–823.

Davies, J. M. (2004). Whose bad objects are we anyway? Repetition and our elusive love affair . . . *Psychoanalytic Dialogues*, 14: 711–732.

Fast, I. (1998). *Selving: A Relational Theory of Self-Organization.* Hillsdale, NJ: Analytic Press.

Gabbard, G., & Lester, E. (1995). *Boundaries and Boundary Violations in Psychoanalysis.* New York: Basic Books.

Gentile, J. (2013). From truth or dare to show and tell: reflections on childhood ritual, play, and the evolution of symbolic life. *Psychoanalytic Dialogues*, 23: 150–169.

Gerson, S. (2004). The relational unconscious: a core element of intersubjectivity, thirdness, and clinical process. *Psychoanalytic Quarterly*, 73: 63–98.

Ghent, E. (1990). Masochism, submission, surrender – masochism as a perversion of surrender. *Contemporary Psychoanalysis,* 26: 108–136.

Ghent, E. (1995). Interaction in the psychoanalytic situation. *Psychoanalytic Dialogues,* 5: 479–491.

Greenberg, J. (1995). Psychoanalytic technique and the interactive matrix. *Psychoanalytic Quarterly*, 64: 1–22.

Greenberg, J. (2001). The analyst's participation: a new look. *Journal of the American Psychoanalytic Association*, 49: 359–381.

Harris, A. (2009). "You must remember this." *Psychoanalytic Dialogues*, 19: 2–21.

Hirsch, I. (1984). Toward a more subjective view of analyzability. *American Journal of Psychoanalysis*, 44: 169–182.

Hirsch, I. (1997). Analytic intimacy, analyzability and the vulnerable analyst. *Free Associations*, 7B: 250–259.

Hirsch, I. (2008). *Coasting in the Coutnertransference: Conflicts of Self Interest between Analyst and Patient.* New York: The Analytic Press.

Hoffman, I. Z. (1992). Some practical implications of a social-constructivist view of the psychoanalytic situation. *Psychoanalytic Dialogues*, 2: 287–304.

Hoffman, I. (2009). Therapeutic passion in the countertransference. *Psychoanalytic Dialogues*, 19: 617–637.

Loewald, H. W. (1979). The waning of the Oedipus complex. *Journal of the American Psychoanalytic Association*, 27: 751–775.

Mitchell, S. A. (1991). Wishes, needs and interpersonal negotiations. *Psychoanalytic Inquiry*, 11: 147–170.

Mitchell, S. (1997). *Influence and Autonomy in Psychoanalysis.* Hillsdale, NJ: Analytic Press.

Ogden, T. H. (1992). Comments on transference and countertransference in the initial analytic meeting. *Psychoanalytic Inquiry*, 12: 225–247.

Renik, O. (1993). Analytic interaction: conceptualizing technique in light of the analyst's irreducible subjectivity. *Psychoanalytic Quarterly*, 62: 553–571.

Slavin, J. H. (2010). Becoming an individual: technically subversive thoughts on the role of the analyst's influence. *Psychoanalytic Dialogues*, 20: 308–324.

Slavin, M. O. (2006). Tanya and the adaptive dialectic of romantic passion and secure attachment. *Psychoanalytic Dialogues*, 16: 793–824.

Slochower, J. (1996). *Holding and Psychoanalysis: A Relational Approach.* Hillsdale, NJ: The Analytic Press.

Slochower, J. (2006). *Psychoanalytic Collisions*. New York: The Analytic Press.

Slochower, J. (2011). Analytic idealizations and the disavowed: Winnicott, his patients, and us. *Psychoanalytic Dialogues*, 21: 3–21.

Stern, D. B. (2004). The eye sees itself: dissociation, enactment, and the achievement of conflict. *Contemporary Psychoanalysis*, 40: 197–237.

Stolorow, R. D. (1990). Converting psychotherapy to psychoanalysis: a critique of the underlying assumptions. *Psychoanalytic Inquiry*, 10: 119–130.
Summers, F. (2000). The analyst's vision of the patient and therapeutic action. *Psychoanalytic Psychology*, 17: 547–564.
Tublin, S. (2002). But always behind in the count: a response to "Sluggers and Analysts." *Contemporary Psychoanalysis*, 38: 445–446.
Winnicott, D. W. (1949). Hate in the counter-transference. *International Journal of Psycho-Analysis*, 30: 69–74.
Wyre, H. K., & Welles, J. K. (1994). *The Narration of Desire: Erotic Transferences and Countertransferences.* Hillsdale, NJ: The Analytic Press.

Chapter 12

A dream as an internal enactment of trauma

The impact on the analyst's self[1]

Sheldon Itzkowitz

People suffering with complex trauma often struggle to keep their dissociated lives and selves hidden. Working with people who struggle this way is extremely challenging. Frequently, we have to deal with many dissociated self-states containing different experiences, feelings, memories, identities, and of course multiple transferences that often occur on different levels of consciousness, including in dreams. Further, we have to deal in response with our many countertransferences, which occur in many levels of consciousness, and can, at times, reflect our reciprocal dissociative processes. As a result, while to some degree we make conscious choices with patients and are free to act in a way that expresses personal agency, to some other degree we are always potentially acting from forces that may exist partly, or fully, out of consciousness.

In this paper, I will discuss my work with Alice, hoping to illustrate how, because of my various identifications and counteridentifications with victimized parts of her, I often did not feel I *had* a choice in how I responded to her, even though on some other level of consciousness I knew I did. In particular, I will discuss Alice's dream or alleged dream and its impact on me. I say alleged dream because it was not clear that it was a dream. The "dream" depicts a rape of one of Alice's dissociated self-states by another. This material is disturbing, and I want to forewarn the reader before he or she continues.

Alice is a 30-year-old woman who suffers from complex trauma and an extreme dissociative disorder. When we began working together, Alice had many different self-states that were unknown or barely known to her or to each other. During the course of the analysis, an awareness of these formerly dissociated states has emerged. Alice is the self-state usually in executive control of her body and responsible for things like making sure she goes to and functions at work, keeping her appointments, and the like. The experience I will discuss involves the different ways in which Alice experiences her self through several of her dissociated self-states or parts. There is Anthony, a 25-year-old, intensely angry, and dangerous self-state who represents Alice's identification with her father who physically and sexually abused her during childhood. The Anthony part of Alice contains sufficient anger that, to protect Alice's other self-states, we had to make use of her capacity for fantasy and trance logic. For the purposes of this paper, one can think of Anthony as occupying an internal space that is separate from other parts of Alice. Anna is a 19-year-old part who is described by Alice and other self-states as a loving caretaker who protects the child parts in Alice's system. Janice is a 25-year-old self-state who holds memories of abuse as well as memories of seeing Alice's mother beaten and abused by her father. Finally, Margaret is an older adult part who holds wisdom and physical pain, and who feels she would welcome the end of life.

I've worked with Alice for six years, in analysis three times a week. At the very end of a Wednesday session during our fifth year of working together, Margaret said, "I had a very strange dream last night. I dreamt that Anthony raped Anna." After hearing this I remember feeling very uncomfortable and confused. It was not only that the material was about rape, but also what this meant in the context of Alice's current life and history. What might Margaret's dream be saying about the Anthony and the Anna ways in which Alice experiences herself? What was the meaning of their engaging in this type of violence?

The following day when Margaret appeared again, she began by talking about her dream, and I asked what she meant by the dream being "very strange." "It was a nightmare," she said. "It was very vivid, not like the usual kind of dreams I have, it felt so real – I'm not sure it was a dream." Margaret spoke haltingly, expressing a deep sense of confusion and sadness while telling her dream. Here it is:

> Anthony went to my childhood home and cut off my father's penis and sewed it on to himself. Then when he saw Anna passing by in front of his cabin he invited her in for a cup of hot chocolate. When she went inside he threw her down and raped her. He raped her with my father's penis.

Margaret, visibly shaken, looked like she was about to cry. I was shaken too. I felt unnerved by the violence and struggled to organize my thoughts while she talked about how upset and confused she felt. I tried to help settle her so that we might look at the dream and understand what it meant to Margaret, since it was her dream.

Suddenly, there was a change in states. My patient's posture changed, she shifted in her chair, sat up, and in a somewhat deeper voice associated with Anthony said, "It wasn't a dream." I was caught off guard when I found myself facing the hard-edged, aggressiveness of Anthony. More confusion found its way into my already rattled state of mind. "What do you mean it wasn't a dream?" I asked. Anthony stared at me and replied, "I raped her!"

I began feeling very angry with Anthony, and the "me" that was in the room with the Anthony part of Alice was surprised and confused at how angry I was feeling. In retrospect I believe these feelings reflected my becoming engaged in Alice's internal drama on a concrete level. I had to exert mental energy to contain my anger and confusion – to keep my composure and remain focused. "How could you have done that?" I asked. Anthony replied:

> I saw Anna walking near my cabin and I invited her in for a cup of hot chocolate. I lied to her! When she came in I dragged her by her hair to the bed and threw her down. I tore off her clothes and I raped her – I fucked her.

There was another switch of states and Anna was now in the room looking very upset and also feeling very confused. She asked, "Did this happen on the inside world or in the outside world?" The one thing I felt sure of and explained to her was that if Anthony did rape her, it could not have possibly happened in the world that both she and I inhabit, and I said so. She asked if Anthony really had her father's penis, indicting her ongoing confusion regarding internal reality and how it relates to the external, consensually validable world – confusion very common among extremely dissociated patients and sometimes their analysts as well. I said, "No," to allay any additional fear and anxiety. Our Thursday session ended, and I was left trying to piece this together.

The dreams of extremely dissociated people can be very different from those of people who are less or minimally dissociative. I hope to show that what felt to one part of Alice, i.e., Margaret, like a dream, felt to the Anthony and Anna parts like reality. Whatever this was, it felt real to Anthony and Anna, and it became real between us for a brief period of time, leading to profound and disruptive feelings in me.

Was this a dream? Was this fantasy? Was the drama between these internal self-states enacting events of Alice's childhood? What did it mean that Anthony believed himself to be a rapist? What did it mean that Anna was unsure if the rape occurred on the inside or the outside world? What did it mean that Anthony raped Anna with Alice's father's penis? Was it easier for Alice's dissociated mind to accept the concreteness of the dream as internal events rather than what they might symbolize? Was this a precursor to Alice's eventual awareness of the horror of her childhood? I was sure of only two things. I was feeling very bewildered and glad the next day was Friday.

The following several days were amongst the most difficult I've experienced during the time I'd been working with Alice. I felt assaulted by a flood of feelings. Throughout the weekend, if I wasn't focused on what I was doing or involved and engaged with family or friends, thoughts and feelings about Margaret's dream and the sessions would appear unbidden in my mind, as if vivified by some external power. I felt invaded, penetrated.

After a while I sensed a swell of feelings gathering inside of me growing in size and intensity and moving upwards from my stomach. I could feel the swell gathering momentum and pushing outward against the walls of my chest. I thought at different moments I was either going to explode or throw up. My mind was racing: "This couldn't happen, one self-state can't rape another self-state, or can they?" Yet this not only seemed real to parts of Alice – it also felt real to me. The idea of Anthony – this nasty, mean, part – assaulting and raping Anna – a kindly, loving, caretaker of the child parts – was frankly disgusting to me. Any kind of rape is repulsive and disgusting to me.

I began feeling hatred towards Anthony. The angrier I got, the more personified Anthony became – or perhaps it was the reverse. Perhaps the dream led to my mind dislodging the Anthony part of Alice and fusing it with the internal image I held of her father. In my mind, Anthony went from being an internal self-state in Alice's mind to being the embodiment of her childhood abuser. Anthony came to life for me and I became, for a while, consumed with rage at this child molester. I fantasized about being a character in a Bruce Willis or Clint Eastwood film. The camera would see me saying:

> I'm gonna get my hands on this guy and kill him. Not with a gun, na that's too easy, I wanna get up close and personal like, so I could look him in the eye and let him know that this is what you get for raping a little girl.

I was furious, beside myself, and totally surprised by emotions that felt alien; I felt possessed, I wanted these feelings out of me.

Whose feelings were these? How did they get inside of me? Why was I feeling murderous rage? Although complicated, I do believe the intensity of feeling that I experienced and had to hold temporarily belonged in part to Alice. She learned from a young age the violent consequences emanating from expressing any form of anger. It was these feelings of anger and rage that Alice dissociated and relocated in the self-state known as Anthony.

But, of course, I was in the picture too. I was there with my history of being bullied as a child, of being Jewish growing up in the shadow of the Holocaust, of being all too familiar with the emotional and physical pain of anti-Semitism, of feeling like an unwanted "other." I was there with my history of being raised by a father who lived with insurmountable and unspeakable guilt for being unable to rescue his mother, his siblings, and their families from the gas chambers of Europe, and my mother whose own pain and anguish often overwhelmed her capacity to be present for me. Perhaps it was these experiences that left me vulnerable to Anthony's aggression and completely identified with Anna's victimization.

But, I am also a father. And being a parent, treating patients who were traumatized and sexually abused during childhood (especially while my children were young) has affected me in many ways. On a very basic, simple, human level, one doesn't stop being a parent, nor should one, while working with victims of trauma. In fact, if anything, I became more sensitive, and attuned to the vulnerability, betrayal, and pain of patients like Alice. And one doesn't stop being a psychoanalyst who treats victims of trauma and abuse, nor should one, while at the playground with your kids, or while being the adult supervising your children and their friends on play dates. Knowing the tortured and brutal experiences my patients suffered during their childhoods made me a more cautious, alert, and vigilant person in general and parent in particular. And perhaps it was the experience of fatherhood that contributed, in part, to the intensity of my anger because of what the rape dream/experience between the Anthony and Anna parts of Alice symbolized – the unthinkable act of a father abusing his child.

When I thought of Anna I was angry with her too. In my mind I was critical of her. I imagined saying, "What were you thinking? What were you doing near Anthony? You know how dangerous he is." Later, when I could reflect on my anger, I felt terrible. I was blaming her for what happened. She after all was the victim, just like Alice when she was a little girl. How could I be angry with Anna? Why wasn't I sad for her? Why was it easier for me to feel anger and not sadness and horror? To be able to feel the sadness and horror, to really feel it as a bodily experience, one would have to hold and imagine the crime as reality in one's mind. Experiencing the unspeakable reality of the victim *with* her as she lives or relives it in the therapeutic relationship allows us to feel the full impact of the horror and sadness. Because Anna did not hold the original trauma as experience, but only symbolically through the internal action with Anthony, I could not fully feel the sadness.

But I also think the part of me identified with Anna wanted to push away the feelings of helplessness that would have come with resonating with her experience. It's my hunch that it was easier to be angry with her and thus distance myself from my own pain and sadness. As I noted above, I am no stranger to feeling helpless, defenseless, and impotent, and some of my most painful encounters with these feelings occurred when I was the same age Alice was when her father began abusing her. And *my* father, who had been through more than his share of tragedy, had difficulty holding and containing feelings of fear, vulnerability, and impotence. On more than one occasion, I saw how a fleeting look of pain or anguish on my father's face disappeared when he lashed out angrily instead. The transformation from fear and anguish to anger and rage was shocking and frightening to me as a child. Yet this did not prevent me from identifying with him as well, and in this instance with Anna, it was easier for me, like my father, to feel anger than tolerate the vulnerability of staying connected to Anna's pain.

I had many thoughts about how to make use of my feelings during our Monday session, and I knew I had to find a way into the unfolding drama of Alice's internal experience. I needed to recognize Anna now as the unseen, neglected, and abused child, feelings that were still dissociated and disavowed by Alice, while at the same time recognizing Anthony as the mean, sadistic abuser. And I had to do this while feeling all of Alice's and all of my own feelings of impotence and rage. My own feelings included the sense that the system of safety we had created together had failed to protect Alice as I had hoped that it would.

When working with dissociated material it is important to keep in mind that what is dissociated is often held and experienced in the mind or the body concretely. Sometimes we are able to hold the symbolic meaning of these concretized experiences while working with our patients. At other times, we become more concretely engaged in the internal drama ourselves. In this example, I was able to enter into Alice's internal world along with Margaret, Anthony, and Anna. However, because of my own particular life history, personal dynamics, and everything else that makes me human, for a brief time I became intensely and emotionally engaged in the drama. This is not an uncommon occurrence when working with dissociation.

As confusion yielded to reflection, I continued to wonder whether this actually was a dream or whether it might be something else entirely. The dreams of extremely dissociated patients can differ from the dreams of less dissociative people. For example, dream characters may reflect different dissociated self-states, both known and unknown; they may be the attempt of a dissociated self-state to communicate its existence to the dreamer and/or analyst. Dreams may express or attempt to clarify the nature of relatedness and relational conflict within the architecture of the dissociative mind. Dream characters may represent different self-states having different experiences, thoughts, and associations to the same dream (Howell, 2011; Kluft, 2015). Or sometimes what is experienced by one self-state as a dream may turn out not to be a dream at all, but that self-state's reported experience while in a hypnoid, trance-like state (see Barrett, 1996).

It occurred to me that the drama being enacted by Anthony and Anna, in what was experienced by Margaret as her dream, the seduction, the pulling of the hair, the aggression and sexual violence, was frighteningly similar to Janice's (the part of Alice who holds the abuse memories) description of what her father had so often done to her. I then began to consider that Margaret needed to experience this internal event, which enacted her early traumatic abuse, as a dream to make it less real and overwhelming.

Anthony presented himself on Monday morning in a way that felt like a caricature of a sociopath. He was arrogant, nasty, and proud of his actions. He pushed, provoked, and taunted me with sarcasm and hostility. I could feel the anger I experienced over the weekend rushing through me again. I could say that I decided to embrace my anger, but in retrospect I don't think I had a choice or could have handled it in any other way. Being gripped by my own feelings in this way was very difficult because I knew many, if not all, of the ways in which Alice experiences herself would be observing how I negotiated my intense feelings. Therefore I had to respond in a such a way that Alice would know I could contain the intensity of my feelings and express them without becoming abusive as her father had, while simultaneously setting limits and boundaries on what is and is not acceptable. I believed it was crucial that I not turn a blind eye, as her mother had, to what her internal experience was and be clear that all the different parts of Alice must respect the integrity of the body. And I had to do all this in a way that would not frighten or (re)traumatize the youngest, child parts of Alice.

There were no chairs flying, no fighting, no screaming, but using a firm voice to make boundaries very clear, Anthony understood that what he had experienced doing and what he felt proud of was *unacceptable and to never happen again!* That no one, on the inside world or the outside world, ever has the right to violate anyone else's body, *ever!* This was a way I "chose" to address the Anthony part of Alice, the part identified with her abuser, the perpetrator, and violator of boundaries. I hoped that by addressing what transpired between Anthony and Anna directly, Alice and her many dissociated self-states would know I wasn't turning a blind eye to her pain. I wanted her to know that she and her body must be respected, and that I would support her need for safety and security.

Switches between Alice's dissociated self-states continued. When Margaret came in, she began asking about her dream. Again I tried to shift her from the dream as a concrete event to consider that she was trying to communicate something we needed to understand. Later, Anna appeared and asked, "It happened on the inside world, so does that make it real?" I understood this to be an indication that this part of Alice was working on distinguishing between internal and external reality; she and Alice were developing the capacity to reflect on her experience in a new way.

Anna and I were working on how humiliated and embarrassed she felt for being hurt and abused. She tried to take responsibility for the rape, explaining, "It was my fault, I was flirting with him." I replied "Flirting can be fun and exciting, but that does not give anyone the right to touch you, hurt you, or abuse you in any way. It never did." This provoked a shift in self-states and Janice was then in the room, remembering and telling the details of her sexual abuse and how her father had begun raping her when she was six. Referring to the experiences of Anthony and Anna, she said, "It was just the way Anna remembers, it's what my father did to me." Janice began sobbing and sobbing, and I felt profound sadness. I was able to *feel* the sadness with Janice because she holds and feels the pain of her past, and because I had shaken off the dissociation of my own.

This became a pivotal moment in the work. Prior to these events, Janice was unable to control her retraumatizing flashbacks of sexual and physical abuse. Subsequently, she has begun to recognize her flashbacks as memories. Bromberg (2006) has written about helping the dreamer be in the dream and in the consulting room simultaneously. In a similar fashion, our work has helped Janice to *feel* her way back into her childhood and remember the nightmares of the past while remaining grounded in the present. Somewhat simultaneously, Alice has become more conscious of the dissociated experiences of her traumatic past, and has begun to say, "I remember." For Alice, the feelings are still too big and too deep, and they remain dissociated. I am hopeful that ultimately Alice will be able to know she can survive having her feelings as they become embedded in the memories of her past.

In summary, I tried to show how, when working with someone suffering from an extreme dissociative disorder, what is sometimes presented as a dream may be an internal acting out of a dissociated experience, or a condensation of experiences of early childhood abuse. The belief that what was experienced in historical reality as a dream serves the function of maintaining the dissociative encapsulation of the traumatic event(s). Thus, self-states unable to process the overwhelming affect associated with the events remain protected, while simultaneously communicating important information about the patient's mind to the analyst.

In addition, I attempted to offer an example of the complexity of the interactive transference–countertransference matrices occurring on different levels of consciousness in the co-participatory analytic process. In particular, I tried to highlight the ways in which these interactions often occur in dissociated states for both patient and analyst and that some of the analyst's "choices" are often powerful, reflexive responses to these forces.

Note

1 I would like to thank Dr. Sarah Schoen for her review of a previous draft of this paper and her helpful suggestions and editorial guidance.

References

Barrett, D. (Ed.) (1996). *Trauma and Dreams*. Cambridge, MA: Harvard University Press.

Bromberg, P. M. (2006). *Awakening the Dreamer: Clinical Journeys*. Mahwah, NJ: The Analytic Press.

Howell, E. (2011). *Understanding and Treating Dissociative Identity Disorder: A Relational Approach*. New York, NY: Routledge.

Kluft, R. P. (2016). Thoughts on working with the dreams of DID and DDNOS patients. In E. F. Howell & S. Itzkowitz (Eds.), *The Dissociative Mind in Psychoanalysis: Understanding and working with Trauma*. New York, NY: Routledge.

Chapter 13

Subjectivity and analysts' personal freedom

Irwin Hirsch

What has been called the "Relational turn" or the "post-modern turn" has, since the 1980s, effectively shifted prevailing psychoanalytic thinking in the United States away from the theretofore dominant view that psychoanalysis is an objective science. How any given psychoanalyst thinks, and what he or she believes, is inherently a function of the subjectivity of that unique individual. From this perspective, a belief in psychoanalysis' objectivity can be just as subjective as the belief that this is impossible. Each major psychoanalytic tradition or school has core theoretical suppositions about both the nature of human development and what constitutes an ideal clinical process. And while it is commonly assumed that most adherents of a given school subscribe to its beliefs and ideals, I suggest in this paper that each psychoanalyst engages with patients in ways that reflect as much the person of that analyst as membership in any of these particular schools of thought. In the negative this may be seen as anarchy, and in the positive, as creativity. Either way, I see this as inevitable and characterizing what Renik (1993) has called "the irreducible subjectivity" of analytic theorizing and of clinical process.

Critiques of psychoanalysis as science and the deconstruction of analytic objectivity began not with the Relational movement in the 1980s but its forerunner, the Interpersonal psychoanalysis of the 1940s. Sullivan's (e.g., 1953), replacement of the analyst as objectivist, blank screen with one whom he termed "participant-observer" was the first and most important step in identifying analytic process as a relationship between two subjective co-participants (see Fiscalini, 2004). Sullivan and his colleagues drew upon anthropology, sociology, and social psychology, swerving away from what had remained for many years an identification with the hard sciences and with medicine. Participant observation is largely based on Heisenberg's principle of uncertainty. Heisenberg was a physicist declaring that, since the observer inevitably influences what is observed, subjectivity reigns, even in the hardest of sciences, and we cannot ever be absolutely certain about what is concluded.

In addition to reconceptualizing psychoanalytic process as intrinsically mutually subjective, Sullivan and his colleagues posited a view of human development based less on universal principles like fixed psychosexual stages (e.g., Oedipal conflict, castration anxiety, sibling rivalry, guilt over masturbation) and more on examining the unique interpersonal history of each individual. With fewer theoretical preconceptions to lean on, it became more difficult not only to know how to proceed clinically but how to understand each unique individual patient. Wolstein (1959) captured this best with his simple credo: "Each patient is unique, each analyst is unique, each dyad is unique." Sullivan's pursuit of analytic work with psychotic patients exemplified the point that one must be careful about making *a priori* judgments about people based on universal ideas about symptoms, diagnoses, and developmental histories. One great value of uncertainty, as disruptive as it can be, is that it will more likely lead to the supreme analytic asset of curiosity (Stern, 1997).

This profound paradigm shift introduced by Sullivan and his colleagues, most prominently Erich Fromm and Clara Thompson, existed, with minor exceptions for many years only in the margins of psychoanalysis. It was not until 1983 when Jay Greenberg and Stephen Mitchell, two analysts trained at the White Institute, which was the first and one of very few prominent analytic institutes in the Interpersonal tradition, published their now classic text, *Object Relations in Psychoanalytic Theory*, that Interpersonal thinking became known to the wider world of psychoanalysis. Though Greenberg and Mitchell's new and broader term, "Relational," was more influenced by the Interpersonal perspective than any other single tradition, the inclusiveness of this term as well as the ways in which it incorporated other traditions (e.g., Object Relational), made it appealing to a far wider audience (Greenberg and Mitchell, 1983).

Greenberg, Mitchell, and a host of writers, some self-identified as Interpersonal though most as Relational, effectively elaborated Sullivan's participant-observer analyst as an irreducibly subjective co-participant, and concepts such as intersubjectivity, two-person psychology, and dialectical constructivism flourished. Assuming that analysts were always countertransferring, this concept drew intense analytic focus. Traditional conceptions of transference distortion evolved into mutual transference–countertransference enactment, with an emphasis on the significance of the analyst's conscious and, most significantly, unconscious involvement in psychoanalytic process. The inherently subjective concept of mutual enactment was embraced by a wide range of analytic traditions in and out of the large Relational umbrella,[1] though distinctive elements of the history of various traditions remain evident in both theoretical/developmental ideas about the origins of enactments and in recommended ways of engaging clinically. Certainly some historically meaningful overlap and divergence can be found among "schools" in their use of this concept, and I have little question that there are different emphases between Mitchell's largely Interpersonally influenced thinking and, for example, middle-school Objective Relations theorists, contemporary Kleinians, Self-Psychologists and post Self-Psychologists and liberal contemporary Freudians.

But, for the most part, it is my sense that most Interpersonally identified thinkers are indistinguishable from what have now become mainstream Relational ways of conceptualizing and working[2] (Mitchell, 1988). And further, whatever distinctions can still be drawn between schools, no theoretical tradition, set of narratives, or preferred way of engaging with patients will ever be proven to be superior to others. Essentially, practitioners think in ways that are most personally resonant to them. We all like our basic ways of theorizing and working better than alternatives and privately think these superior, though upon reflection they can be said to be superior *only for us*.

I have suggested elsewhere (Hirsch, 2008, 2015) that analysts' preferred ways of thinking and working are based on a combination of personal and intellectual aesthetics, unique individual personalities, and identifications with personal analysts and/or teachers. Though many of us do remain at least somewhat loyal to the traditions in which we were raised, there may still be vast differences among members of each tradition, since personality and taste will always prevail, especially with regard to the way we engage with patients. In what follows I will articulate and briefly discuss nine dimensions of subjective preference that distinguish analysts, often somewhat independently of their identified traditions, from one another. While I will try not to, I will inevitably resort to a degree of "either/or" thinking. Further, while I am aware that some of these dimensions may seem to capture undesirable splits that would ideally be bridged or integrated, I also believe that our personal biases often outweigh our attempts to transcend them, and to some degree we will all, at times, fall into categories. Further, along each of these dimensions, I suspect that my own personal biases will be quite evident.

First, some of us are attracted to the hard sciences and to matters technical, while others find the humanities and social sciences more appealing. For the former there is greater likelihood of interpretive understanding and explanations of patients' development that can be very complicated and abstract. In the latter, there is usually more emphasis on description than explanation, and interpretations are more likely to sound common-sensical and pragmatic. Patients are thought about more novelistically – that is, in the way novelists may capture people. The first group may criticize the second for being superficial and insufficiently deep, while the latter may accuse the former of intellectualization and science or physics envy (see Levenson, 1972; Mitchell, 1988). I have suggested elsewhere (Hirsch, 2008, 2015) that the psychoanalytic profession from the beginning seemed to be burdened with a self-consciousness about being insufficiently scientific, often resorting to convoluted, explanatory conceptions that are unnecessarily complicated.

Second, some of us are temperamentally quiet and reserved and others more expressive and gregarious. Independently of theoretical prescriptions, this dimension alone may lead to vast differences in ways of engaging with patients. Individual practitioners may find theoretical reasons why one way is better than another in order to reduce conflict about one's own interpersonal strengths and weaknesses. Very reserved analysts may be critical of the intrusive elements of more active engagement, seeing it as interfering with the analytic ideal of patients expressing themselves without influence. Active verbal engagement may be viewed as narcissistic, self-centered, and competitive. More verbally engaged analysts may dismiss very quiet colleagues as cold and emotionally distant – hurtful to patients in this respect and too rigidly wedded to traditional analytic protocol. They may claim that excessive reserve sets a bad example for patients, discouraging them from being more emotionally expressive and verbally open (Renik, 1993).

Third, some analysts are inclined toward viewing patients as fragile and easily injured, while others see them as resilient and not benefitting from being treated as if they were delicate. The former group may try overtly to be gentle in manner and be very careful about broaching sensitive topics. Conceptions of timing may be central, along with the proclivity to judge that patients may not be ready to address certain material. Dealing with themes that emerge in the transference is more likely to be put on hold, and the patient tends to be assumed not to welcome the observations of the other. The term "need" is likely to be invoked, e.g., the patient "needs" to be held or contained. The latter group will often pay less attention to issues of timing, assuming that if a patient raises something explicitly or implicitly, this indicates a readiness to address it (Singer, 1965; Gill, 1982), and the same is true for the tendency to address issues in the transference as they appear. In this context there is no attempt for the analyst to engage or to speak in a manner that is not of normal tone. The term "need" is less likely to be invoked and the term "wish" is more likely to be used, e.g., the patient wishes to be held but this may or may not be the best thing for the analyst to do at this moment (Mitchell, 1988). Fundamentally, those analysts with this latter vision do not view well-intentioned interventions as likely to be profoundly damaging. The former group criticizes the latter for being insensitive to vulnerability and, because of this, more likely to retraumatize patients. The latter group is critical about the former's tendency to pathologize patients and, in so doing, treat them as even weaker than they may already feel. There also exists the charge that many analysts have a stake in seeing patients as "sick" as a way for the analyst to feel in a stronger and "healthier" state him or herself (Hirsch, 2014).

Fourth, and closely related to the above, is the conflict between emphasizing the degree to which patients have been hurt by important others and, conversely, viewing patients as unconsciously orchestrating and repeating in contemporary life the very hurts they sustained earlier in life. One view focuses on patient as almost exclusively a victim, the other on patient as unconscious agent in recreating a troubled future destiny. The former group may be more inclined to be empathic with patients' wounds and not at all actively question what the patient may be doing to invoke these wounds currently. To do otherwise would amount to blaming the victim, and piling new hurt on to old injury. Patients are not seen as healed enough to hear that they may be active agents in their current life in ways they were not when they were children.

The latter group believes that it is pathologizing for patients in most life situations to experience themselves in current life primarily as victims, since this implies that they have little control over life at it exists now.

This group argues that, although patients may feel soothed and comforted by analysts' exclusive empathy for their victimization, they will not likely change unless they can recognize how they unconsciously recreate their past miseries in their current lives. Further, this group of analysts posits that people may be all too comfortable in familiar unhappiness, and excessive empathizing with this misery can reduce the desire to move on from this well-known, albeit unhappy, state. These analysts are more likely to resonate with what Freud originally identified as the domain of psychoanalysis – not inevitable and ubiquitous sadness, tragedy, and unhappiness, but the misery that we ourselves unconsciously bring on. This said, every analyst knows that empathy with patients' subjective experience of their own lives is an absolute necessity. Conflict between respective points of view arises when one subgroup of analysts perceive the other as putting excessive emphasis on either empathy or on challenge of patients' experience of themselves.

Fifth, as Hoffman (1998) has thoroughly discussed, each analyst attempts to strike some balance between adhering to the more conservative tenets of historically standard psychoanalytic rituals, on one hand, and the injection of spontaneous commentary on the other (see also Tublin, 2011). Though we invariably engage differently with each unique patient, we all lean one way or another along the continuum of ritual and spontaneity. Those of us who adhere more closely to ritual may criticize the embrace of spontaneity as a form of analytic self-indulgence. They may view such analysts as insufficiently willing to take a contemplative back seat to patients' freedom to express themselves, perhaps even suppressing this freedom by usurping the expressive dimension. Those analysts who embrace spontaneous expressiveness are likely to see an excess of adherence to ritual as too rigid – perhaps reflecting a need to live by rules and regulations.

Sixth, along somewhat similar lines is the controversy over analysts' deliberate disclosure of affective states. However, spontaneous commentary is not synonymous with deliberate self-disclosure, though these can be conflated. One may make spontaneous comments or observations to patients without deliberately disclosing affective states. Indeed, the latter phenomenon remains the most controversial issue in analytic practice. Many analysts who embrace the value of spontaneous commentary are still reluctant to disclose affective states. One reason, not commonly acknowledged explicitly, is that the expectation that we will answer patients' questions about what we are feeling may leave us unduly exposed and anxious.

Just as the use of the couch and thus not being visually observed has been calming and liberating for many analysts, so too has the ritual of not being expected to talk about one's feelings. And of course, as with other forms of spontaneity, there is the argument that analysts' expressions of feelings are likely to exert excessive influence on patients and reflect narcissistic indulgences. Those who advocate a "judicious" use of deliberate disclosure claim that outlawing this mode of expression is too restrictive: Patients often know what we are feeling in any case and it is too *gamey* to withhold confirmation of what patients sense and perceive. Such withholding of verbally expressed affective states is seen as creating undue asymmetry in the analytic relationship.

Seventh, some analysts view many personal problems as endogenously based and may focus on the alleged biological and neurological roots of personality. This belief is most clearly present when dealing with patients who function less effectively, e.g., people with long-standing depression, those considered Aspergian, or borderline, or in any way psychotic. For such practitioners the value of diagnosis is obvious, not only because it places a limit on what can be expected from analytic work, but because it can dictate technical application, i.e., prescribed ways to treat such categories of patients. This follows from a medical model of psychoanalysis, and its proponents argue that failure to acknowledge the endogenous bases of personality not only avoids awareness of research literature, but is naïve and grandiosely quixotic. On the other end of this controversy are those who eschew biology and neurology as important factors in personality development. Rather, who we become is a function of our history of relationships with others and the internalization of life experiences. Viewing even severely dysfunctional individuals as predestined to be this way is far too limiting of human potential and can take the easy way out of what is a very difficult analytic task. While it is usually acknowledged that analytic work with more severely troubled people is more difficult than with high-functioning patients (see Searles, 1979; Hirsch, 2015), this is seen more as a function of entrenchment and adaptive self-protection than it is the result of anything endogenous. Analysts who view things in this way are likely to accuse their conceptual adversaries of being overly dependent on clear structure (e.g., diagnostic certainty) and may be envious of the "real doctors" in the medical profession.[3]

Eighth, some analysts place great value on retreat into private reverie during sessions, believing both that the occurrence of the retreat and the content of the reverie will be invariably informative about the patient. Others believe that, although the nature of the analytic interaction may provoke retreat, the content of the retreat and the amount of time spent there may often have little to do with any given patient. The former subset of analysts accuse the latter group of having insufficient faith in unconscious-to-unconscious communication and of adhering too rigidly to rational modes of analytic engagement. The alternative argument accuses the reverie celebraters of rationalizing their self-interested retreats, while simultaneously assuming that they reflect an unconsciously influenced profound connection to patients (Hirsch, 2008).

Ninth, an extension of this difference is the view that psychoanalysts by and large are an altruistic breed, in contrast with what may correspond with Sullivan's (1953) long-ago declaration that we are all more simply human than otherwise. Some analysts, for example, tend to be highly nurturing in ways that may lead them to feel that they are abandoning self-interest and only responding to what is best for patients. Others may not be especially nurturing, but may believe that they can uniformly stay pointedly attentive and engaged as consistent servants of the analytic process. Those more skeptical of a dominant altruism point out that holding such a self-deceptive view elevates analysts to a higher personal and moral plane than their patients. This, in turn, is unconsciously communicated to patients, and as well, reflects an element of denial that contrasts with the analytic ideal of acceptance of *all* facets of self-states and personal shortcomings.

I have noted elsewhere (Hirsch, 2008, 2015) that psychoanalytic process is best served when analysts are intensively and affectively engaged with their patients and are comfortable with the theoretical narratives and theories of therapeutic action that most resonate personally. Each of us is likely to have strong feelings about the advantages of our preferred theories and ways of working and this is as it should be. Try as we might to be flexible and reflect on our own preferences regarding the dimensions I have outlined above, who we have become as people and as professionals will inevitably prevail. As long as we are not excessively rigid in our beliefs and willing to try adapting to the idiosyncrasies of each individual patient, our personal commitments lead to both comfort and involvement. They are part of what puts us in a position to be productive. Indeed, each of our unique ways of working *is* superior to some alternative precisely because it best suits each of us as individuals. This degree of subjectivity creates muddle and confusion for those looking in from the outside, though I believe that it creates the basis for an important sense of security for those of us on the inside, and thus probably for our patients as well. Subjectivity reigns in every dimension of this most unscientific profession and it can be no other way. If this is thought to be a shortcoming in our field, we can only make the best of it.

Notes

1 The Interpersonally identified Levenson (1972), gave birth to this concept, referring to this phenomenon as "transformation," and asserting that the analyst must *unwittingly* become part of the patient's problem in order to help resolve it. It was Jacobs (1986), unaware of Levenson's writing, who first used the term "mutual enactment."

2 For a more thorough discussion of the juxtaposition of Interpersonal and Relational perspectives, see Hirsch (1998).

3 Parenthetically, the value of medication is less of a controversy than one might expect. Many analysts who eschew endogenous explanations of personality may be sanguine about medication because this can temper noxious symptoms. They would argue that psychology provokes biology and neurology. In other words, our biology or neurology have not caused our personality but are profoundly influenced by our affective states. For example, low serotonin levels do not cause depression; rather, when we are depressed, serotonin declines. Of course, this whole arena remains an area of profound difference among clinicians.

References

Fiscalini, J. (2004). *Coparticipant Psychoanalysis.* New York: Columbia University Press.

Gill, M. (1982). *Analysis of Transference (Volume 1).* New York: International Universities Press.

Greenberg, J. & Mitchell, S. (1983). *Object Relations in Psychoanalytic Theory.* Cambridge, MA: Harvard University Press.

Hirsch, I. (1998). Further thoughts about interpersonal and relational perspectives. *Contemporary Psychoanalysis,* 34: 501–538.

Hirsch, I. (2008). *Coasting in the Countertransference: Conflicts of Self-Interest between Analyst and Patient.* New York: Routledge.

Hirsch, I. (2014). Narcissism, mania and analysts' envy of patients. *Psychoanalytic Inquiry,* 34: 408–420.

Hirsch, I. (2015). *The Interpersonal Tradition: The Origins of Psychoanalytic Subjectivity.* New York: Routledge.

Hoffman, I. (1998). *Ritual and Spontaneity in the Psychoanalytic Process.* Hillsdale, NJ: The Analytic Press.

Jacobs, T. (1986). On countertransference enactments. *Journal of the American Psychoanalytic Association,* 34: 289–307.

Levenson, E. (1972). *The Fallacy of Understanding.* New York: Basic Books.

Mitchell, S. (1988). *Relational Concepts in Psychoanalysis.* Cambridge, MA: Harvard University Press.

Renik, O. (1993). Analytic interaction: conceptualizing technique in the light of the analyst's irreducible subjectivity. *Psychoanalytic Quarterly,* 62: 553–571.
Searles, H. (1979). *Countertransference and Related Subjects.* New York: International Universities Press.
Singer, E. (1965). *Key Concepts in Psychotherapy.* New York: Basic Books.
Stern, D. B. (1997). *Unformulated Experience.* Hillsdale, NJ: The Analytic Press.
Sullivan, H. S. (1953). *The Interpersonal Theory of Psychiatry.* New York: Norton.
Tublin, S. (2011). Discipline and freedom in relational psychoanalysis. *Contemporary Psychoanalysis,* 47: 519–546.
Wolstein, B. (1959). *Countertransference.* New York: Grune & Stratton.

Part V

Body tyranny

Hyperawareness and hyperdeadness with eating-disordered patients

Chapter 14

Fear, shame, courage

Body-to-body interactions as we move towards untapped imperfection

Jean Petrucelli

Madeleine L'Engle once said, "When we were children, we used to think that when we were grown-up we would no longer be vulnerable. But to grow up is to accept vulnerability . . . To be alive is to be vulnerable." In this paper, I will share a personal story and two clinical vignettes to illustrate how fear, courage, shame – the mutuality of our experiences in body and mind – speak to the underbelly and emotional tenor of much of our work with eating-disordered patients. These emotions exist in between states of hyperawareness and hyperdeadness. These states emerge in our eating-disordered patients' struggle against their own desires: wanting, longing, hunger, yearning, and the vulnerability of reaching with one's appetite towards the world of others is subverted.

Our eating-disordered patients are trying to bear what feels unbearable. Barraged by culture, or tempted by the fruit of an "other," when these patients engage in the silent disordered eating battle in their heads, even the simplest experience creates a *mélange* of inner turmoil, shame, and body tyranny. For a patient suffering from anorexia, whether or not to lift the fork to her mouth begins the debate. If she manages to talk herself successfully into doing so, the end result remains: she can only taste shame. For patients suffering from bulimia, there is often a history of chaos in the family which contributes to these patients' development of pseudomaturity. Parentified children do not learn to self-soothe; instead they become caretakers to defend against their own neglect. Their inner voices call them "fat pig, lazy bitch, loser" – harsh, shaming, critical judgments towards the self. In both anorexia and bulimia, unprocessed emotional hurt and pain stay trapped in the body, and the maladaptive attempt at a solution is to numb that pain with an eating disorder.

But before returning to the pain and solution of the eating-disordered patient, I want to offer a personal story. It begins with a phone call I received after leaving for work one Friday from my significant other/soulmate, who opened with, "I guess you didn't get my message *yet* because you are *way* too calm." Of course, *no matter what I might have been doing*, he now had my full attention! "Well," he continued . . . when I was leaving the house this morning I saw something fly by – *in the dining room*. I think it was a small bird or a sparrow, but I was late for my train so I left." With stunned disbelief, I muttered, "You left a *wild* bird flying around in our house?" "Yeah . . . sorry," he said. Now this story could go in several directions (anger or forgiveness, just to name a few), but I'm going to stick with fear, courage, and shame.

Let's begin with shame. Now he *knows* I'm terrified of birds. In fact, to confess, I am a "Chicken Little" around most animals – unless they are in a jar. When my fear of animals comes up with my patients, and it inevitably does, they often delight in seeing the look on my face and laugh at my being afraid. And, of course, in spite of my fears – or, perhaps, because of them – an abundance of small, medium, and large canines (although size is subjective) have crossed the analytic threshold of my office. Yes, I admit it: I'm afraid of dogs, too.

But back to the bird. I remember exactly where I was sitting when I was told about our uninvited houseguest and could feel the shift in my body-state begin. Panic rose in my chest, dizziness, near syncope, sweat, my heart pounded with dread. The thought of this wild creature spending several days in my house, while we were away for the weekend had me in a complete tizzy. What was I going to do? What if I was the first one back to the house? How could I face this bird alone? What if this bird had decompensated and become psychotic? What if other birds had come in? What if they were now conspiring? Was I to become Tippi Hedren[1]? Should we sell the house?

Now let's go to courage, although not mine. In my panic, I called my neighbor to ask for the name of an exterminator. My neighbor is an amazing woman who was recently diagnosed with multiple myeloma cancer and had just undergone a series of chemotherapy treatments and bone marrow transplants. When I tell her about the bird, she gets all excited and with a giggle says, "I have your key. I'll go over to your house. I've been a prisoner in my house for weeks – I could *use* an adventure!" Armed with a small broom she proceeds to track my imprisoned two-legged winged animal, which by the way, was no sparrow but a flicker, in fact, a nine-inch woodpecker, throughout various rooms and floors in my house. This *nine-inch pecker* headed towards a closed window and got stuck in the *window* treatments (Freud could have a field day). With an unfailing sense of purpose and confidence, my neighbor tore away the curtain and guided this *wild monster* (now a *Tyrannosaurus rex* bird in my mind) to safety – his or her natural habitat – the outside.

I'm waiting with bated breath in my New York office when she calls and says 'Done!" I have tears of gratitude and relief for no longer having to live in the anticipated *terror* I was feeling of going home. As I am thanking her profusely, she stops me and says,

> Actually I want to thank you – the timing of your call was impeccable. I was in the middle of a heated argument with my mother, and I finally mustered up the courage to tell her, for the first time in 59 years, how much shame I have carried and lived with, because I felt that she had forced me to live my whole life in fear . . . It was from the small things – like making me wear a bathing suit cap swimming in the local pool when other girls didn't . . . because chlorine, to my mother, of course, was poison . . . to raising me to be a girl who should never want anything *more* for herself – no career – *nothing* to build *my* self-esteem – I was raised to be afraid of change, the world is scary. The message was just find a man, get married, and he will take care of you! *You* called me at the moment that I realized, in this argument, that my mother would *never* be able to hear me and could only be defensive with me . . . She couldn't take responsibility or understand my shame – *she* would never change . . . but I – I could feel the change in me.

I am listening intently and then blurt out, "Well today you are *my hero*! I called you for help, and you came through." We laughed, but she kept insisting that I had really made *her* day and that *I* needed to accept this, because ironically, until today, she had never had the guts to tell her mother what she really felt. And the clincher, she said, occurred as she was running out of her house – to rescue *my* house. Her mother yelled out, "Don't go over there alone!" to which my neighbor yelled back, "*Just try and stop me*!"

Why am I telling this story? The simple answer is because it's linked, for me, to the two clinical moments I will discuss below and how emotions such as fear, shame, and courage show up in body-to-body interactions – consciously, viscerally, and unconsciously. The more complex answer is that, with the story I've just told, I'm hoping *you – the reader – felt* what I did, and you'll simply "*get it.*" For me, the mutuality of the feelings that occurred in this exchange with my neighbor captures the *felt experience* of many aspects of our work with eating-disordered patients. It shows up in clinical moments when we give, take, and share a part of ourselves in ways we can't anticipate, until we do it.

Our eating-disordered patients are often fighting for dear life, and they present challenges in how they engage us and communicate with their bodies. We see bodies that feel in sync, and out of sync. Our patients compare, contrast, and create cacophonies in their heads, which become *our* therapeutic arena. From Lady Gaga to the Dalai Lama, bodies tell multiple stories about the self and communicate a range of affects and desires. Patients bring us not only their mental anguish but their distressed bodies as well (see, for example, Chapter 17, by Orbach) as the body itself sometimes tells a piece of their narrative. Here are two examples.

The moment Willomeena walks into my office I know I am in for it. Like an unstoppable force of nature, this diminutive 5-foot-tall, 45-year-old woman, *marches straight into* me, and with the strength of Hulk Hogan bear hugs me to the count of ten and doesn't let go! It's an attack hug. I can barely breathe. This is her greeting after a two-week break, and although she had "threatened" me with this "attack" before, I was still unprepared for its intensity, force, and duration. It was an act of both love and aggression, ripe with defiance against our understood boundaries, and blazing with confidence in her ability to succeed in its execution. I am first caught unaware and feel rendered helpless. I react with stunned curiosity, thinking, "Boy, she really wasn't kidding."

After successfully recovering from full-blown anorexia, Willomeena was diagnosed with tardive dystonia and then tardive dyskinesia – both severe movement disorders that might have been averted. There was a neurobiological underpinning for the dystonia but the tardive dyskinesia resulted from a prior treatment where she was misdiagnosed and over-medicated. This was a tragic error that, while taking a devastating toll on her psyche, took an irreparable toll on her body.

The aggression exhibited in Willomeena's attack hug is layered and complicated. The tightness of her embrace embodies the anger towards those who wronged her and didn't protect her. It also embodies her wish to have me both feel her pain through holding her aggression and constriction, as well as get her pain – perhaps even take her pain – as her body demands its release by squeezing it out and putting it in me. She may have also needed to "know" if her actions would undo me, or drive me to retaliate as others had. When I asked her what she was thinking that made her *want* to do this, she told me it was an act of love.

But love is problematic, as her history reveals physical abuse, numerous battered relationships, humiliations, and unspoken bargains for acceptance. Willomeena's anticipated terror of the other's capacity to humiliate, torment, and shame her has made it difficult for her to engage with others in the thing she wants most: a powerful struggle that allows her to find out what *she* is made of, but without destroying the other. In one fell swoop of this crushing hug, Willomeena and I enact numerous scenarios and relational demands: her demonstration of power and desire to dominate, her need to render me helpless, her plea for help and comfort, her wish to merge, her wish to destroy, her desire to possess my body, her desire to have a functioning body, her wish for me to feel her pain, and her false bravado that defensively masks her fear. But each encounter suggests a new potential direction for us to explore. When she hugs me, do I hug her back? And how hard?

Willomeena recovered from anorexia only to lose confidence in her body through a movement disorder. In losing confidence in her body, she lost confidence in herself. Re-finding some confidence in her impulses – in her desires – was part of our work.

I had to allow a certain degree of thoughtful flexibility around the frame and her need to "use" me, without conveying that I was letting her do *just* what she wanted because I had *given up* on her. In other words, if I colluded in letting her do *just as she wanted*, when it was not something I felt comfortable with, I would risk repeating the historical pattern in which her mother would be punitive and resentfully withdraw. So, if I were going to hug Willomeena back, I couldn't give her a limp fish hug. At the same time, I wanted to address the use of her aggressive energies in her body, the importance of respecting boundaries, and help her understand the impact she has on others. Perhaps this is a tall order, but it is only by keeping each of these in mind that I feel I can help her live *with* her aliveness and not feel shame.

In Willomeena's mind, boundaries are conventions waiting to be transcended and one may transcend any convention if one can conceive of doing so. Her belief, like her love, is a force to be reckoned with and understood. She needed me to hold her anger and shame and to witness her courage. And she used her body to overtly convey this. For her, there is no hope other than defiance. Defiance is her aliveness, expressed through breaking body boundaries. I had to respect her defiance while helping her see how the way she expressed it affected me.

So I let her hug me, and *sort-of* hugged her back. She looks at me then, waiting to see what I'll do. I ask her to tell me the first thought that came to mind about hugging. She shares with me a story about her father, who was not officially diagnosed as bipolar yet came across clearly so. In his manic phase, he would hug her, squeeze her tight, and – *she didn't like it* – but it was the only connection she had with him. She says,

> My father would hug me, hurt me, disregard me. And then I married a man who mauls me and takes it as a personal rejection if I say, "Please don't squeeze me so tight." Without asking, my husband grabs my breasts, while I'm changing, and he thinks that's sexy! If I say no, I feel guilty.

This opens up the door for us to talk about the idea of respect for the body and body boundaries – hers, mine, and ours – and how she might want to be treated by others. We explore what it feels like to have and want ownership of one's body. To value the body, one must first experience others valuing it and you. Willomeena then reveals how she wakes up her 17-year-old son and 13-year-old daughter. She gets into bed with them each morning but stays on top of the covers. Her son reaches over and hugs her. She says, "I'm scared of him having an erection and I've recently become really aware of that – you are helping me rethink the meaning of my morning hug ritual." This had never occurred to her or come up in our sessions before.

Fast forward a few years, after this summer's break with her body progressively falling apart and failing rapidly, Willomeena leaves me a message before our return, telling me to be prepared. This year, she warns me, she is going to *sit in my lap* for the entire session (a double session, I might add). But this time, when she enters the room she sits down in the chair and with a twinkle in her eyes says, "I had you scared, didn't I?" (And as I have already described above, it's not hard to scare me.) On the one hand, Willomeena still needs me to know that anything from her is possible. On the other hand, she now trusts in us and can play with her words. Her body, once the vehicle for all communication, has begun to take a back seat, as her faith that *her* words can truly reach and impact me has developed more in our work together.

The same, however, could *not* be said for my patient Lola, who struggles with binge eating and bulimarexia. Bulimarexia is a syndrome in which the symptoms of both bulimia and anorexia are present, characterized by distorted body image, excessive weight loss, and use of forced vomiting to compensate for periods of binge eating.

In our second meeting, Lola, fresh out of residential treatment, is raring to go and out to do business. Her style of deception and guardedness is pervasive as she demonstrates with her body an overcompensation in physical action for her feelings of vulnerability. Lola, like Willomeena – like so many eating-disordered patients – has lost faith in the human reliability of the other. Thus, as a general rule of thumb, she never really develops sustaining interpersonal relationships or progressively withdraws from any that do take root. Lola's withdrawal takes the form of a false self-presentation of friendliness that is palpably disingenuous. It also represents a test: will I see through this façade and call her on it while understanding that the purpose is to hide her single most important and only steadfast relationship – her secret retreat to food? Now that Lola is out of a residential treatment setting, and "free" to do as she pleases, I am about to discover that "whatever Lola wants, Lola gets." She is prepared for me to react against a decision she has already made, and to prove her point she needs to take out "the big guns" and flash her advantage.

Lola comes in to this particular appointment with the idea of a scheduled surgery to finally correct the size differential of her breasts. I listen intently and simply ask, "When did you make this decision?" She takes this as a criticism or a suggestion that I don't believe her about the size of this problem, sight unseen. In an unparalleled, one-two Brandi Chastain (the US soccer player, for those of you who might not remember) move, her shirt is up, only this time, bra off, she argues her point with "*See? Can't you see the size differential?*" Her "bodacious" breasts were now within inches of my face. I mustered a measly, albeit nonchalant, "OK, I see your point, but . . . "

Indeed, what is the point? For Lola, so early in our relationship, I felt her communication, shocking as it was, was most important as a signifier of what she needed to know I could tolerate and accept *about* and communicated *through* her body, about her body's need to break the rules, even as she was threatening to subjugate it surgically to social convention. Bodies can contain unconscious aggressive impulses, whether in an "attack hug" or an unexpected unveiling of a body part. But it's not only aggressiveness communicated in Willomeena's, or Lola's body-to-body interactions, but their conflicted longings as well.

As therapists, how we *feel* our patients bodily – the contagiousness of belly laughter, yawns, and mood states, such as a nonchalant demeanor – can also offer insight into the meanings of various body-states. Sometimes these body-states or body reactions are defensive in nature, like the experience of unstoppable laughter triggered by inappropriate circumstances. Is it a dissociated reaction to surprise, incongruity, or historical trauma? And why is it so contagious? Body-states, like affect states, attest to the power of relatedness in articulating their meaning. After all, we can't tickle ourselves. Bodily and emotional influence is always at play. Does empathy start with the unconscious synchronization of bodies? If that is true, then our role as therapists may be to join and accept the patient first in a bodily dimension before helping her consciously reconstruct how she would feel if she were in someone else's shoes.

Eating-disordered patients think with their bodies, and working in the register of the body is profoundly important. Embodied cognition has profound implications for working with these patients because it implies that the mind is not only connected to the body but that the body influences the mind and therefore influences one's ability to self-regulate internal emotional states (Balcetis & Cole, 2009). Patients will communicate their fear, their courage, and their shame through their body-states (Petrucelli, 2015). Imitation and influence occur as patients involuntarily "enter" the bodies of those around them, sometimes strengthening a bond, while other times creating envy and aggression. I've written elsewhere that the power of the clinical encounter resides in the analytic couple's ability to regulate relatedness (Petrucelli, 2004, 2010, 2015). But, with our eating-disordered patients, this relatedness is as much between bodies as it is between minds.

As Susie Orbach (2009) has poignantly written, "Bodies desire to be loved, accepted or admired in some way that they have never known." Embracing the pleasure and aliveness of our bodies builds confidence and is something altogether different from objectification. At the same time, to know oneself is only possible through the eyes – through the felt, bodily experience – of the other. For each person the expressive and symbolic meaning of one's own body changes with changes in one's self and body-state. Understanding one's affect states, disconnects, and desires in the experience of mind and body is critical in trying to remain consciously embodied and relationally attuned.

And this brings me back to the bird episode with my neighbor and our contrasting and shifting bodily and mind experiences. My neighbor was taught to live in fear, and yet she proved courageous in the face of my fearfulness. At 59, she was seeing herself differently and we both saw something differently through the "eyes" – and through the felt bodily experience of each other's experience and therefore, of each other. To me she was heroic, not just in battling cancer, but in her unquestioning desire and bravery to help another and I was helpless and hesitant – the scaredy cat – afraid of a bird. Historically, my neighbor thought of me as capable and strong in my "athletic" body and typically not one to be afraid. But in our moment of reaching out to each other for help, we were vulnerable together without shame, and through this shared experience, we both felt accepting of ourselves and admiring of each other.

I think this is akin to what can happen when we let a patient use us, when we use ourselves to recognize the patient, and when, together, we find a way to recover. This means feeding our patients, feeding ourselves, and feeding the relationship. Only then is the treatment full, and only then can the patient feel that there is hope. Willomeena and Lola both wanted me to fully experience *their* experience and in *their* own bodily ways, they found the perfect way to do it.

It is easy sometimes to forget how much courage is needed for an eating-disordered patient to take us into *his or her world.* And it is also hard at times to live with the body and affective states elicited in us when we take in our patients' shame and fear. Fear immobilizes. Shame destabilizes. Courage revitalizes. If we stay open to what bodies tell us, then we can, with our patients, begin to process the mutual experience of holding another's mind and body, another's body and mind, *in mind.* This in turn creates new relational ground. This is ground on which we can not only kill two birds with one stone, we can also say a bird in the hand is worth two in the bush because, after all, a *bird* in the house is still *better* than a mouse.

Note

1 For those of you too young to remember or too old and have forgotten, Tippi Hedren was the actress from the 1963 Alfred Hitchcock movie, *The Birds.*

References

Balcetis, E., and Cole, S. (2009). Body in mind: the role of embodied cognition in self-regulation. *Social and Personality Psychology Compass,* 3 (5): 759–774.

L'Engle, M. (n.d.) Quotes.net, STANDSS4 LLC, 2015. Available online at: http//www.quotes.net/quote/14957 (accessed June 24, 2016).

Orbach, S. (2009). *Bodies*. New York: Picador.

Petrucelli, J. (2004). Treating eating disorders. In R. H. Coombs (Ed.), *Handbook of Addictive Disorders: A Practical Guide to Diagnosis and Treatment* (pp. 312–352). Hoboken, NJ: John Wiley.

Petrucelli, J. (2010). Things that go bump in the night: secrets after dark. In J. Petrucelli (Ed.), *Knowing, Not-Knowing & Sort-of-Knowing: Psychoanalysis and the Experience of Uncertainty* (pp. 135–150). London: Karnac Books.

Petrucelli, J. (2015). Mermaids, mistresses & Medusa: getting 'inside out and outside in' the relational; montage of an eating disorder. In J. Petrucelli (Ed.), *Body-States: Interpersonal and Relational Perspectives on the Treatment of Eating Disorders.* London: Routledge (pp. 13–34).

Chapter 15

What we talk about when we talk about food

Judith Brisman

Angelina is an amalgam of one patient, of all my patients. She is quick-witted, playful, introspective, and impossibly adept at deflecting any connective embrace. In our sessions, there are always problems to tackle, family issues to discuss, work crises to navigate. But the biggest problem, Angelina insists, is her weight. When Angelina entered treatment at age 27, she was 240 lb and 5' 4". She hoped to lose 80 lb, following bariatric surgery from which she had already lost 60 lb, and then, for years, had plateaued.

Because I am known as a specialist in the field of eating disorders, when patients work with me, they come with an expectation that I am going to help them change their eating behaviors. Trained both as a psychoanalyst at the William Alanson White Institute and as an expert in addictions (my first job was in the alcoholism outpatient department at St. Vincent's Hospital in Manhattan), I have from the start grappled with the intricate play between direct intervention with symptomatic behavior and exploration of what might lead to the development of these behaviors in the first place.

And so, with patients like Angelina, I have argued for an approach (Brisman, 1992, 1995) that immediately embraces the patient's language (that of eating, food, and weight) as the therapist slowly, quietly, over time, introduces her own language, that of analytic inquiry.

This kind of therapeutic work involves a focused and detailed questioning regarding the food and bodily obsessions and, at least at the start, a seemingly behaviorally oriented technique that allows for ongoing and direct management of the eating behaviors. With Angelina, for example, this meant tracking, session to session, when she ate, what she ate, what felt OK, what didn't. Initially, Angelina did not ever think about what she was eating. Food was air. She never noticed when a breath was taken. Just paying attention was a critical first step.

When a more detailed understanding of the eating patterns emerges, the work then involves a direct exploration of what behaviors the patient can engage in before turning to food. This may include the introduction of self-care and self-soothing behaviors, the use and presence of other people, exploration of what one is feeling or thinking before eating, communication, distraction, even planning regarding the food itself. What is the patient willing to do before turning to the food? I have the patients write this down; we're maddeningly specific. The language and world of the patient take center stage.

Angelina, like many of my patients at this early point, had no way of caring for or listening to herself that didn't involve food. The only alternative to eating she could think of was to literally leave the room if she could, or get a glass of water, so that she could, for a moment, remember the part of her that wanted to be mindful of what she was feeling and thinking – and what she would eat next. This wasn't easy. There was nothing besides the food to quiet her ever-pulsing feelings. She was lonely; the food was her friend. The highs that one experiences from falling in love, having a life adventure, deeply connecting with another person – all had, lifelong, been replaced with the high of eating whatever she wanted. For Angelina, eating was a moment of liberation, freedom, excitement, embrace. It enveloped her life. Taking the water, stopping, listening . . . and literally breathing were the flat-footed initial alternatives to the ever-present possibility of bingeing.

With all patients (as long as they are engaged and willing), "contracts" are made, transitional objects of sorts, in which agreements are established between therapist and patient regarding the substitution of "alternative behaviors" for disordered eating. An overt pact is negotiated that involves the patient's attending to needs or emotions, instead of bingeing at very specific moments in time – the minute someone gets home from work, the hour before bed, the walk to work. And the more specific the negotiation, the better (think of Sullivan and the detailed inquiry). Angelina contracted for one night a week to get the water and pay attention, to feel, before she ate. That was not a minor step.

I want to emphasize that, despite the introduction of specifically concrete therapeutic action, the goal of treatment is not merely symptomatic change (though one certainly hopes for that). More expansively, the goal is the eventual exploration of what happens between patient and analyst as this concrete directed work evolves. Herein lies the potential for analytic conceptualization, the introduction of the language of the therapist. In that regard, the emphasis is not primarily on interpretation of internal conflict or inner life. Rather, the focus of interpretation and exploration is on what actually happens between two people. "What is going on around here?" Levenson (1983, p. 53) asks in an iconic representation of the interpersonal analytic exchange. What happens when two people are in the room, when they make an agreement together? When and how is the other embraced, discarded, kicked out? Often a contract can spark healthier eating patterns and self-care. But when the contract gets broken (or even when it's kept), what has happened? And why? Herein lies the potential for inquiry. Herein lies the introduction of psychoanalytic technique.

The work with Angelina got off to a running start. She couldn't explain why, but she knew she was eating less. Was it our contracts, reporting in to me, the possibility that prior to even our first session, she had already decided she was ready to take things the next step? It was hard to know. But in a dizzying jump forward, Angelina found herself losing weight weekly. Angelina lost 30 lb. I quietly cheered.

A couple of months later, however, and now into the weekly rhythm of treatment, Angelina hit a wall – though I didn't initially know it. A work crisis erupted for her. A dog was bought. A brother became ill. The focus on weight silently disappeared as life issues catapulted to the foreground. There was just too much else going on to talk about food.

As Angelina plummeted into a swirl of worry about life decisions, I too found myself in a vortex of worry. I worried that Angelina wasn't getting the best of me. We had had to change her appointment time due to a new job, and I was tired when I saw her, distracted. I worried that I was seeing her too late in the evenings (mind you, we're talking 6 p.m., not 9). I started a furious attempt to rearrange the session time so that I could be more alert. But early-morning meetings were logistically out of the question for Angelina and new job responsibilities precluded a midday appointment. We just couldn't come up with a time that felt right.

Clearly, at this point, I had no idea what we were doing in our work together. And in terms of the food and the weight, I certainly didn't know if Angelina's weight was steady. Was she was OK with things the way they were? Was she in trouble? I would look at her body to see how we were doing. Maybe she was losing weight and didn't want me to intrusively ask. Maybe she wanted to surprise me. I thought her pants were loose. See, we *were* working. But maybe this was how she looked before. I felt delusional. I couldn't ask – Angelina was so worried about so much else at the time. I couldn't reach her. I felt dead.

And so we labored on. I heard about the ongoing crises in Angelina's life; we juggled times, switched meetings, missed meetings. Only over time did I realize that I had to pay attention to the fact that the sessions were deadeningly hard for me. Something had to give.

And so one session, as a new crisis arose that I knew would now be the focus for weeks on end, I dared to say the unspeakable. I stopped talking about what we were talking about when we talked about food – which was indeed anything but food. I talked about the food itself.

I told Angelina that, as important as the life events were, I felt like I was missing her. We hadn't spoken about eating in weeks. I didn't know if she had lost weight or gained, if she was in trouble and losing nights to bingeing. Most importantly, I had no idea who she was – even though she often cried in the sessions and was clearly moved by the life issues we were discussing.

Oddly, as soon as I said what I did, it wasn't hard to talk at all. Angelina was right there with me, somewhat stunned but attentive, aware, and with a cascade of memories and images that took us immediately to a new place. She indeed hadn't been paying attention to the food – or to me. She knew the sessions were dead. We spoke openly and at length about the disconnection. It was the first I learned that a television set had been her babysitter and that her deepest relationships had been with TV characters who were reliably and endlessly there for her. She loved these people deeply. But she noted a TV screen couldn't love back. I told her how furious it made me inside when I couldn't reach her, how alone I felt, how I thought moving the sessions would help. Angelina cried and talked deeply about what it was like to be her. She told me how angry she has been when I initially pushed her forward with the eating. I had taken away everything she knew and now she was alone, as though she was stranded on an alien planet with no one in sight. She knew what it was like not to be able to reach someone.

Over the next sessions, Angelina was critically insightful about her retreat to a secret safe place where no one can reach her, the world in which she grew up. I've told her that I don't know one thing she thinks about me. I'm a TV character – and I am her, as a child, watching the TV characters. My experience is that I sort of don't exist. She holds no mirror for me; when she looks at me, I have no idea who she is seeing. And I, in turn, have wondered if what I have been mirroring back to her is not herself, but her body. Angelina told me she lives in a glass prison. In these moments, we shatter the glass.

And so we move on. Angelina has asked that we don't focus on the weight for now. She needs to get her bearings. She maintains the initial weight loss, but she is not ready yet to move forward. This, by the way, has been a common experience with patients. Weight is lost and then, unexpectedly, the patient comes to a halt. Other issues emerge in the work together. Often though, over time, the patient reinstates the work with the food and weight, either directly with me again, or now with other outside support – nutritionists, trainers, programs, and sometimes with the help of medication such as Topomax. The work of healthier self-care takes a next step forward.

With Angelina, after the sessions I reported, I had a different experience of her body. At least for a moment, her weight felt less important – it was *her* body, not mine, and she had to figure out what to do with it. The weeks moved forward, with a sense that we had been through something important together. Yes, there have been new avalanches of life crises; no question, there are yet again moments when I feel the black, deadening dullness of what it's like encased in a television set.

But there also is now that anchor of the more engaged place that we visited together. Now it is Angelina, not just me, who can say that she knows we are back in the glass prison. She can tell me that she needs to be there that day; she needs the safety. She reassures me (yes, me) that we will return to working directly on our relationship – and with the food. She tells me why she needs the retreat. And for these moments, a connection between the two of us is tentatively back, the glass wall momentarily opens, and I don't have to peek at her body to find out how we are doing. Angelina reminds me that we will continue to speak the unspoken, and we dare to move on.

References

Brisman, J. (1992). Bulimia in the late adolescent: an analytic perspective to a behavioral problem. In J. O'Brien, D. Pilowsky & O. Lewis (Eds.), *Psychotherapies with Children: Adapting the Dynamic Process*. Washington, DC: American Psychiatric Press.

Brisman, J. (1995). Addiction. In M. Lionells, J. Fiscalini, C. Mann & D. Stern (Eds.), *Handbook of Interpersonal Psychoanalysis* (pp. 537–554). Hillsdale, NJ: Analytic Press.

Levenson, E. (1983). *The Ambiguity of Change*. New York: Basic Books.

Chapter 16

"So must we to others call"

Anorexia, dissociation, and the analyst's neglect

Susan Sands

When my anorexic patient Jill was in an inpatient eating disorders program, she was asked to do an art piece about herself. She crumbled up a sheet of paper and placed it inside a small cardboard box. When asked to describe it, she said, "I'm empty inside, and I can't get out what's inside." What a paradox. Empty – yet not empty. Something in there, wadded up, trashed, and unknowable, that she can't recognize or open up. In my view, anorexia is one of the most severe dissociative disorders, because it operates so pervasively and incessantly in the patient's life that neither traumatic memory nor genuine desire can penetrate its symptomatology.

Now in her late 40s, Jill has been struggling with severe anorexia since her early 20s, rising above her usual 86–88 lb only a couple of times when hospitalized. Because I am discussing a particularly chronic and challenging case, I will not be describing towering, even moderate, therapeutic success. Instead, I hope to show how Jill and I have been able to make some small progress by working through a particularly daunting enactment which allowed her to come to know more about the crumbled-up inside her and to unspring herself a bit from her constrictive box.

More theoretically, I will be describing: (1) how anorexia may be understood as an attempt to self-regulate through the repudiation of need and desire; (2) how the anorexic individual dissociates need and desire in three ways – a self-object relationship with food and the process of eating (or not eating), a subjugating relationship with the body, and the projection of need and desire on to the Other; (3) how a particular enactment can often emerge, in which the analyst's oscillating states of worry and neglect arise in reciprocal relationship to the patient's alternating states of needing or not needing; and (4) how understanding this enactment can help the patient emerge from her anorexic cocoon into life.

Jill

Jill's early family environment was painfully permeated by the themes of this book – the unknowable and unspeakable. When she was a senior in college, she received the shocking news from her mother that her father had another family – including two daughters – during most of her childhood. Her mother had always known. Jill immediately recalled her father's many late-night phone calls from the rec room, seeing him in a car with another woman when he was supposed to be out of town, and all the Christmases and Thanksgivings when he was supposedly away on business. She also gained a new understanding of her mother's deep depression, passivity, rage, and isolation.

Jill's early life had been marked by profound loneliness and invisibility. She was often left in her crib alone at home with a neighbor "on call." She would pound her head against her bedroom wall incessantly until her mother made her stop and was finally given her own room so that her head banging would not bother her sister. There appears to have been little or no comfort. Jill also vaguely remembers inappropriate sexual behavior by her father – a French kiss, showering together, his walking around naked. She also experienced relentless guilt about having "more" than her depressed, helpless, self-punishing mother.

When Jill entered treatment, anorexia was her only complaint. "I feel stalled," she said. "I take my body to the edge, then flip back." She was depressed, brittle, taciturn, and profoundly self-negating. She was underemployed as a childcare worker and in a distant, non-sexual marriage. "I have nothing to say," she told me. "What I say is not profound or interesting. I am boring." And yet I did not find Jill boring. I sensed something alive in her. She also reminded me, in her prudish, conservative style, of a favorite aunt of mine.

She soon began to reveal acute panic experiences that she'd been having since high school, involving a terrifying fear of death and what she called "eternity," "the blackening of the sky," "floating in black empty space," "falling into darkness." She said, with a shiver, "I can't even think of black holes." I told her I thought these are fears of being cut off from human contact – the most terrifying thing we can imagine. Her fears as a child were so vague, so unknowable; there was nothing to attach them to. When I told her that we would "try to put words to them," she reacted with alarm, saying, "If I felt that panic here, I'll want to go right through your window." It was clear that Jill's anorexia functioned in part to create a somatic container for overwhelming annihilation anxieties. She also used numerous obsessive-compulsive disorder behaviors, like folding her pajamas in a certain way, to ward off anxieties about terrible things happening to family members.

Jill's betraying, lying father reappeared during the treatment in the form of her husband, who, it emerged, had a secret drinking habit. Jill became hyperaware of his behavior and would snoop and find liquor bottles in his shop or the trunk of his car. She would then plunge into states of helpless rage and fear, during which she would grill and berate him for lying to her. I said to her, "A man doing sneaky things, then lying about it . . . A man doing something that feels dangerous, which could destroy the family . . . This time around, you want to make sure that someone sees what's going on and names the truth." Our understanding of this enactment with her husband has given Jill an unmistakable, visceral experience of how she felt with her father growing up and has thus helped to lift a dissociative veil.

Three ways the patient attempts to subjugate need and desire

In working with anorexia for almost 30 years, I have come to understand that these patients are always negotiating three related, self-regulatory "relationships" as part of their do-or-die campaign to subjugate both need and desire (because need is barely experienced in anorexia, it cannot be elaborated into desire or appetite). The first is a self-object relationship to food and eating (or not eating) – a theoretical arena developed primarily by self psychologists. The second is a subjugating relationship to the body, which has been mainly the province of object relations thinkers, who have typically associated the body with the Bad Mother. The third is a projective relationship with the Other, an avenue first explored by Harold Boris (1994). I believe that all three relationships must be explored in treatment as well as in any complete account of eating-disordered psychology.

In the first relationship, the patient's disavowed need and desire are directed obsessively toward the forbidden food, and this connection substitutes for the missing bond with a self-regulating object or self-object (Sands, 1991). Food is fantasied as an Other over whom the patient has omnipotent control. But this strategy alone is not enough to subdue the needy self. The patient must also dissociate, displace, and concretize her intolerable affect states in the *body* where they can be controlled and attacked by means of starvation (or compulsive exercise or bingeing, purging, or other self-harming activities). When relational need is displaced to the body, it becomes not-me, and the patient's conscious experience of self can remain strong, admirable, self-sufficient, and invulnerable (Sands, 2003); she can preserve the illusion that the body can live without any contribution from the outside. Thus an eating disorder is always paradoxical; it offers a narrow avenue for attending to basic needs and desires at the same time that it attacks and subjugates them. And there is a third, less autonomous, way that the eating-disordered patient seeks to rid herself of desire, need, appetite, and this is by projecting it and experiencing it as emanating from the analyst. It is the analyst who wants the patient to eat and to stop harming her body, not the patient. This last avenue – because it is the most relational – can offer the most hope.

The most important point here is that when eating disorders (or other addictive activities) are used to split off and subjugate need and desire, the banished longings are particularly difficult to access in treatment (Sands, 1991, 2003, 2007). Jill's well-established solitary system of bodily subjugation was so "effective" that her conscious experience of need and desire had virtually disappeared, making it initially impossible for her to form a developmental transference to a new, good object, what I have called a "transference of need." Because her emotional longings had been detoured into her body, where they were ruthlessly attacked, or gratified somewhat through the obsession with the forbidden food, or projected and experienced as emanating from me, they were not as available to be mobilized in her relationship *with* me. She had developed what we might very loosely call a "positive transference" to the anorexic activity and a "negative transference" to her body. In cases like these, the analyst often feels a particular deadness, a peculiar absence of transference or enactment. We do not feel swept up in a drama but feel instead that nothing much is happening. Of course, this is itself an enactment, which, when understood, can begin to move the action into the analytic relationship, where the long-renounced needs and desires can become intersubjectively elaborated.

A perplexing enactment

I will now turn to a discussion of an enactment that began to unfold early in our work together. About five months into treatment, Jill said, "I'm so afraid you'll give up on me . . . everyone gives up on me." Her former therapist had fallen asleep during sessions and her former psychiatrist had terminated their relationship, citing her resistance to treatment. She had tried many different therapists, groups, outpatient and inpatient programs, 12-step programs, and all had, in her view, given up on her. Not surprisingly, her fear of my giving up has permeated our work.

At the same time, of course, she continued to push me away. I have not been able to get her to come in more than once a week and even that has felt like too much – too much money, too much time, too much focus on herself. "I have to do this on my own," she says. If she or I need to miss an appointment, she will not reschedule, leading sometimes to long separations, from which it takes us many weeks to recover. When I urge her to consider an intensive outpatient or inpatient program or group, she reacts with brittle anger, saying she can't, she's tried that. It doesn't work. When I try to talk about our relationship, she looks away and dismisses what I'm saying with lightning speed. The paradox she presents – "stay away/don't give up on me" – is her particular variant of what Norman Fischer (1989) first identified as the "pull–push" dynamic of the anorexic, and it is wearing on me. She comes out of her little cardboard box for a minute, then wads herself up and puts herself back in.

At times, I am aware of a growing fatigue, an increasing willingness to just go along with her agenda. I am less likely to ask about her eating and weight, less likely to call her internist. I give up trying to get her to come in more often. I wonder what more I can do with someone so rigid, so controlling, so "concrete," so "chronic." But the truth is that, during these periods, I am "coasting" (Hirsch, 2008). I am neglecting my patient. Jill is becoming invisible to me too. Yet, at other times, I become quite frantic with worry. I consult with colleagues, search the literature, become obsessed with finding local resources. I demand she make eating agreements, exercise agreements. I tell her we can't do this alone and attempt to make her go into a treatment program. I tell her I can't really help her unless she comes in two, preferably three, times a week.

I have written previously (Sands, 2003) about this potentially dangerous form of enactment, in which the analyst becomes, alternately, overly worried and overactive, then oblivious and neglectful, in the face of the patient's brutal anorexic regime. We find ourselves shifting back and forth between two distinct states – one an anxious need to control the patient and force her to take care of her body, the other a state in which we "forget" about her frightening physical condition and become lulled into believing that we are engaged in treatment while all the while the patient's vicious bodily subjugation continues to operate silently outside of the office. I have suggested that the analyst's oscillating states of worry and neglect arise in reciprocal relationship to the patient's alternating states of needing or not needing.

In order to grasp this dynamic, we must remember that the patient's deepest needs are sequestered in her body, where they are being brutally subjugated. If we fail to hold in mind her poor ravaged body, we are neglecting that part of the patient that needs us most. When the patient's bodily subjugation is most severe, she is most out of touch with her need for us, and we feel helpless and useless and can become neglectful, which can push her deeper into her bodily subjugation. Or the cycle can begin with a vacation or other separation on our part, which the patient responds to with increased bodily tyranny, and so on. In short, the patient's dissociated need helps to evoke our dissociated neglect, which then helps perpetuate the patient's dissociation of need in an endless cycle – an example of what Phillip Bromberg (2006) calls the interaction of "not-me" states of patient and analyst. These particular dissociative dyadic cycles do not usually feel like what Anthony Bass (2003) has called "capital E" Enactments – that is, "discrete and unique events with their implication of mutual and bidirectional, unconscious influence" (p. 627). Rather, with hindsight, whole treatments can often be seen as one big enactment, in which the patient's not-me states of desire can remain sequestered indefinitely if we do not know what to look out for.

Coming to life

Returning now to Jill, I find myself becoming more able (at least in retrospect) to recognize and track my oscillations between worry and neglect and to see how my neglect is helping to perpetuate the disavowal of her needy self. It is also more consistently clear to me that we cannot possibly make headway with her coming in only once a week or less. But what to do? Each time that I bring up her coming in more often she responds with such brittle affect that, despite my best intentions, I find myself reflexively backing away. I fear she will break – either break in two or break out of treatment. I remind myself of the words of Boris (1994), who cautions us not to *want* too much from our anorexic patients – who find "wanting" in themselves or in us intolerable – but, rather, to offer interpretations as "food for thought," "set out but not served" (p. 178). I also decide to speak more from my heart.

When Jill once again tells me vehemently that she has to get through the anorexia by herself, I gird my loins and tell her that I do not want to leave her on her own as she had been left as a child, and I add that I feel committed to her for the long-term. She responds with her first show of tears, telling me I am the only person who has ever believed in her.

But moments of sweet connection like this, while extremely moving to me, do not seem to stick to her ribs. A few weeks later when Jill is again expressing despair about ever getting better, and I suggest that it would be easier to make progress if she had more contact with me, she reacts venomously. I have made the mistake of wanting something from her. I take a deep breath and say to her, "I know you hate it when I bring up two times a week, but when I stop bringing it up, I think I'm neglecting the scared, lonely little girl in you; I'm leaving you alone in your room." Without missing a beat, she says,

> I don't know why I thought of this, but there was a little girl with emotional problems on the playground today, trying to get into a game but disrupting everything for the other kids. I removed her. She went over and sat by herself, mad, and I let her stay by herself. But then later I thought, you should have gone and talked to her.

"Yes," I say to her, "you can feel how much you would want someone to come after you."

The next week, Jill brings in a dream, a very short one:

> I am getting into a car, an old car of mine, like from my family growing up, and I was driving, but I couldn't open my eyes. Somebody was with me, maybe a dog, maybe a person, I don't know. I am struggling and struggling to get my eyes open, and then I wake up.

When I ask for her associations, she says softly yet matter of factly, "well, some animals are born with their eyes closed." I am stunned by her association to birth, rather than death, given the danger in the dream, and by her sudden imaginative connection to her unconscious life. Then I suddenly feel tearful and intensely maternal and protective. I say, "Newborn . . . and not yet equipped for a dangerous world." She nods, and after a brief silence, says that when she was lying in bed that morning with her husband, all she wanted was for him to hold her. I have never heard an expression of desire like this from Jill before. In the sessions following this interaction, she begins to speak more about her longing for and fear of having more human connection, and she actually gains a few pounds.

But several months later, she has shifted back to her stoic, self-sufficient stance with a vengeance. Her "anorexic voice" is again loud inside her, her weight has dropped a bit, she is refusing to get more help from me or anyone else, and I am once again struggling with my own hopelessness and inertia. I have to summon my forces to try again. I tell her that I think it's terribly hard for her to take in enough from me to sustain her. She looks at me blankly and changes the subject. I feel myself drifting. I make myself ask her if she heard me. She says very sharply and petulantly that, yes, she heard me and that she just can't do that. She doesn't want to talk about it any more. I feel muted and surprisingly afraid to push ahead. I brace myself and tell her, "I think it's very hard for you to let yourself *have* very much of me – just as it's hard for you to have as much food or sleep or vacations or money or your 'own time' as you need." I see a flicker of interest, and she says, "Right. I don't even let myself have tea every day."

The next week, when we are well into the session, Jill tells me that when she was listening to music during her church group, "I felt like I was with you here in this room and I felt overcome with emotion. I don't know what this is. I almost called you. I just wanted to hear your voice." I say, "You wanted more," and she says, "Yes! I usually don't, but this time I did." A few days later I receive an email from her saying, in part, "Here is the song that I mentioned on Monday. I realize that this song is about God. However, some of the words bring to mind the kind of relationship that can exist between therapist and client." I wept as I read it. The song, entitled *Hosea*, begins by asking someone to return with all their heart and avoid letting fear keep them apart, noting that whilst trees are tall and straight, they bend nonetheless, and that they should do the same to others that call out to them. They have waited a long time for the other person to come back home to them and be able to live deeply in a new life together.

A few weeks after sending me the song, Jill tells me calmly that she wants to come in twice a week and to see a nutritionist regularly. "That sounds like a very good plan," I say calmly, secretly leaping for joy.

At the time of this writing, she has gained 9 lb. While I find myself indulging some "cure" fantasies, I am also reminding myself that, given her history, her future remains unpredictable.

Waking up

Jill and I had to live for a long time in that awful gray zone of working together without really doing the work. During this time, I found my states shifting between terrible worry about her ominous physical condition and a kind of obliviousness as she maintained her rigidly closed and self-sufficient stance. Her extreme dissociation of need helped evoke my "neglect," the dissociated part of myself, which, in turn, helped perpetuate her repudiation of need, and so forth. This cycle replayed, of course, the emotional neglect of Jill's childhood and her tragic response to it. In retrospect, it is clear that Jill needed to (unconsciously) test me again and again to see whether I would give up on her like everyone else had or whether I could care enough to pull myself out of our mutual torpor and go after her. Only then could she believe that I truly wanted more of her, and only then could she want more of me.

Jill's dream of driving with her eyes closed and her subsequent waking association to birth contain many of the metaphors which emerge in treatment as dissociative barriers begin to become more permeable: opening one's eyes, waking up, being born, coming alive (Sands, 2010). These experiences of psychic birth are accompanied by intense anxiety, as the patient feels thrust into the world as a kind of newborn – raw, wet, vulnerable, and unequipped for the challenges and responsibilities of adult life.

During these times of "waking up" from dissociation, the patient must often wake *us* up too – as Jill did so powerfully with her dream association to birth and with the song *Hosea* – to procure the early maternal holding needed to withstand the terror of crumbling defenses and the emergence of dependency and desire. The patient's "cries," like those of a newborn infant, activate intensely maternal and protective feelings in us, rooted no doubt, in part, in the biological imperative to preserve new life. Her sequestered longings (which have long been concretized and subjugated in her body) slowly make their way into our conscious, somatic experience. We feel the patient's need for us *viscerally*. Our ability to receive, with open heart and mind, the patient's intolerable need states helps her slowly become "desomaticized" (Krystal, 1988) – that is, lifted out of her body and into the relational mind of the analytic dyad, where they can be thought about, symbolized, and transformed into appetite and desire.

References

Bass, A. (2003). "E" enactments in psychoanalysis: another medium, another message. *Psychoanal. Dial.* 13, 657–675.

Boris, H. (1994). *Sleights of Mind: One and Multiples of One.* New York: Jason Aronson.

Bromberg, P. (2006). *Awakening the Dreamer.* Mahwah, NJ: The Analytic Press.

Fischer, N. (1989). Anorexia nervosa and unresolved rapprochement conflicts: a case study. *Int. J. Psycho-Anal.* 70, 41–54.

Hirsch, I. (2008). *Coasting in the Countertransference: Conflicts of Interest Between Analyst and Patient.* New York: Routledge.

Krystal, H. (1988). *Integration and Self Healing: Affect, Trauma, Alexithymia.* Hillsdale, NJ: Analytic Press.

Sands, S. (1991). Bulimia, dissociation and empathy: a self-psychological view. In C. Johnson (Ed.), *Psychodynamic Treatment of Anorexia Nervosa and Bulimia* (pp. 34–50). New York: Guilford.

Sands, S. (2003). The subjugation of the body in eating disorders: a particularly female solution. *Psychoanal. Psychol.* 20, 103–116.

Sands, S. (2007). Review of Philip Bromberg's *Awakening the Dreamer. Psychoanal. Dial.* 17(5), 741–751.

Sands, S. (2010). On the royal road together: the analytic function of dreams in activating dissociative unconscious communication. *Psychoanal. Dial.* 20, 357–373.

Chapter 17

The anguished body

Susie Orbach

When Jean Petrucelli, the co-editor of this volume and the architect of the conference that inspired it, rang me to ask whether I'd be part of the panel on body tyranny, I was on the bus to Bond Street, one of London's premier shopping streets. In common with hundreds of others, I was on a mission to find something lovely for my body. Every inch of Bond St is devoted to dressing the body (save for Sotheby's). So body consciousness or body awareness could be thought to be high. Which is why I was astounded at the number of people, the number of bodies who bumped into me or me to them.

Yes, there were too many people with too many packages on streets once built for horses and carriages and a small population. But that is really not a sufficient explanation for the jostling and apparent lack of body awareness that meant that someone's arm would be flung across my breast without him having even registered there was a human body he was bumping into, or my bulky package of boots went flying into the person in front of me because I was being shoved at from behind.

The desire, compulsion even, to decorate and signal who we are and how we wish to be read as a body dramatically clashed with this stunning lack of body awareness, and it got me thinking about bodies in space, dissociated bodies, the hyperawareness and hyperdeadness of bodies today, and the way I might frame some remarks for this collection of papers.

Patients who come with eating difficulties and discuss them are not so very different from my patients who come with other kinds of issues: loss, anxiety, confusion, deadness, fear, and so on. These patients, too, may have eating and body image problems of equal severity, but they fail to bring these issues into the therapy, as they are not something they believe it possible to change. Like gravity, they take these problems for granted. For both these groups, body difficulties are constitutive of self. They obsess about their dismay with friends; body preoccupations, food terror, and body hatred are part of their identity. Both the undisclosed eating-disordered patients and those who come specifically to address eating and body image issues suffer with extreme body anguish and thus link in with my reflections on those people on Bond Street.

To say that the general population has disordered eating is to state the obvious: girls not eating during the week, throwing up in bathrooms, 50 per cent of 9-year-olds dieting; women in old-age homes obsessed with weight for their whole lives; gyms full of people reshaping bodies; cosmetic surgeons doing a brisk business in everything from breast, chest, and cheek implants to labiaplasty, leg extensions, toe breaking, fat suctioning, and so on. These ways of being are not considered or diagnosed as being about body dysmorphia or eating difficulties. These behaviours are considered normal, even praiseworthy. Over three decades ago, when I wrote *Fat is a Feminist Issue* (Orbach, 1978) and *Hunger Strike* (Orbach, 1986), such behaviours were oddities and a cause of great concern, not the quotidian experience of millions. Today such behaviours form part of the cultural space we all occupy in which the making of bodies is a personal production and indeed is invoked as a site of power and empowerment. You can have the body you want, exhort the journalists, copywriters, beauty makeover shows. These, perhaps inadvertent, but nevertheless powerful merchants of body hatred ensure that body transformation is a central agenda destabilizing corporeality for girls and women – and increasingly boys and men.

For bodies to be so readily available for attempted transformation, they must be felt to be either fundamentally wrong or in need of bettering. Like the neurotic mind that compulsively seeks self-improvement alerting us to its discontents, the dead or hyperaroused bodies that bump into each other on Bond Street as they search for a way to clothe themselves are alerting us to the body and *its* discontents. This is not the body as receptacle for the mind's troubled conflicts that can't be borne, but the body as author and agent of its own discontents.

As bodies are mined and colonized for profit in ways which have individuals feeling they are doing right for themselves when they engage in drastic procedures or extreme eating/non-eating behaviours, we need to ask ourselves as analysts deep questions about the psychological development of the body. What is unfolding that so frequently renders this body abject, either hyperanxious or alexithymic?

This idea that the body has a psychological history of its own is a difficult one to get our minds around. I spoke about it at this conference nearly a decade ago and was struck by senior analysts' misinterpretation of what I was saying. I don't think it was wilful or ungenerous. I think it was a foreign idea. Indeed, even though I have been living with it and theory making about it for several decades, I still find it quite hard to get my head around it myself. I don't think it is because it is wrong. I think it is because we have become so used to the mind–body problem posed in hierarchical terms, and so much of our skill as analysts is to see the hystericized links between mind and body, that if we reverse the hierarchy or try to talk about the body as a body, not only as a deposit for the contents of mind, we find ourselves unmoored. When we are unmoored, we seek ideas that confirm what we already know. Like our patients, we can become reluctant to think and feel new things, but in this brief paper, I want to suggest that an understanding of the "hyperized" body states of arousal or deadness can be illuminated by regarding the construction of the body in the same way as we revisit, expand, reshape theory on the construction of mind in the process of trying to meet our patients daily in our consulting rooms.

I agree with Sands (see Chapter 16) that we need to address the anorectic patient's body. Yes, it can be thought of as a container, but I don't want to limit myself to that lens, for there are multiple ways I might attempt to address this body: (1) I think about the history of the body and how it was received by the bodies that interacted with and raised it. (2) I think about the body of the mothering person or people that became the foundational body from which the individual apprehended her body. (3) I think about the way the mothering person felt about the body of the newborn and the developing child. (4) I think about what the mothering person's bodily expectations and desires were for that developing child. (5) I think about what the child experienced in the body-to-body relation with the mother. (6) I think about the child's perceptions of the mother's body. (7) I think about the early feeding relationship. (8) I think about how the woman Sands describes, now 55, might have perceived her mother's own eating and relation to her body.

In other words, I think about the body in ways not dissimilar to how I might think about psychic biography. How, I ask myself, did the relational field become internalized in the body history of this individual? This kind of inquiry allows me to get a sketch of how she or he comes to have her or his particular body experience.

Simultaneously I notice how the body of that person comes to therapy and engages with my body, and how my body opens or closes itself to the corporeality I am offered in the room. My body countertransference is as much a part of the intersubjective field as is the more commonly addressed affect-laden countertransference responses we have become used to scrutinizing in our work. What I feel viscerally in response to the body of the individual I am working with is, for me, a crucial part of the clinical picture alerting me to the nature and kind of troubled body I am with.

I might feel nothing. I might feel that I am sitting with a no body; a kind of vacuum where I would expect in social intercourse to sense the body of another. I might be sitting with a body that pushes up against mine – a body that moves too closely into my space. I might be sitting with a 50-year-old body that comes to each session in incongruous outfits – a Playboy bunny look one day, a business woman the next, a tough-looking hiker the next. I might be sitting with someone whose bodily impact on mine is to make me feel very much larger than I am, or very much smaller, Alice in Wonderland style. I might be sitting with hyperdeadness or hyperarousal, or my body might be being obliterated as I described the bodies on Bond Street – no room for the body of another, only room for the body of the other.

Whatever is aroused in me during the session – and I have had many strange body countertransferences from feeling on fire, to feeling I was purring, to wanting to throw up – is a clue to me about the question of how we get a body. It is a clue to me about the kind of bodies that we and our patients inhabit, and the kind of bodily provision that is being asked of me as a therapist.

Am I being asked to witness the impossibility of the individual having a body? Am I being asked to provide a nurturant body big enough to offer the patient's body a home? Am I being asked to provide a proxy body, a kind of physical body the other can use while she deconstructs a defensive or false body that has produced hyperarousal as a way to feel it exists? Am I being invited to view a body desperate to be seen and acknowledged? Am I invoked into experiencing envy towards the patient's body – an envy that may tell me about her own relation to her mother's body? Am I pulled to experience the deep sadness that means where body could be, only abjection and despair are?

All such questions may occur when working with people with troubled eating. While the focus of diagnosis is customarily on the structure of the individual's psychopathology, I want to extend that diagnosis to the body too. I want to argue that, whatever schema or theoretical orientation we work with, we might want to take a look at the body per se. We might ask ourselves: is this a dissociated body? Or if one is of an attachment-based perspective, is this a disorganized body? Or, is this a borderline body? Is this a neurotic body? Is this a split-off body?

In asking these kinds of questions I am trying to address the troubled bodies I see and I experience in my consulting room. Over my years as an analyst, I have endeavoured in many ways – we have all endeavoured – to give or release our patients' minds and hearts of the complexity and richness denied to them by their truncated existences. I believe that our patients with severe eating troubles are also seeking to have complex and rich bodies which are able, adored, tired, thriving, ageing, and conflicted.

Mothers pass on not just their psyches to their daughters, they pass on their bodily sense of self. The way a baby is held, soothed, fed, put to sleep, swaddled, and so on will form the physical core of her corporeality. These bodily interactions create psychic foundations and they create corporeal foundations. The way in which these behaviours are carried out, combined with the mothering figure's sensitivity to her own and her baby's body, will form the template for that baby's body security or insecurity.

Today the body is being mined for profit. Big profits. The US growth rate, that's to say the GDP for the second quarter (Q2) is 1.6 per cent.[1] For a beauty company such as L'Oréal, the growth figure in the United States is 5.4 per cent in the same quarter. L'Oréal and its sister industries don't get figures like this simply through their skilled application of exploiting visual culture and huge expenditure. In part, of course, they do, because a marketing budget is the greatest cost for the goods being sold. But they couldn't do it if they hadn't targeted women in really sophisticated ways. They could not do it if identity had not come to be predicated on looking good, and looking good had not come to be something felt to be so highly difficult to achieve without huge expenditure and preoccupation.

The industries that colonize bodies have a Trojan horse in each home: the unhappy and destabilized bodies of many, many mothers today. This is not to blame mothers. This is to say that, at the same time that beauty has been democratized and made into an imperative, beauty ideals have narrowed to one limiting aesthetic. The consequence is that body anxiety is inevitably rife. That body anxiety, which is an anxiety every parent would wish to protect their child from, unintentionally enters the early feeding and body-to-body relationship. In so doing, it creates unstable bodies on the search to find body peace. This is a peace that is restless and finds expression in hyperarousal or hyperdeadness; in the slippage between being visible and invisible; between the longing to do away with the body and the desire to exhibit it; or in the attempt, as in anorexia, to repudiate the body one has by creating out of oneself a body one can admire.

The body becomes a Winnicottian false body, pumped up by intense attention to keep it going, to enliven it, to make it real to the person who inhabits it. Tragically, the efforts often fail, for without deconstructing the deadness and accepting it in the consulting room – in the therapy relationship – it is an alienated body waiting to be invited in to grow down and grow up.

Note

1 4.5 per cent, 5.4 per cent (first figure is Q1, second 2 is Q2) like-for-like sales as opposed to reported.

References

Orbach, S. (1978). *Fat is a Feminist Issue.* New York: Paddington Press.
Orbach, S. (1986). *Hunger Strike.* New York: Norton.

Part VI

On being naked

Self-revelation, secrecy, and shifting truths

Chapter 18

Dissociation among psychoanalysts about sexual boundary violations[1]

Mark J. Blechner

Dahlberg (1970) published an important and brave exploration of sex between psychotherapists and their patients. He had difficulty getting it published, and the topic continues to be fraught with anxiety, suppression, and inconsistency. The disconnection between the official and private attitudes of members of our profession toward sexual boundary violations continues to receive little attention. In this paper, I hope to open a dialogue bridging the gap between private and public views about sex between psychotherapists and their patients and to thus make a topic that causes us all great distress and confusion something we can speak about more openly.

If I had been asked 30 years ago what my views were about sex between analysts and patients, I would have answered simply that it must be absolutely forbidden. My thinking was based on the essential pact that we clinicians make with our patients. For their own good, they can and should talk about whatever feelings emerge in the transference, including sexual feelings. We, in turn, guarantee that it is safe to do so; we will use our patients' revelations to help them explore their psyches, but we will not act on their sexual fantasies, or ours. Without this safeguard, there can be no wide-ranging analysis of transference. And since we know that early experiences can be reenacted in psychoanalysis, it is especially important that we resist the temptation to violate this trust. For people who were sexually abused as children, the prospect of exploring these experiences in psychoanalysis and having such exploration lead to sexual reenactments can be doubly traumatizing.

The absolutist position

I would call my view the "absolutist position." There are many reputable people, past and present, who would agree with the absolutist position, including Hippocrates. The Hippocratic oath includes the following passage: "Every house I shall only enter for the sake of my patients' wellbeing, refraining from every intentional harm and all seduction, especially from love relationships with women or with men, be they free or bonded" (Van Emde Boas, 1966, p. 215).

Masters and Johnson, the renowned sex researchers, were also absolutists and raised an alarm about patient–therapist sex (Masters & Johnson, 1970). Their patients, who had sexual problems, reported a startling number of experiences with psychotherapists who, recognizing the vulnerability of their patients, initiated sex with them. Indeeed, Masters and Johnson argued that therapists who have sexual relations with their patients should be prosecuted for rape. Since then, we have the unflinching viewpoint of psychologist Kenneth Pope and his colleagues (Pope et al., 1993), who wrote:

> Under no circumstances should a therapist ever engage in sexual intimacies with a patient. No matter what the situation. No matter who the patient. No matter what the patient has said or done. No matter how the therapist or patient feels. Therapist–patient sexual intimacies are in all instances wrong and must be avoided. In all situations, it is solely the therapist's responsibility to ensure that he or she never engages in sexual intimacy with a patient. The locus of responsibility for the therapist's behavior in this regard can never be shifted; it remains always and completely with the therapist.
>
> (p. 180)

That is the absolutist view; I still subscribe to it, although I recognize that it has its own problems. I have come to realize that many people, some quite respected clinicians, privately do not hold to the absolutist view. They usually do not publish their points of view, and so most people could be unaware of these alternative perspectives. For instance, I was involved in discussions of an ethics code for a psychoanalytic institute, in which the issues of sexual ethics needed to be clarified. There were several analysts, some of them quite senior, who held what I would call the "relativist view." They said, "You know, sometimes those relations work out well. The patient and therapist marry, and the marriage is a happy one." I was startled by this argument; it seemed beside the point. The principle of adhering to sexual boundaries in psychoanalytic treatment is not dependent on whether the relationship works. It is based on maintaining the safety and integrity of transference exploration.

Even if one holds to the absolutist view, are there distinctions to be made? There are people who are well-meaning analysts who, in a single instance, fall in love with a patient and choose to spend their lives with that patient, whatever the consequences may be. They do it once; the relationship may work, or not, and the analysts may seek to remain part of the profession. Should they be differentiated from analysts who are "multiple sexual boundary violators," clinicians who repeatedly exploit the transference to seduce patients? They use their power in the analysis to try to keep this abuse secret, and they use their power within the profession to do the same and hold any judgmental colleagues at bay. In one instance, an analyst who committed a serious sexual boundary violation retained his position as director of a prestigious psychoanalytic institute for decades. The effect of such analysts on their patients is destructive, again and again, yet they may continue to sustain a positive clinical reputation. When their deeds are made public, they may blame the patient or exonerate themselves with justifications like "the patient knew about transference," as if abstract knowledge about transference protects the patient from exploitation of the transference (Simon, 1991; Herman, 2012; Honig & Barron, 2013).

One could argue that multiple sexual boundary violators should be shunned by the profession and disciplined by the law. Yet, in actual practice, many of them face no serious penalties, and quite a few manage to hold on to positions of authority (Gabbard, 1995). The legal courts are severe with sexual boundary violators, but the record of our profession enforcing its own principles is weak, uneven, and unfair. The punishment may be milder if the offending analyst is aggressive and threatens a countersuit, and harsher if the analyst is meek and repentant. Andrea Celenza (2007) calls this "rampant punitiveness" and has questioned whether some overly harsh and shaming punishments come from guilt about not having adequately prosecuted perpetrators who were more frightening.

One problem of the absolutist position is that its very harsh stigmatization of all sexual boundary violators may discourage open discussion of the issue. Paradoxically, talking about sexual boundary violations can be punished more harshly than committing a sexual boundary violation (Dimen, 2011). Several psychoanalysts who have spoken publicly about there being a problem in our profession with sexual boundary violations have been threatened with punishment, as law professor Leonard Riskin (1979) has pointed out. The message seems to be, "Keep quiet; don't talk about it."

The "supportive of sex with patients" position

Given the reluctance to condemn and to punish sexual boundary violators, is there another way to respond other than ejecting them from the profession? One alternative might be to require that any practitioner who has sexual relations with his patients must be open about it. He must recertify as a psychosex therapist and inform his patients in the first session that he sleeps with patients and that they have a right to know this in advance. If they then choose to work with a psychosex therapist, that is their prerogative.

At first glance, this proposal might seem preposterous, but it has some precedents. In 1966, psychiatrist James McCartney published an article entitled "Overt transference" in the *Journal of Sex Research.* He argued that some patients need a real sexual experience within the treatment in order to proceed to mature heterosexuality. He noted that a man can sometimes find professionals who will allow him to work on his sexual development (by which I think he meant prostitutes), whereas such resources are less available for women. Therefore the psychoanalyst should fill in and give her what she needs, as he had done with dozens of his female patients.

However problematic this proposal may be, McCartney deserves credit for being clear and straightforward – he was open about his approach; he even would meet the patient's husband or family at the start of treatment to explain it.[2] Nevertheless, after McCartney delivered his paper describing his practice, he was expelled from the American Psychiatric Association. However, McCartney's expulsion may have been imposed more to protect the profession and the organization than to punish a breach of ethics, since the Ethics Committee wrote: "There comes a point at which the offender so outrages social sensibilities that the peer group must act to protect its own integrity" (Riskin, 1979, p. 1008). If he had merely kept the information to himself instead of giving a paper on it, he might have been left alone. The message, once again, was: Keep quiet; don't talk about it.

We could call McCartney's position the "supportive of sex with patients" position. Officially, this position is an outlier in our field. We may assume that therapist–patient sexual relations are damaging. But how true is that? Do any patients find it benign, even useful to sleep with their therapists? The patients who have been damaged are likelier to go public with their experience, perhaps suing the therapist, perhaps going into treatment with another therapist. But if a patient finds the sexual relationship with the therapist useful, we are much less likely to hear about it.

At one of my lectures, I mentioned this problem and wondered out loud about whether we were not hearing from people who had benefited from sexual relations with their therapist. After my talk was over, a woman came to speak with me. She did not identify herself by name, but she told me,

> I am one of those people. I went into therapy with a sexual problem; my therapist had a sexual relationship with me, and I no longer had the sexual problem, with him and afterwards. So for me the experience was useful.

Martin Shepard (1971), outspoken about the "supportive of sex with patients" position, claimed that "as many people are aided by intimate involvements with their therapists as are hurt" (p. 207). The fact is, though, that Shepard was wrong. Research shows that sexual boundary violations are harmful much more often than helpful. A survey of the literature (Taylor & Wagner, 1976) found that 47 percent of patients who had sexual contact with their therapists found it harmful, 32 percent found it mixed, and 21 percent found it helpful. Pope and Vetter (1991), in a more systematic survey, found that it was harmful for 90 percent of patients who had sex with their therapist during treatment.[3] For those who had sex after the treatment was terminated, 80 percent found it harmful.

The percentage of psychotherapists who have had sexual contact with their patients has been estimated to be between 2.5 percent of women and 9.4 percent of men (Pope et al., 1986). That is almost one in ten male therapists. Why are sexual boundary violations so frequent? There are many answers, the simplest being that these therapists are unable to find satisfactory relationships outside the consulting room. Dahlberg (1970) noted that sexual boundary violators tend to be older, widowed, single, divorced, or in troubled marriages, and lonely. The average age of therapists he studied was 50, and the average age of the patients with whom they had sexual relations was 30. We all have sexual and romantic needs, and if our needs are not well satisfied in our lives outside the consulting room, would we not be more likely to seek satisfaction within the consulting room? If we are not physically or emotionally attractive to most people, or have our own inhibitions or character quirks that make romantic relationships difficult for us, how tempting is it to use the rose-colored haze of the transference to feel more attractive to a romantic partner lying on the couch? The answer will depend on many factors, including character, fear, and one's education and role models.

When it comes to role models, we have another problem. Part of the trouble is that sexual transgressions are so common in the history of psychoanalysis. The list of psychoanalysts who have had sex with patients or married them reads like a *Who's Who* of our field: Carl Jung, Sandor Ferenczi, Erich Fromm, Frieda Fromm-Reichmann, Wilhelm Reich, Victor Tausk, Otto Fenichel, Harry Stack Sullivan, Karen Horney, and many others. I know of no instance where Freud had actual sexual relations with a patient. In his writing, Freud took the absolutist position (Freud, 1910, 1915), but in practice, Freud violated his own principles, especially in the Frink case. Horace Frink, an American psychiatrist, went to Vienna to be analyzed by Freud (Edmunds, 1988; Warner, 1994). Frink was married but was having an affair at the time with one of his patients, Anjelika Bijur, a very wealthy woman. Freud encouraged Frink to leave his wife and marry his patient, which was disastrous for everybody concerned. So, starting with Freud, we have a long-standing dissociation between the official condemnation of sexual relations between analyst and patient, and a hidden acceptance or even support for them.

The "empathic-sentimental" position

We teach the theories and principles of the major figures in psychoanalysis and rarely mention when they had sexual relations with their patients. Perhaps our training programs need to acknowledge this fact and open up more of a discussion with psychoanalytic candidates about sexual feelings in treatment. We need to teach and take seriously the prescience of Searles' (1959) observation that sexual and romantic feelings and fantasies are common in the psychoanalyst, especially towards the end of a successful treatment. Searles wrote:

> Since I began doing psycho-analysis and intensive psychotherapy nine years ago, I have found, time after time, that in the course of the work with every one of my patients who has progressed to, or

> very far toward, a thoroughgoing analytic cure, I have experienced romantic and erotic desires to marry, and fantasies of being married to, the patient. Such fantasies and emotions have appeared in me usually relatively late in the course of treatment, have been present not briefly but usually for a number of months, and have subsided only after my having experienced a variety of feelings – frustration, separation-anxiety, grief, and so forth – entirely akin to those which attended what I experienced as the resolution of my Oedipus complex late in my personal analysis – specifically, about five years ago.
>
> (Searles, 1959, p. 180)

Searles provided an unusual perspective on erotic countertransference; if understood and handled correctly, it was not necessarily a problem. It may be a sign that the psychoanalyst has done good work, and it is near the time for termination of the treatment (Brockman, 2008; Blechner, 2009).

Despite the challenges, we need to discuss why sexual boundary violations have occurred so often in the history of our profession and the unspoken or unconscious attitudes that may support such boundary violations, even while they are officially condemned. One of those attitudes is that many analysts feel empathy for romance and true love. We could call this the "empathic-sentimental" position, and it competes, sometimes unconsciously, with the absolutist position. Psychotherapists want people to be happy in their love lives, and it is often a goal in treatment.

Consider the example of Frieda Fromm-Reichmann. She had been raped during her medical studies, a terrible trauma (Hornstein, 2000, p. 69). At the age of 36, when she was still Frieda Reichmann, she had never been married and had no children. This was considered shameful for a woman, certainly for someone from an Orthodox German-Jewish background. Frieda began psychoanalyzing Erich Fromm, an attractive, brilliant man who was 11 years younger than she and came from a similar religious background. She claimed they fell in love, ended the analysis, and married. Some people felt or continue to feel: isn't it wonderful that Frieda got a chance at love with Erich? Yet most people also avoided speaking about it, betraying their ambivalence. Hornstein (2000, p. 401, n. 24) notes in her biography of Fromm-Reichmann: "I found it extraordinary that every person I interviewed knew this fact [that Erich had been Frieda's patient before marrying her] but claimed never to have discussed it." Their belief seems to have been: Keep quiet; don't talk about it.

Hornstein is herself ambivalent about the relationship; she alternates between ethical concerns and the empathic-sentimental position. She says that almost everybody fell in love with Erich and suggests that Erich seduced Frieda. Lawrence Friedman (2013), in his biography of Erich Fromm, suggests that Frieda seduced Erich. The fact that there is a debate about who seduced whom in a psychoanalytic treatment reveals the tendency to romanticize these situations in the empathic-sentimental position.

Daniel Mackler (2006) has taken a different stance in an article: "An analysis of the shadow side of Frieda Fromm-Reichmann." Also from the absolutist tradition, he writes:

> It is the patient's inalienable right to *try* to seduce his therapist, just as it is the therapist's inalienable emotional responsibility to analyze the (not-so-) hidden message in the patient's behavior – for the sake of her patient's growth. If the therapist goes along with the patient's attempted seduction – no matter what the time period or what the therapist's analytic style – it is really the therapist seducing the patient in disguise, in an equally disguised attempt to have the patient meet her own ancient unmet childhood needs.
>
> (p. 10)

From this point of view, no matter what the situation, the analyst is letting down her or his patient if there are sexual relations, and the patient may be traumatized in ways that may not be immediately obvious. Dahlberg (1970, p. 121) cites Raymond Sobel: "The determinants of whether the therapist acts out are his inner states rather than the seductiveness of the patient. The latter is always with us."

Fromm-Reichmann seems to have espoused this viewpoint herself. In her classic text, *Principles of Intensive Psychotherapy* (1950), she stresses near the beginning of the book how important it is for the psychotherapist to be sure to have adequate sources of personal gratification in life outside the consulting room, in order to avoid seeking such gratifications from patients. She writes:

> Sexual gratification has been quoted as another goal of satisfaction in man's life. The therapist has to safeguard strictly against using the patient, actually or in fantasy, for the purpose of lust, so that sexual

> fantasies with regard to the patient or the partners whom the patient mentions, or identifications with the patient or his partners regarding their sexual experiences, do not interfere with the psychiatrist's ability to listen. . . . A psychiatrist who is lonely must see that his own need for physical contact does not interfere with his coming to the correct conclusions about patients' needs.
>
> (Fromm-Reichmann, 1950, pp. 9–12)

In summary, we need to be clearer about where we stand as a profession on sexual-boundary violations. We need to relax the unspoken but powerful ban on discussing this issue, in current clinical work and in the history of psychoanalysis. Our message must shift: Don't keep quiet; please speak about it. We must resolve the dissociation between what we say publicly and think privately and believe unconsciously. Only when this gap is dealt with can we hope to find a way of dealing with sexual boundary violations – which often, if not always, harm our patients – that is honest and effective.

Notes

1 An earlier version of this chapter was published in the *Contemporary Psychoanalysis*, 2014, 50 (1–2), 23–33.
2 It is hard to believe that the husbands or families of female patients gave consent to such treatment and agreed to pay for it.
3 This is quite close to the finding of Dahlberg (1970). In his relatively informal survey, in one case out of nine (11 percent), the sexual interaction between psychoanalyst and patient had no apparently harmful effect.

References

Blechner, M. (2009) Erotic and antierotic countertransference. *Contemporary Psychoanalysis*, 45: 82–92.
Brockman, R. (2008) The slippery slope: touch in dynamic psychiatry. *Journal of the American Academy of Psychoanalysis and Dynamic Psychiatry*, 36: 403–414.
Celenza, A. (2007) *Sexual Boundary Violations: Therapeutic, Supervisory, and Academic Contexts*. Lanham, MD: Aronson.
Dahlberg, C. (1970) Sexual contact between patient and therapist. *Contemporary Psychoanalysis*, 6: 107–124.
Dimen, M. (2011) *Lapsus linguae,* or a slip of the tongue? A sexual violation in an analytic treatment and its personal and theoretical aftermath. *Contemporary Psychoanalysis*, 47: 35–79.
Edmunds, L. (1988) His master's choice. *Johns Hopkins Magazine*, April: 40–49.
Friedman, L. (2013) *The Lives of Erich Fromm*. New York: Columbia University Press.

Freud, S. (1910) The future prospects of psycho-analytic therapy. *Standard Edition*, 11: 139–152.

Freud, S. (1915) Observations on transference-love. *Standard Edition*, 12: 157–171.

Fromm-Reichmann, F. (1950) *Principles of Intensive Psychotherapy*. Chicago: University of Chicago Press.

Gabbard, G. (1995) The early history of boundary violations in psychoanalysis. *Journal of the American Psychoanalytic Association*, 43: 1115–1136.

Herman, C. (2012) Sex with patient caused no harm, doctor says. Suit alleges negligence, violations of consumer law. *Commonwealth Magazine*, January 26.

Honig, R., & Barron, J. (2013) Restoring institutional integrity in the wake of sexual boundary violations: a case study. *Journal of the American Psychoanalytic Association*, 61: 1–28.

Hornstein, G. (2000) *To Redeem One Person is to Redeem the World: The Life of Frieda Fromm-Reichmann*. New York: Free Press.

Mackler, D. (2006) An analysis of the shadow side of Frieda Fromm-Reichmann. *International Society for Psychological and Social Approaches to Psychosis (ISPS-US) Newsletter*, 7(1): 10–12.

Masters, W., & Johnson, V. (1970) *Human Sexual Inadequacy*. Boston, MA: Little, Brown.

McCartney, J. (1966) Overt transference. *Journal of Sex Research*, 2: 227–237.

Pope, K. S., & Vetter, V. A. (1991) Prior therapist–patient sexual involvement among patients seen by psychologists. *Psychotherapy*, 28: 429–438.

Pope, K., Keith-Spiegel, P., & Tabachnick, B. (1986) Sexual attraction to clients: the human therapist and the (sometimes) inhuman training system. *American Psychologist*, 41: 147–158.

Pope, K., Sonne, J., & Holroyd, J. (1993) *Sexual Feelings in Psychotherapy*. Washington, DC: American Psychological Association.

Riskin, L. (1979) Sexual relations between psychotherapists and their patients: toward research or restraint. *California Law Review*, 67: 1000–1027.

Searles, H. (1959) Oedipal love in the countertransference. *International Journal of Psychoanalysis*, 40: 180–190.

Shepard, M. (1971) *The Love Treatment*. New York: Wyden.

Simon, R. (1991) Psychological injury caused by boundary violation precursors to therapist–patient sex. *Psychiatric Annals*, 21: 614–619.

Taylor, B., & Wagner, N. (1976) Sex between therapists and clients: a review and analysis. *Professional Psychology*, 7: 593–601.

Van Emde Boas, C. (1966) Some reflections on sexual relations between physicians and patients. *Journal of Sex Research*, 2: 215–218.

Warner, S. (1994) Freud's analysis of Horace Frink, M.D.: a previously unexplained therapeutic disaster. *Journal of the American Academy of Psychoanalysis*, 22: 137–152.

Chapter 19

Seducing patients into treatment

When the naked truth feels too revealing

Sandra Buechler

Stephen Mitchell once wrote,

> Consider the hopes of the obsessional patient beginning treatment. He is not interested in giving up his life's work of controlling everything that happens in his experience and that of those around him . . . Of course, the analyst does not say anything like: "Look, I understand that you are hoping I will help you repair and perfect your obsessional approach to living, but I can help you give all that up and find a much fuller and more meaningful life." If the analyst did say something like that, the patient would likely leave, and rightfully so.
>
> (Mitchell, 1993, p. 208)

In this passage, Mitchell (1993) told the truth about some dangers of blurting out whatever we may be thinking. No matter how fervently we believe that "the truth shall set ye free," clinical experience drives home the complexity of balancing this priority with others in the initial stages of the work. But, when does this process shade into seduction? When do omissions become lies? When have we endangered, or even forfeited, the integrity of the work, and our own professional integrity?

In some psychoanalytic circles, I think it has become reflexive to pathologize the clinician who hesitates to say something to a patient. All too easily, particularly if the clinician is in training, he or she is labeled as uptight, withholding, controlling, cowardly, lacking the ability to confront, and so on. Yet, I believe, we are all making judgments, moment by moment, about what it might be helpful to say, and what might be countertherapeutic, although many of these decisions are made on a less than conscious level. Are we omniscient, and able to be sure about these judgment calls? Of course not. Might our omissions stem from our own characterological limitations? Of course. But, I feel it is important to respect that at least *part* of the developing clinician's motivation may be a desire for the patient to stay in treatment long enough to get a sense of its potential to enrich his or her life.

I have always said that free association is the privilege of the patient, and not the analyst. Every moment of every session we face conundrums. What to confront, and what to silently contain, is one of them. Helping less experienced clinicians develop the courage this takes requires us to give full respect to how difficult this task is, without oversimplifying it in any way, or privileging one side of the conundrum over the other.

A young man in an arts-related profession enters treatment with an analytic candidate, who is in supervision with me. The patient is anxious, depressed, has difficulty concentrating, and is confused about whether or not he wants to continue in a relationship with his current girlfriend. My supervisee is very eager to increase the frequency of his sessions, for practical reasons, as well as out of a genuine wish to engage him as fully as possible in an analytic process. Early in the treatment, it becomes clear that, while this patient's career is blooming, his relationships tend to crash and burn. His therapist is very concerned that the treatment relationship will follow suit.

The patient is wary from the start. He asks how treatment will help him concentrate, whether the therapist will tell him what to do about his girlfriend, whether she will give him concrete guidance, whether he can know more about the therapist's personal life. He compares his experience to reports from friends about their more "hands-on" treatments. He wonders if, by participating in this treatment, he is, once again, trying to please a woman, to his own detriment.

The patient's attendance is sprinkled with cancellations. My supervisee wonders whether or not she should frame the cancellations as expressions of resistance. Should she confront his unrealistic expectation, head on? How much should she explain about the process, and what is it likely, and unlikely, to provide? At times explaining feels like trying to sell him on the treatment she can offer. Being silent can sometimes feel like tacit acceptance of his premises. Confronting him with possible meanings of his interpersonal behavior feels doomed to precipitate a premature termination.

A few months into treatment, the patient complains that he is not getting better. The treatment is not having results. He wants an objective view of the material he presents, and he wants the therapist to organize him. He feels that he is just venting. He wants to be transformed. There is no clarity. Later on in the session, he becomes pessimistic about his future, predicting that it will be more of the same.

The therapist tries to reach him, by describing what seems to recur in his relationships, including with her. He alternates between challenging her, and criticizing himself as a patient. He asks her if she is different with other patients. Maybe the two of them are not a good fit. He follows this speculation with an even more pointed question. "Have you ever told a patient, I don't think I can help you? Would you ever say that to me? Would you tell me if things weren't going well?"

What is the naked truth, here, and how much of it should be spoken? Should she tell him how unsure she feels with him, how much he puts her on the spot, how afraid she feels that he will leave? How much should she admit she just doesn't know about the probable outcome of their work? The therapist struggled with these questions every session. This treatment lasted almost a year, I would say, largely because of the tremendous effort and skill of the therapist. I think the patient benefited greatly, but it ended much too prematurely. Would the outcome have been different if she had addressed his confrontations earlier, or more directly, or less directly, or more consistently? I really don't know, but I will say she did a valiant job, emotionally connecting with him much of the time, staying in touch with her own frustrations, curiosity, anger at his provocations, and compassion for his struggles. On paper, their work can be seen as failing to fully develop. But, by being non-defensive and truly engaged herself, I would say she grappled admirably with how and whether to address his many questions and doubts.

Just what are the naked truths we tend to avoid, especially in the early stages of the work with our most challenging patients? Here are some, from my perspective.

First, although analysts vary in the extent to which we believe in focusing on defenses, most analysts would view some of the patient's goals as, themselves, reflecting issues to be analyzed, but we tend not to announce that, especially early on. For example, when the patient (mentioned above) wanted to find ways to better control his girlfriend, my supervisee and I understood his *need for control* as a *symptom* of his obsessive compulsive character, rather than joining him in viewing *the limitations of his control of his girlfriend* as the problem. Should the clinician have made this more explicit in the first few sessions, and taken the risk he would leave without getting a sense of what their work had to offer? Would another clinician have seen it differently, or responded differently, even if he or she shared this point of view? On what basis do we make these decisions?

Second, we really have no idea how long a treatment will take or, concretely, how the patient's life will change as a result of it. How explicit should we be about this, if the patient raises it in the first session? A third thorny truth raised in this case is that we can't spell out exactly what we will do, in order to have a specific outcome. That is, it would be hard to explain cause and effect in treatment, in advance of the process. For example, this patient would have liked his therapist to tell him something like, "We will make a list of the pros and cons of your relationship with your girlfriend, add them up, and come to a conclusion about what to do. Then you will not feel conflicted." At what point should the clinician clarify the disparity between what the patient hopes for, and what we are likely to be able to provide?

A fourth, related issue is that patients and analysts are often unable to formulate how any particular session was of benefit. There is no way to predict when fruitful insights or emotionally meaningful interchanges will occur, and what impact they will have. Some of therapy's benefits may accrue well after the treatment terminates.

Fifth, whether or not we will be able to work well with someone may be unclear to us in the initial phase. What makes a good match between patient and analyst is mostly intuitive. It is certainly not as clear cut as, for example, in medicine where a cardiologist can say she just doesn't work with dental problems. This opens us to the possibility that our judgment about treating someone might be colored by our own needs to fill our practices. How much should we share about uncertainties about the match, and about our own motivations for seeing it as we do?

This, in turn, bears some relationship to the sixth issue, which is how a particular patient will fit with the individual clinician's marked differences in how much personal information we disclose. Frequently we share less of this material than the patient would like to hear.

The seventh is that many patients enter treatment hoping to feel more happiness, optimism, and certainty about their decisions. In my experience, at the end of the work, people are not necessarily happier, more optimistic, or more certain about their choices. While, hopefully, they understand themselves better, and may function in better sync with themselves, as the work progresses, glimpses of how their lives might have been less burdened by defensive operations frequently *sadden* my patients, at least for some period of time. In many cases, over time, they realize more fully that some missed opportunities are irretrievable. Many actually end treatment with a heightened sense of life's fragility, uncertainty, the shades of gray between right and wrong, the voluminous ways a human being's impact can differ from his or her conscious intentions, the stark limitations of time, and, more generally, a greater appreciation of life's inherent difficulties. I wonder whether any of this could be usefully communicated in the first sessions. Perhaps omitting mention of these frequent outcomes doesn't warrant the term "seduction," but I think what we call it is less important than the recognition that it could be counterproductive to try to reveal in early sessions some of our best guesses about what a new patient is likely to experience as the treatment unfolds.

Lastly, the eighth "truth" – friends and partners who seemed satisfactory before treatment may seem unsatisfactory afterwards. It may feel as though they are too narcissistically self-involved, or too superficial, or unable to engage in profound conversations, or too involved in the internet, pills, alcohol, or other diversions. Like the warning on a pack of cigarettes, should we tell entering patients that this process may be hazardous to your relationships?

I am sure that this is not an exhaustive list. Stephen Mitchell's words, that opened this chapter, come to mind again. I think that if we were to spell out some of these naked truths in early sessions, perhaps fewer patients would enter treatment. While I would guess that most of us do not lie, when directly confronted by patients' questions about the way therapy works, the time it takes, the feelings it often evokes, and the benefits they can reasonably expect, there is probably much that we deliberately leave out. Whether consciously or not, on some level we judge what to share based, possibly, on what we think the patient can hear, and still give treatment a chance. But how do we know what the patient can and can't hear? And are we then lying by omission? Are we hoping to seduce patients to stay long enough for their goals to evolve, and to see what they can gain from the work, so as to be willing to bear treatment's practical and emotional limitations, challenges, and costs?

Let me be clear: I believe that psychological treatment helps many patients enormously. I count myself among those who have greatly benefited from it. I believe my own life was greatly enhanced by being in treatment. I love this work with all my heart. But I see therapy itself as invented by each dyad. It is a vital part of my own interpersonal psychoanalytic orientation that there are no pre-set, invariable goals, techniques, or insights relevant to all patients. I don't think everybody needs to understand their wish to marry one parent and kill the other, although some people do need this. I don't focus as much on dreams with some patients as I would with others. In short, early in treatment, I couldn't tell a patient the naked truth about how we will work together because, except in the most general terms, I don't know how we will work until we invent it together. This answer, while truthful to me, would not satisfy many prospective patients in an intake.

I have never knowingly lied to a patient. That is not what I am talking about. But, generally, I think there needs to be a dialectic in therapy between confronting and containing, just as there needs to be a dialectic between ritual and spontaneity, as discussed by Irwin Hoffman (1998). I am not merely alluding to the list above, of what I called naked truths that we often can't communicate in first sessions. Much more broadly than that, I am harkening back to Winnicott's (1949) paper, "Hate in the countertransference," where he recommended that some of our thoughts and feelings should, at times, be held in storage.

Of course, once again, we are hardly omniscient, and very frequently don't feel we know what the patient can find useful, whether to share our thoughts and emotional responses, whether to hold them in temporary storage, or simply keep them to ourselves. And yet, like so much else in treatment, and the rest of life, we must choose, since not deciding is also a choice.

At the same time it is crucial, in my view, that the patient believes in our absolute allegiance to the truth, in our cherishing truth, and in our unimpeachable personal and professional integrity. I have sometimes thought of treatment as a process of radical truth telling. We ask this of our patients, and they, rightly, expect the same from us. But what do I communicate to them when, for example, I face decisions about what to tell insurance companies about our work? Often, if I report all I believe to be true (including, perhaps, that I think our work will take at least five years, at three times per week), I will lose needed coverage for the patient. Do I give the patient a diagnosis that reflects what I really think is accurate, or one more likely to get reimbursement? What message does my patient thereby infer about my attitudes toward the truth?

Many situations in training can be seen as opportunities for candidates to reflect on the question of what to share, and with whom. For example, the candidate may try to please, or at least not lose the patient by bending. That is, he or she may bend over backwards to fit the patient's scheduling needs, needs for a reduced fee, needs for emotional support, wishes to bend the usual frame, and so on. Afterward it can be challenging to report all of this "bending" in supervision. Even for candidates determined to be honest, forthright, and non-defensive, disclosing all the bending can be difficult.

Speaking for myself, as a patient, I remember many times I needed to believe my analyst was telling me what she really thought, without censoring those "naked truths" that might bring me pain, or shame, or any other feeling. I didn't want her to hold them in storage, or to feel she knew better than I did whether I was ready to hear her truths about me. So, again, we have a conundrum. As in the rest of life, we make choices without knowing their outcome, and we focus on one truth at the expense of others. Every session is another opportunity to realize how little we know. Is there such a thing as the naked truth, about my responses in a session, about what can be expected in treatment, about which goals are defensive strategies and whether, nevertheless, they should be adhered to? If I think a patient's life would be enhanced by staying in treatment, does that entitle me to hold off on expressing some naked truths? I have no definitive answers to these questions, and, perhaps, I never will. But just as adherence to some rituals gives added meaning to spontaneity, I think a background of considering and sometimes not uttering our words gives heightened meaning to those moments when, throwing caution to the winds, we do bare all the naked truths we can possibly consciously uncover in our own minds and hearts.

My final point is that facing the complexity of our task takes tremendous courage, and I think we should more fully address the development of that courage in training. I think the courage it takes is to understand that in any session the stakes may be high, while also being aware of the complexity of our task, and the limitations of our knowledge, and to nevertheless keep going. It wouldn't take courage if simply aiming to confront, or to contain, or to obey ritual, or to cultivate spontaneity, was enough. What takes courage is that clinicians live in a world of conundrums, where a containing moment may sometimes nurture both participants' capacities to engage in a tough confrontation the next moment.

In the fourth century BC, Aristotle defined courage as the observance of the mean between excessive fear and excessive rashness. He went on to say we should especially value bravery in response to sudden events, since bravery in unforeseen danger springs more from character, as there is less time for preparation. He suggests that one might resolve to face a danger one can foresee, from calculation and on principle, but only a fixed disposition of courage will enable one to face sudden danger.

I suggest that clinicians face the possibility of danger every hour, so we must nurture that fixed disposition of courage in ourselves. I am reminded of something I often say to supervisees. If you were lost in the woods, and could find no clues about which direction to take, what would you do? Well, the surest thing is that you can't stand still. You have to choose a direction, and start putting one foot in front of the other. And, whether we like it or not, that is often our position as clinicians. Clinical work demands of us the rash timidity to bear the responsibility of being lost, yet still have the courage to keep going.

Regardless of our degrees and certificates, and no matter how much experience we have, in every clinical hour we still need to be brave; to approach, with rash timidity, the daunting task of being a clinician; to embrace the paradox of knowing we feel lost in the woods; and yet choose to keep walking until we come to a clearing.

References

Aristotle (4th century, BC). *The Nicomachean Ethics. With An English Translation.* transl. H. Rackham. Cambridge, MA: Harvard University Press Loeb Library Edition, 1926.

Hoffman, I. Z. (1998). *Ritual and Spontaneity in the Psychoanalytic Process.* Hillsdale, NJ: The Analytic Press.

Mitchell, S. A. (1993). *Hope and Dread in Psychoanalysis.* New York: Basic Books.

Winnicott, D. (1949). Hate in the countertransference. *International Journal of Psycho-analysis,* 30: 69–75.

Chapter 20

The "scandalous patient"

Disgust, fascination, and compassion

Sue Kolod

In writing this paper, it became clear to me that the topic of "scandal" and treating the scandalous patient falls into the "unspeakable" category encompassed by the three U's – *Unknowable, Unspeakable, and Unsprung.* In what follows, I will begin with my story of helping to organize a panel and series of papers on the topic of scandal. I will then discuss scandal in general and offer a clinical example that illustrates the countertransference reaction of disgust on the one hand, and fascination on the other. Finally, I will place this reaction in the context of the therapist's reactions to a patient who may have engaged in scandalous behavior.

The process of organizing a "scandal" panel gave me an experience-near sense of the problem of dealing with the "scandalous patient" and why these clinical experiences may be "unspeakable." This is because, in talking about them, the people speaking, as well as those listening, become implicated in the process. When thinking about who might participate on the panel that inspired these papers, it seemed important to include someone who had been at the center of a scandal him- or herself. Rather than talking about the issue, in the best tradition of interpersonal psychoanalysis, I wanted to have a person who could speak from personal experience, thus reducing the distance between "us" and "them."

I considered individuals who had scandalized their psychoanalytic institutes by becoming involved with a patient or former patient, and a person who has been at the center of many scandals and leads a pro-pedophile organization and has been jailed several times. But the conference committee felt that it would be perceived as giving these people a platform which they did not deserve. Putting such individuals on a panel could be seen as endorsing their scandalous behavior unless they specifically had reformed or been rehabilitated.

Eliot Spitzer was interested when I invited him to speak at a psychoanalytic conference. But after he heard what the topic would be, he realized he would be out of town that weekend (even though I had asked him more than one year in advance). I asked a friend who knows John Edwards whether he might be interested, and she replied that he might, but it wouldn't be good for him.

So, it seems that talking to scandalous people about their experience falls into the "unspeakable" category as well. Here are some assumptions about engaging with individuals who have been involved in a scandal: (1) The scandals are an embarrassment, and those who commit them should not talk about what they did. (2) Ostracism is the appropriate response to a member of a community who engages in scandalous behavior. (3) If the person is willing to come forward and talk about his or her experience, it is either "not good for them," or it is considered vulgar, self-serving, or potentially damaging to them or their community; (4) In hearing out the scandalous person, the listener becomes scandalous him- or herself. (5) The one exception to this is if the (scandal-committing) person is asking for forgiveness, sees the errors of his or her ways and is trying to be rehabilitated.

What is "scandal"? From the Merriam-Webster definition, scandal derives from a Greek word for "snare," implying that one is "snared" into moral failure. It was originally a term used to denote a discredit brought upon religion by "unseemly conduct in a religious person," especially if it encourages a lapse of faith in another (www.merriam-webster.com/dictionary/scandal). Today, scandal has a spectrum of meanings, including discreditable or immoral conduct, damage to reputation caused by such misconduct, and malicious or defamatory gossip, whether or not well founded. "Scandal" and "slander" share the same root.

Clearly, there is a relationship between scandal and boundary violation, but not all boundary violations result in scandal, and likewise, not all scandals involved boundary violations. Scandal is historically and culturally relative. What causes a scandal in one generation might not in the next, and acts that were scandalous at one time would not be today. Think of Oscar Wilde and Joan of Arc. Sex outside of marriage, particularly if it produced a child, was scandalous at one time – Hester Prynne and Tess of the D'Urbervilles are examples from literature.

Likewise, there are acts that did not cause a scandal in earlier times that would today. For example, Sullivan's methods of treating gay men at Sheppard Pratt in which he encouraged physical contact between the patients and staff did not cause a scandal at that time. Even more scandalous by today's standards would be Sullivan's initiation of sexual contact with his private patients and his relationship with James Inscoe, who was either a patient or an underage hustler (or both) when they met. It was not even considered an ethical violation to have sex with a patient until the 1979 revision of the Ethical Principles of Psychologists that defined "sexual intimacies with clients" as unethical (Wake, 2011). Sex abuse of children in general and in particular in the clergy did not cause a scandal until fairly recently because it was ignored and unreported.

Abby Stein was involved in the planning of the scandal panel and was supposed to be a presenter on this panel. She had to withdraw because of illness and died about one year later. In her wonderful paper, "The Sex Monster," she examines how "deep splitting triggered by our own sexual desires and fears has fueled a contemporary hysteria that vilifies strangers, who may not have even committed any serious crimes" (p. 497) and makes the point that we all have disowned parts of ourselves that wish to do harm. These disowned parts are easily projected on to the alleged perpetrator who is experienced as repellent and alien. Stein writes, "In the presence of perpetration we may be repelled but we are also excited. In an odd way, people who have done awful lurid sexual things to others are not just interesting – they are downright sexy" (Stein, 2011, p. 512). I experienced those combined countertransference reactions, of disgust/outrage on the one hand and fascination/titillation on the other, in the case I will now describe.

I received a call from a man I will call Frank.[1] When Frank called, he was obviously in great distress, as he had been arrested for sexually molesting his seven-year old granddaughter. He was taken from his home in handcuffs and incarcerated. Subsequently, he was fired from his job as a substance abuse counselor at a metropolitan hospital because of the arrest. Although this "scandal" never reached the media, it was indeed a scandal in Frank's family and community.

The charges were subsequently dropped when his granddaughter recanted, but at the time Frank called me, his file was still open in the Administration for Children's Services (ACS) and he was only permitted supervised visitation with his granddaughter. Frank was not mandated for therapy. He was seeking treatment for two reasons of his own: one, he was suffering and traumatized as a result of the arrest, incarceration, and loss of job. He was profoundly depressed – crying all the time and unable to enjoy anything in his life; and two, his lawyer told him that if he could obtain a letter from a therapist, saying he did not fit the profile of a pedophile, that would help in getting his file with ACS sealed.

In truth, I was somewhat fascinated by the thought of working with an alleged pedophile and agreed to meet with him for a consultation. As Stein observed, the possibility that someone might have committed lurid sexual acts imbues that person with a kind of glamor. When we met, I was relieved and a little disappointed to see an ordinary-looking, 68-year-old man who was visibly suffering, which contributed to my sense that there was no reason to refuse to work with him if I could be of help. We began psychotherapy on the condition that Frank not ask me to advocate for him with ACS, with his family, or in any court-related hearings. I told Frank I would not write a letter for him or be engaged in anything related to his court appearances. My reason for this condition was my awareness going into this treatment that there was no way for me to know that he did not, in fact, molest his granddaughter. I suggested that if he was seeking therapy primarily to get a letter, there were other therapists who might be willing to do that for him. He insisted that he wanted therapy not only to get a letter, but because his life had been ruined by this accusation, and that he was profoundly depressed and traumatized. We decided to work together, but in fact, Frank persisted throughout the first year of treatment in trying to get me to write a letter for him, which made me quite angry.

The story Frank told me was this: his granddaughter, who I'll call Esther, complained to her father, Frank's son, that, "Grandpa lifted my skirt." Frank vehemently denied having molested Esther. In fact, he told me that she frequently flipped up her skirt, and he told her not to do that. He also told me that the two of them often played in his bedroom with the door locked. She insisted on locking the door, according to Frank. She liked to play a game in which Frank tied her hands with a belt and she escaped. When I commented that this was an odd and somewhat suggestive game, Frank agreed and said he had been uncomfortable with the game but Esther insisted.

Esther's parents were divorced, and she lived with her mother, who Frank described as borderline. Esther herself was having emotional problems – Frank told me she lied frequently – and was in therapy. When Esther complained about Frank lifting her skirt, her father told the mother who told the therapist. The story grew into one in which Frank is depicted as touching Esther's vagina while masturbating.

Frank and I worked together for two and a half years. During this time, his symptoms of posttraumatic stress disorder (PTSD) and depression, including rumination, obsessive thoughts about revenge, and an inability to enjoy anything in his life, abated. I was never completely sure whether or not Frank was a pedophile, or at the very least, a child molester. But in order for the treatment to be therapeutic, it became clear to me that I needed to maintain an open and non-judgmental attitude on this issue. Frank often related dreams or memories that could be viewed as implicating himself as a perpetrator; for example, the story about tying up Esther. When this occurred, I found myself trying to get Frank to confess that he might have in fact, behaved inappropriately with her. I felt that Frank might feel better if he admitted this to me but always ran up against a brick wall when I pursued this line of inquiry.

There were times when I experienced strong negative feelings towards Frank: disgust, suspicion, and apprehension, in particular. But was this because there was something disgusting about him or just that he had been accused unfairly of doing something that disgusted me? And there was that feeling of fascination as well. Frank was the (potentially) "exotic other." This combination of disgust and fascination made me very uncomfortable throughout the time we worked together. I found that I was distant with Frank; more suspicious and less likely to ask pertinent questions. For example, I was reluctant to inquire into Frank's sexual life and fantasies, a subject that was clearly relevant.

Although there was much more to Frank and to this treatment than the scandal, I found myself drawn repeatedly into the question of whether or not he did it. The pull of the scandal, the question of his guilt, and the issue of whether or not to try to get Frank to confess were overwhelming at times. I felt that if I didn't find a way *both* to imagine Frank as guilty of the charge *and* to still experience him as a suffering human being, I could not be helpful to him.

In an attempt to overcome this countertransference problem, I contacted several people in the mental health field but could not find anyone who seemed at all sympathetic towards a person who might be a perpetrator. Finally, I did something very unorthodox: I consulted with Tom O'Carroll, who is himself an unapologetic pedophile and an expert on the subject of pedophilia. He has written several books on the subject (O'Carroll, 1980, 2010). I contacted him rather than a clinical supervisor because I wanted to discuss the issues with someone who would not be disgusted, fascinated, or suspicious. This was one way I was attempting to bridge the gap between "us" and "them." Here is our email exchange[2]:

> SK: I've read several chapters in your book, *Paedophilia: The Radical Case*, which is very interesting and well written. Clearly, your pedophilic interests are completely ego-syntonic. I cannot agree that it is ok to have sex with children and am not interested in debating this with you. Neither of us will convince the other. I do have a clinical question. [I summarized the case for him and then told Tom that my patient seemed to be looking for a therapist willing to testify on his behalf that he "didn't do it." How can I help this person, I asked him.]
>
> TO: Hi Sue, thanks for your very interesting question, which reminds me that therapists have the hugely responsible job of dealing with real people and their difficult problems. I am pleased you apparently feel I might have something useful to say. I am not sure that I do, but I am very happy to give it a try. First, though, you say: I cannot agree that it is ok to have sex with children but am not interested in debating this with you. That's fine by me and very understandable. I can tell you, though, that I am by no means convinced that "it is ok to have sex with children" in present circumstances. I do maintain there is nothing intrinsically harmful in it, but the extrinsic sources of harm are immense in the present state of our culture, and cannot be ignored.
>
> That said, let me turn to your question: "How can I help this person?" This phrasing contains the optimistic assumption that you can indeed help, but that is not necessarily the case. He might be in greater need of a lawyer than a therapist: someone willing and able to fight his corner in court against the child protection people. The charges were dropped, after all. Why should a citizen who has never been convicted of a sexual offence (I presume this is the case) have to prove his innocence? Proving a negative is notoriously difficult. Your client has a huge stake in convincing you of his innocence, and that may be the only reason he is continuing in therapy. Although you have told him you will not testify in court, it sounds as though he has not given up hope that you will. Or he may hope for some sort of endorsement

> from you that will enable him to regain the respect of his family and community – and restored relations with his granddaughter. If the guy was "fessing up" to paedophilic interests I'd probably be suggesting you could introduce him to certain literature, and perhaps to an organization such as B4U-ACT. But that is not the case.
>
> SK: Hi Tom, To hone my question a bit, I keep wondering if he'd feel better if he could speak openly to me about what really happened. This may be very naive on my part – he seems genuinely horrified at the accusation.
>
> TO: Hi again Sue. He might [feel better], but perhaps that would put you in a difficult position in the long term. It might also make him permanently nervous about what you could eventually reveal (not that you would). Of course you want to know the full picture, but I'm not sure it would be wise to press for this.
>
> SK: Hi Tom, You've been extremely helpful. I'm convinced that it might do more harm than good to press.

Subsequent to this email exchange, I stopped trying to get Frank to admit to anything. Once I relinquished responsibility or interest in getting him to confess, I found that I was able to empathize with him. My feelings of apprehension, disgust, and fascination towards him were less acute, although they didn't disappear entirely, as I'll show later. My exchange with Tom O'Carroll helped me to "de-fetishize" my patient and to see him as "more simply human as otherwise" (Sullivan, 1947). I realized that my job was to treat him for PTSD and depression, not pedophilia. But although I was able, for the most part, to put aside the question of whether or not he "did it," I still, at times was drawn into this speculation.

I have used transcripts from my therapy sessions with Frank for teaching purposes and every time I do so, the participants also become preoccupied with whether or not Frank was guilty.

After two years, Frank's depression had lifted and his PTSD symptoms had abated. He was no longer consumed with fantasies of revenge and had begun to enjoy life again. In the last six months of the treatment, I finally confronted my own resistance to inquiring about Frank's sexuality. Frank was quite attached to me and I sensed the beginning of an erotic transference that I was uncomfortable about exploring. This discomfort with and avoidance of exploring an eroticized transference had to do, I think, with fears that I would uncover something disturbing in Frank's sexuality or feel that he was fetishizing *me*. Indeed, at this stage, my earlier fascination with this part of Frank had mostly dissipated, and I think our having developed a good relationship and connection led me to avoid trying to uncover the perversity I had suspected all along.

In fact, when we began to explore his sexual fantasies and his interest in pornography, Frank mentioned that he had found the book, *The Story of O* (Reage, 1954), to be very exciting. He went on to say that it was the female protagonist's utterly submissive attitude that turned him on. This, of course, made me think of the incident of tying up his granddaughter. The more we explored his sexuality, the more ambiguous it became as to whether or not he could be guilty of molesting his granddaughter.

I had a number of countertransference dreams about Frank that illuminated my strong, complicated reactions to him. For example:

> I'm with a group of people and Frank is kind of like my date. He starts embracing me – it's really disgusting and I push him away. He becomes very despondent which makes me feel guilty. I feel sorry for him. He is lying on a bed face down, very depressed. I lie down next to him and put my hand on him to comfort him.
>
> I am going to be kidnapped by Frank and I'm very frightened.
>
> I am involved with Frank in a sexual relationship and want to get out of it. I feel no attraction for him. In fact, I'm repulsed by the idea of having sex with him. But since I agreed to (initiated) it I feel responsible.

I am intensely involved with Frank, in these dreams. As I think about them now, they indicate my ambivalence about becoming an object of attraction to Frank and my misgivings about being attached to a person who may have committed perverse sexual acts. This is despite the fact that I had put aside the matter of his guilt, at least in my conscious mind.

Frank often mentioned that he really enjoyed our sessions and, although he was feeling a lot better, he knew it would be difficult to say goodbye. Through dreams and associations Frank expressed closeness and even romantic feelings towards me. Frank reported this dream:

> I have a younger girlfriend. I'm infatuated with her. I'm still married to Marcia and am leading a double life. Her friend says, you have to

> either make a commitment to her or give her up. (SK: How did you feel in the dream?) She made me feel good, young. The dream was mixed good and bad feelings.

Of course, as with many things Frank related, this could also refer to romantic/sexual feelings about his granddaughter. That was the kind of ambiguity inherent in this treatment. But mostly, we talked about this dream in terms of his feelings of closeness and aliveness in relation to me and to the treatment.

In the last month of treatment, Frank expressed gratitude for the work we did together but also referred back frequently to his continued puzzlement over whether or not I believed in his innocence. Whenever this question arose, I validated his sense that there was some ambiguity in my mind. The combined countertransference reactions persisted throughout the treatment, although less acutely. Despite my ambivalence and his disappointment that I was not completely convinced of his innocence, we both felt quite warm and loving toward each other, and I told Frank the door is always open if he wants to come back.

The combined countertransference reaction of disgust and outrage on the one hand and fascination/titillation on the other that I have highlighted in my work with Frank is likely quite common when treating a person who has been engaged in sexual behavior that has resulted in a scandal of some sort, be it boundary violations with a patient or sexual transgressions of others sorts such as pedophilia, rape, or paraphilias. This can be disturbing and result in distancing, seeing the patient in black-and-white terms, becoming moralistic, or seeing the patient as the "exotic other." At a later date, when preparing for the scandal panel, I contacted Tom O'Carroll again and asked him a series of questions about his own scandal and reactions to scandal in general, O'Carroll remarked,

> As for helping patients who have been involved in a scandal, it depends what you mean by "help" and what you regard as scandalous. As I understand it, you are pledged to *help* your patient, if possible, rather than *reform* him necessarily. For any patients who are at all like me, even the slightest hint of being judgmental or coercive is likely to be extremely counterproductive. The one-size-fits-all approach of forensic CBT programs seems to guarantee this type of reaction, at least with a certain type of offender, like myself.

I'd like to end with a quote from Andrea Celenza:

> Recovery from boundary violations depends on two interrelated factors: One – probably the most important involves the attitude of the transgressor, both toward the transgression itself and his/her openness to and capacity for rehabilitation. The other is the attitude we hold toward fallibility – both the patient's and our own.
>
> (Celenza, 2007)

In other words, when treating the "scandalous patient" it is important to remember that the situation cannot be characterized as "us" and "them" – it is only us.

Notes

1 I want to thank this patient for giving me permission to use case material.
2 I want to thank Tom O'Carroll for giving me permission to publish our email exchange.

References

Celenza, A. (2007) *Sexual Boundary Violations: Therapeutic, Supervisory and Academic Contexts.* New York: Jason Aronson.

O'Carroll, T. (1980) *Paedophilia: The Radical Case.* London: Peter Owen.

O'Carroll, T. (2010) *Michael Jackson's Dangerous Liaisons.* Leicester: Troubador.

Reage, P. (1954) *Story of O.* France: Jean-Jacques Pauvert.

Stein, A. (2011) The sex monster: dissociations as parallel process in the response to sex offenders. *Contemp. Psychoanal.* 47 (4): 497–518.

Sullivan, H. S. (1947) *Conceptions of Modern Psychiatry.* New York: The William Alanson White Psychiatric Foundation.

Wake, N. (2011) *Private Practices: Harry Stack Sullivan, the Science of Homosexuality and American Liberalism.* New Brunswick, NJ: Rutgers University Press.

Chapter 21

The scandal within psychoanalysis itself

Paul Lippmann

This paper is about psychoanalysis, itself, as "the scandalous patient." It has always been our strength and our responsibility, while exploring the lives of our patients, to be able to turn around – to face, reflect on, and analyze ourselves as best we can. With this in mind, it's incumbent upon us to recognize that there are several aspects of the institution and practice of psychoanalysis that hint at its darker shadows.

Even during these difficult days for our field, such self-examination in no way detracts from a deep acknowledgment and appreciation of the genuine strengths and virtues of psychoanalysis; quite the opposite. One of the central virtues of psychoanalysis is its insistence on honest self-analysis. There are features of our training procedures, our relation to money, our complex engagement with secrecy and power, our hidden neediness, our hidden nastiness to one another, our well-rationalized ways of holding on to patients, our inevitable – but often destructive – capacity for hiding and pretense that together form the underbelly of our mostly helpful therapeutic activities. In our efforts to be of genuine assistance to persons in difficult emotional circumstances, we often engage in painful, heroic, and moving interaction with our patients. The shadow side, however, holds an often-unspoken scandal.

Psychoanalysis is no stranger to scandal. Let us bear in mind that psychoanalysis, itself, was born of a scandal. To study and practice psychoanalysis, in the early years, was to bring the potential for shame on to oneself, one's family, one's acquaintances. It was not a profession for those who sought status, security, money, or academic position. One hundred years ago, it was the province of pioneers, free thinkers, dreamers, explorers, eccentrics. *And mainly, it should be said, these ideas were advanced by a collection of Jews.*

That was the real scandal. In Vienna, in the midst of a darkly anti-Semitic period in that city's life, and just a few decades prior to the entire destruction of the Jewish world, these adventurous and brave Jewish doctors, these free-thinking mind doctors, dared to speak of children's sexual minds, of the sexual secrets hidden in family life and in society, of the unconscious, of the power of the irrational, of the deepest truths found in dreams. These were, to say the least, distasteful and alarming notions in Victorian Vienna, but the scandal was that these Jews were turning the world upside down and inside out in their daring and brazen intellectual revolution. The scandal (or *scahndahl*, as it was pronounced) was psychoanalysis, itself. That is, our ancestors were the scandal – a group of misfits, revolutionaries, visionaries, schemers, tricksters, neurotics, and worse – selling weird ideas as essential to healing the ills of a gullible people; a cult of Jewish doctors continuing their age-old, destructive mission of be-spoiling innocent Christian civilization – or so many thought.

Of course, contradictions abound. These early pioneers, although mindful of the potential dangers of being thought of as perverse Jewish sexual cultists, lived and worked in an atmosphere of greater personal freedom than is often found in contemporary psychoanalytic circles. As they explored and learned about the new ways of thinking and healing, emotional and sexual entanglements with patients were not uncommon. Family and personal interconnections on and off the couch were richly intermixed. The contemporary atmosphere of more rigid and often righteous boundary concerns has been the result both of large-scale changes in cultural values and of changes in ideas about the appropriate and the permissible in psychoanalytic practice. Our pioneers were experimenting and learning as they went along. Attitudes of superiority and rectitude adopted by many contemporary therapists when they view the early bumps in the learning process of the earlier generation of pioneer analysts are not a sign of current progress, but of unfortunate narrowness.

It should be said that, in the contemporary psychoanalytic world, again in seeming contradiction, relational openness and flexibility are often paradoxically joined with the puritanical – as if there is some correct, or even superior, way to be in human relationships – and the atmosphere, despite everyone's intentions, can seem more cautious, more paranoid, chillier, than the more relaxed atmosphere of the early days. This is compounded by being in the age of HIPAA compliance, of the bureaucratization of correctness – all in the purported interest of the patient. *Fat chance.*

The earlier, more relaxed atmosphere is well described, for example, by Stanley Couch in a paper on his analysis with Anna Freud (1995), and also by Young-Bruehl in her wonderful biography of Anna Freud (1994). In those days, it seems the analytic business began and ended at the door to the analytic office. Inside that door, analyst and analysand did the work of analyzing. Outside that door, both participants were equal citizens, regular people, fellow patients. It was not required of the analyst that he or she demonstrate a superior kind of humanity, a deeper capacity for relationality, being a better spouse or parent or a sunnier human being, all of which are unfortunate and impossible requirements for therapists in our own times. This more contemporary set of values often results in a falseness – a public posture – that creates an unreal atmosphere both in the relationship between patient and therapist and in the relations between therapists. Life is hard enough without this layer of pretending to be a higher form of being. And yet, there is an implicit requirement that we act more relaxed, more successful, more happily situated, and less neurotic than we may actually feel. Rather, our public lives, our overt personalities, our spouses, lovers, and children are marketed as an advertisement for our work.

Some patients prefer flesh and blood, more real and possibly flawed analysts. They often need their analysts to have gone through tough times so they can better understand the depths of struggle. But most wish their healers to be more or less healed. There are many potential analysts who hide past experiences with severe depression, suicide, hospitalization – no matter the depth of resulting self-understanding or personal growth. I believe this shame and prejudice will change over time, because people with scars often make the best therapists. The image of analyst as damage-proof, as above the fray, as cool and confident, while understandably appealing, has its costs. It results in part from a misguided idea of what is at the heart of analytic therapy, i.e., an analyst who knows, who interprets, who stays to the side (at best), or above (at worst), who observes, who never sweats. Such prejudice against analysts who have experienced significant psychological suffering, while, on the one hand, reflecting the beliefs in objectivity that characterized our ancestors' times, on the other, has little to do with the original creative spirit of adventure and exploration that animated our founders.

Indeed, a collection of conformist, careful, unadventurous analysts and students may seem safer for the life of an institute, but it is deadly for the life of our field. And institute leaders who care more about institutional and organizational politics than what is roaring about in our contemporary world are also deadly for our field. Psychoanalysis can no longer afford business as usual, or assume that attempts to conform or fit in with the mainstream will be better for our discipline or the people we want to serve. That is not what will help us bring our strengths to a suffering world. Rather, it is – in yet another contradiction – attempts to fit in that are most likely to leave us justifiably marginalized. It is time to join the resistance, to reclaim our outlaw status, to turn away from efforts to justify our existence to malignant insurance panels, HIPAA rulings and credentialing institutions, and to reimagine our basic goals, purposes, and methods.

Now let me return to scandals. I have had my share of interest in patients who have been scandalous. Indeed, our days are filled with stories of scandals: transgressions, sexual infidelities of all sorts, lies, substance abuse problems that endanger unwitting others, boundary violations, both historical and present-day, lovers, or their families.

We analysts are a funny group of people, who know about these things and are required to keep secrets. Again, we were born a scandalous field, and daily we witness and listen in on and advise persons involved in scandal, and even participate in conferences in which we discuss our response to scandal. In some ways, we are a bunch of *yentas,* interested in and alive to various forms of gossip, privileged to hear the dirt, the real scoop, the goings on behind closed doors. But it's more complicated than that. Keeping quiet about what one knows, in order to safeguard privacies, has many ramifications. In the supermarket, the patient's secret lover looks over at us from the nearby checkout lane, knowing that we know and brazenly daring us to look him or her in the face, or looking away in fear and shame.

Keeping secrets is not a simple matter. Some are good at it, some not. But, in general, what is the effect on us and our community of so many secrets? So much hooded and veiled knowledge? Does it not create an unnatural atmosphere where knowing and not knowing on all sides make it difficult to have a simple, straightforward conversation? We all keep secrets here and there. It is part of learning how to be a private and public person at the same time. But in our field, it has become the water in which we swim. It is part of the definition of who we are and how we are to conduct ourselves. This is not a complaint. It is our job. We get paid for it. The question is: How does it actually affect us? What does it do to us and to our relations with one another and with the public at large? At what point do we become too skilled at artful lying? Or allow the compartmentalization required in clinical work to contribute to our silence in public discourse on the important moral and human dilemmas of our day?

To my mind, the individual scandals – the stories of scandal – that we hear in our consulting rooms, as interesting as they may be, pale in comparison to the scandals that lie at the heart of psychoanalysis. I believe built into our profession are forms of witting and unwitting participation in a series of violations of decent human conduct, albeit rationalized, justified, and swept under the rug. These include:

1 The refusal in America to follow Freud's lead in allowing non-MDs to study and practice psychoanalysis, which has been both harmful to the liberating spirit of psychoanalysis and to the personal, professional and economic lives of legions of individual practitioners. This has begun to change in recent years, but these changes to the increased openness across institutions have been forced economically, rather than arising from the result of serious institutional change.
2 The system of moving up in the hierarchy as supervising and training analysts is filled with an ugly history. The failure to be honest about these interests does no service to a profession that professes and advertises the deepest kind of honesty. The hypocrisy should be embarrassing to us all.
3 The following is but one of thousands of small examples. I'm chatting with a colleague. I have learned, from one of my patients, that my colleague's spouse just received a diagnosis of incurable cancer. My colleague knows from one of his patients of a minor tragedy that has crossed my life. Neither piece of information has yet hit the street. Neither of us can speak of these matters since these are secrets from the couch. And yet we converse in almost natural sounds and rhythms, about institute matters and life in general in ways that seem intimate. We may feel deeply for the tragedies of each other's situations. We may even feel *Schadenfreude.* But whatever we feel, the dance of pretense goes on. In yet another insoluble contradiction, the psychoanalytic edifice would collapse without this secrecy and guaranteed confidentiality, yet the lack of realness and naturalness is an enemy to the root ideals of psychoanalysis. Perhaps there is no other way to do it. But I believe we need to rethink the fundamentals of psychoanalytic practice and institutionalization if we are to move to a way of being

with each other that is less weird, less strangulated and filled with pretense. These are among the reasons that organized psychoanalysis is so awful compared with the often wondrous adventures of talking in meaningful depth between analyst and a patient.

4 The powerful role of money in psychoanalysis has been a powerful secret. Our method, as advertised, and maintained by our national and international organizations, including sessions three or four times a week, is a treatment that, while clinically powerful, is only at this juncture available to the rich. While many analysts reduce their fees substantially early on in their practice, and while some continue to do so over time, successful analysts often stop seeing patients at reduced fees, and the market is such that even $200 for a 45-minutes hour is often too low a fee for many analytic clinicians. Given the usually paltry coverage by insurance carriers and their intrusion on patients' privacy, most analysts refuse to participate in insurance programs if they can. Our justifications for our high fees at times reflect our own financial burdens and ambitions, but at times are excessively self-serving. That analysts want to make money is not surprising in a culture so devoted to material success. However, our origins have to do with a very different set of ideals. This conflict in all its complexity needs to be aired more openly. Our hiding the money part of things is part of the scandal.

5 The way we are trained to get and keep patients is deeply problematic. While there are those patients whose interests are served by lengthy treatments, it is also the case that we can rationalize via concepts, methods, and techniques keeping patients with us when it is not clear that this is what they need. This problem is more obvious in those whose practices are lagging, and inevitably interfaces with the complexity of money's role, noted above. But it's also the case that "the relational turn," and with it the critique of prescribed technique and linear models of cure, at times has ways of holding on to people that far exceeds some of the excesses of the "one-person" and classical psychoanalysis. Now this is not to say that long-term treatment has no positive effects. Nor is it to say that holding on to patients has inevitably negative consequences – indeed, there are those patients whose lives are much improved, or who would not have lives at all, but for the ongoing connection to their therapists. But these are not the cases I'm addressing here. Further, in our Institute training, the need for purposes

of graduation to get and hold on to "analytic patients" is felt early and inevitably emphasizes candidates' needs to meet requirements in an expensive and onerous training experience.

I could go on in this vein. But enough is enough. Mostly, my hope is to initiate discussion of these problems. Psychoanalysis is at a crucial crossroads. Our origins prepared us for a major contribution to world culture. In 1900, Freud and Jung and their students were called upon to help heal people within Western culture who were struggling with the alienation attendant to the effects of the Industrial Revolution and the demise of the old forms and structures within economics, religion, community, and politics. Over 100 years later, psychoanalysis has fallen from grace and has little voice in central dilemmas found in modern living. For example, our home in the natural world is fast disappearing. The ecological crisis is upon us. The virtual, electronic, digital universe is gaining great influence.

We need a new psychoanalysis, based on our extraordinary intellectual history and tradition, one that addresses the real world and the plight of real people. But, we must now begin by facing ourselves and the ways in which we have separated ourselves from our finest ideals and from the central problems of our times.

References

Couch, A. S. (1995) Anna Freud's adult psychoanalytic technique: A defence of classical analysis. *International Journal of Psychoanalysis*, 76 (1), 153–171.

Young-Bruehl, E. (1994) *Anna Freud: A Biography*. New York: W. W. Norton.

Part VII

Unsafe surprises

Evil, mortality, diversity, and other strangers

Chapter 22

Psychoanalysis, the uncanny, and the banalization of evil

Edgar A. Levenson

As psychoanalysis has, at least for many of us, drifted away from its focus on fantasy (the roiling Unconscious of Freud) towards the more pragmatic interpersonal/relational matrix, we have become less aware of, and pay less attention to, manifestations of the uncanny. Everyone has had experiences with the uncanny, but it is more easily experienced than described. "Uncanny" can mean anything from a mild experience of dislocation, or *déjà vu*, on to sheer terror. I want to start with a story of my own experience with the uncanny – particularly its relationship to that ultimate uncanny, Evil – and then go on to discuss the consequences of this shift for psychoanalytic therapy.

In 1949, during and after the airlift, when the Russians cut off Berlin from the West, I was, among my other medical officer duties, the American officer for Spandau prison. Spandau held a number of the Nuremberg prisoners who had not been hanged, but given long or, in the case of Rudolph Hess, life sentences.[1] Being there stimulated in me a great deal of interest in the Nazi movement and in its individual participants. I offer this autobiographical bit to emphasize that, despite the difficulty of morally and psychologically struggling with my contact with Nazis I should hate, I found them to be largely very interesting, formidable and, dare I say, agreeable.[2]

This was in striking contrast to the following episode that took place in La Paz, Bolivia, in 1967. La Paz was, at that time, a rather small dreary Indian town at 11,000 feet, with a tiny ex-pat population. I entered a small restaurant. There were two large Nordic men sitting at a table. One looked up at me, quite pleasantly, and I experienced what can only be described as a severe physical shock! I was absolutely jolted by the experience of what felt to me like a contact with some mythic Evil.

As I later discovered, Klaus Barbie, "The Butcher of Lyon," a monster of a sadist and killer, was present in La Paz at that time. He slipped out of Europe in 1957 (with the help of the CIA) in the aftermath of World War II, obtained Bolivian citizenship under the name Klaus Altman, and lived there quite undisturbed until 1971. He was then extradited to France, where he died in prison in 1991 at age 77.

I do understand that at Spandau prison I wore the uniform, and I had the power. Also, these prisoners were the most benign of the Nazi hierarchy. But even then, my experience in La Paz feels not merely uncanny. It felt – dare one say – telepathic. I do believe it really *was* Barbie – although obviously I can't prove it. It doesn't matter; the experience was certainly real. Oddly enough, there was something *pleasurable* about it, exciting – rather like hearing a ghost story. I had no explanation for why scary and exhilarating should be so co-mingled until, as I shall elaborate, I re-encountered Sullivan's explication of the uncanny.

In any exegesis of the uncanny, of course, one must start with Freud's 1919 essay on the uncanny, the *Unheimlich. Unheimlich* translates as "not familiar." But, as Freud points out, its opposite, *heimlich,* has two meanings. First, what is familiar, and second, what is hidden or kept out of sight: *ergo* forbidden. The uncanny, then, is "that class of the terrifying that leads us back to something long known to us, once very familiar" (pp. 370–371); or, "when the primitive beliefs we have surmounted seem once more to be confirmed"(p. 403). It is not an entirely satisfactory exegesis. Although Freud's Oedipus complex, castration anxiety, and vagina dentata surely suggest something approximating uncanny terror, those do not seem to be addressed. At least in this particular article, the focus seems to be on the uncanny experience of the "double" – the me that is not-me.[3]

Kristiva offers a theory of experience-close horror based on the concept of "abjection," referring to the human reaction (horror, vomit) to a threatened breakdown of meaning caused by the loss of the distinction between subject and object or between self and other (Kristeva, 1982): "There looms within abjection, one of those violent, dark revolts of being . . . opposed to 'I'" (pp. 1–2). And Lacan in his 1962–1963 seminar, *L'Angoisse*, stays close to Freud's vision of the double (Lacan, 2004).

But, despite the absence of the cornerstones of Freud's theory in his *Unheimlich* essay, Freud brilliantly conflated his theory to Greek mythology, a European cultural heritage that exploited its intense uncanny affects. In Sophocles' *Trilogy*, the focus is not really on the incest; it is on our helplessness and terror in the face of the gods' implacable and inhuman intent and man's hubris in trying to evade it. Oedipus's lament echoes touchingly across the centuries, when, in *Oedipus at Colonus*, the second book of the *Trilogy*, he complains, how could he know she was his mother? How was it his fault (Sophocles, 1941)? The gods' vengeance was transgenerational. Poor, dense Oedipus the "puzzle-solver," as Tiresias mockingly called him, paid the price for a transgression committed by his father, Laius.[4]

Sullivan presented a far more extensive and detailed exegesis of the uncanny. In addition to the "good-me" and "bad-me," Sullivan described one additional infant state, the "not-me." The "not-me," he believed, was manifested as the unknown, the uncanny, the unintegrated, because it is dreadful and beyond representation:

> The not-me is literally the organization of experience with significant people that has been subjected to such intense anxiety, and anxiety so suddenly precipitated that it was impossible for the then relatively rudimentary person to make any sense of, to develop any true grasp on, the particular circumstances that dictated the experience of this intense anxiety.
>
> (Sullivan, 1953)

This state is accompanied by intense anxiety such as occurs in nightmares and schizophrenic experiences. Consider Sullivan's famous spider nightmare, which describes a terrifying and extremely disorganizing experience of a spider (Sullivan, 1953). Note also that, according to Sullivan, "not-me" and its destabilizing affect is an interpersonal event – it is not a reaction to an internal state (Sullivan, 1953, pp. 334–336).

Sullivan then does an astonishing thing. He establishes a hierarchy of the uncanny, running from "*awe*, to dread, to loathing and horror" (Sullivan, 1953, p. 315). Sullivan goes on at length to describe experiences of awe that are powerful and aesthetic: "awe-some," like the Cathedral at Chartres, or, say, a vision of the Virgin Mary. How did he grasp that progression from awe to terror, the strange confluence of magic and the uncanny, how the extremely disrupting experience of sheer terror makes the experience of the uncanny seductively attractive? Rainer Maria Rilke, in his poem *Duino Elegies*, put the mystery very beautifully:

> For beauty is nothing but the beginning of terror which we are barely able to endure, and it amazes us so, because it serenely disdains to destroy us. Every angel is terrible.

I will turn now, as a clinical vignette, to a dream, not just about uncanny experience, but also something akin to theological Evil. The session prior to the dream centers on this man's profound fear of women betraying him by having ardent sex with someone else. In the process of the telling, he experiences intense severe nausea, quite unlike his usual blandness. That night he has the following dream:

> He is in a room in a hospital (simultaneously his home) with his oldest son, his mother/wife and baby in the next room. They are evil in some terrible way. He has to go in and slit their throats to save himself and other children. He sees gristle, windpipes, and blood pouring out everywhere. Blood has soaked the carpet. He must cover it up. Then they are alive, coming after him, zombies, he sees his wife's/mother's eyes going blank behind heavy goldfish-bowl glasses. He awakes in horror!

I have heard many dreams as horrific as this from rather placid, reasonably put-together patients. Sullivan much preferred to finesse any confrontation with uncanny affect or content, since he considered uncanny dreams and nightmares to be momentary psychotic episodes. Contrary to Sullivan's expectation, my experience has been that these dreams are frequently presented blandly – offered up rather like stool specimens – immediately disowned and dismissed, even though, in the dream itself, the affect was overwhelming. Does the patient's response perhaps depend on the analyst's "contagious anxiety"? Is it not occurring in interaction with me because I am less anxious about the patient being anxious; or is it dissociated because I am *more* anxious?

Why are we so inured to the uncanny? You cannot imagine how little visual stimulation we had in the 1930s, when I was a child. We cherished the comic strips, book frontispieces, the arrivals of picture magazines (*Look* and *Life*). There has indeed been a shift from the written to the visual, an incremental increase in visual stimulation, and a progressive desensitization to images of horror, now commonplace on television and the cinema.

All that was certainly true, but also there has been a paradigm shift from Modern to Postmodern, with the latter's cultural relativism, its refusal to countenance categorical distinctions like Good and Evil. The shift, I believe, is largely about the flight from an Evil that transcends "the absence of good." The uncanny is unquestionably in the psychoanalytic domain, but Evil is, strictly speaking, a theological concept. Nevertheless, the traditional Manichean/Augustinian dichotomy, which postulates a split between Evil as a real presence and Evil as an absence of good, still has great relevance for psychoanalysis, even in our Postmodern times. As Delbanco said:

> [despite] the shriveling of the old words and concepts, we cannot do without some conceptual means for thinking about the sorts of experiences that used to go under the name of evil . . . We certainly no longer have a conception of evil as a distributed entity with an ontological essence of its own, as what some philosophers call " presence." Yet something that feels like this force still invades our experience and we still discover in ourselves the capacity to inflict it on others. Since this is true, we have an inescapable problem: we feel something that our culture no longer gives us the vocabulary to express.
>
> (Delbanco, 1995, p. 9)

The death camps were not run by people whose mothers didn't love them enough. The consequence of "opening the eyes," seeing what really took place, what people are capable of, is more than can be endured without emotional flattening. As Stalin is reputed to have said, "A single death is a tragedy; a million deaths is a statistic."

The Freudians' strongest objection to the new interpersonal view was, I believe, its failure to take imagination seriously, bowdlerizing the power of destructive aggression and its fantasy manifestations. If your mother loved you – if there were no attachment issues – would there be no destructive Oedipal fantasy, no castration anxiety, no penis to envy, no terror of the "Dark woman," the vagina dentata, the castrating mother? Are these terrors inherent to the psychic structure or the secondary consequences of emotional deprivation?

One value of engaging the powerful affects of the uncanny is that it brings into the patient's awareness the intense anxiety that, from the interpersonal perspective, leads to avoidances in the present. The present, for all of us, is a Swiss cheese riddled with "absences" – inattentions, blind spots, dissociations that make it impossible to grasp the immediacy of one's experience. It is true that the intensity of the anxiety, and its subsequent avoidances, is based in childhood experience, particularly of helplessness and despair; but the bringing into awareness of these anxieties does not assure the patient of a wonderful present. Rather, it equips the patient to know what is going on around here, and – most neglected perhaps – what he or she is *capable* of. Uncanny experience may be not entirely contagious – not entirely relational, as Sullivan thought it to be. It may also be a reflection of human interiority, a capacity for, and even exultation in, the potentials of inhumanity.

Well past the impotence of childhood, one might be able to change the otherwise incorrigible present, come to terms with it, or maybe reconcile to failures and disappointments. Freud dreaded the likelihood that American psychoanalysis would be utopian, espouse a feel-good banality. On the occasion of the Clark lectures, he is reported to have told Ferenczi and Jung, "They don't know that we are bringing them the plague!" Perhaps in our cozier, more *gemütlich* vision of the psychoanalytic process – by viewing the uncanny, the truly Evil pleasure in destructiveness, as being "an absence of good" – we are, as Irwin Hirsch put it, "coasting in the countertransference" (Hirsch, 2008) and, in consequence, diminishing the meaning of being human. Dostoyevsky in *Notes from the Underground* puts the question:

> And what makes you so cocksure, so positive that only the normal and the positive, that is, only what promotes man's welfare, is to his advantage? Can't reason also be wrong about what's an advantage? Why can't man like things other than his well-being? Maybe he likes suffering just as much. Maybe suffering is just as much to his advantage as well-being. In fact, man adores suffering. Passionately!
>
> (Dostoyevsky, 1961, p. 117)

It is a telling caveat for those of us who believe that love and repair are enough. As Freud tried to warn us with his much-disputed Death Instinct, life is a lot more complicated than that.

Notes

1 Speer, Hess, Dönitz, Raeder, Funk, Von Schirach and Von Neurath were the seven prisoners in the dank ancient fortress. All were eventually released, except for Hess, who hanged himself after his last prison mate left.
2 This was an extremely common experience. Guards, officers, diplomats became very sympathetic and involved in helping the Nazi prisoners (e.g., smuggling out notes, etc.), except for the Russians, who would have preferred to shoot them on the spot!
3 Freud based his essay on writer E. T. A. Hoffman's story *The Sandman*, which contained a "doubled" doll, Olympia.
4 Parenthetically, I believe that Freud's use of the Greek concept of hubris, its obstinacy in the face of obvious warning of disaster, carried with it anticipations of the death instinct – the desire to self-obliterate, or be destroyed – as a psychoanalytic correlate of Evil.

References

Delbanco, A. (1995). *The Death of Satan: How Americans Lost the Sense of Evil.* New York: Farrar, Straus and Giroux.
Dostoyevsky, F. (1961). *Notes from the Underground.* New York: Signet Classics.
Freud, S. (1919). The uncanny. *The Standard Edition of the Complete Psychological Works of Sigmund Freud*, vol. 17. London: Hogarth Press, 2001.
Hirsch, I. (2008). *Coasting in the Countertransference: Conflicts of Self-interest between Analyst and Patient.* New York: Analytic Press.
Kristeva, J. (1982). *Powers of Horror: An Essay on Abjection.* New York: Columbia UP.
Lacan, J. (2004). *L'Angoisse.* Paris: Seuil.
Rilke, R. M. (2001). *Duino Elegies*, transl. Snow, E. New York: North Point Press.
Sophocles (1941). *Oedipus at Colonus.* New York: Harcourt, Brace.
Sullivan, H. S. (1953). *The Interpersonal Theory of Psychiatry.* New York: W.W. Norton.

Chapter 23

Hate and destruction at (and behind) our door

Emily A. Kuriloff

Twenty-first-century psychoanalysts no longer believe in their therapeutic neutrality. Still, we recognize that we are not always able to know when and how our own context – our subjectivity – enters the analytic process. Ironically, our own participation in the interactive matrix often eludes self-reflexivity. As D. B. Stern (2010) reminds us, "The eye does not see itself," perhaps most pointedly when we are required to see our least valorous, more destructive or hateful selves. On the other hand, finding bias in the words and acts of our more distant foremothers and fathers feels easier, although nuance and complexity are lost in the absence of their lived experience. It is with such challenges in mind that I explore the impact of hateful and destructive experiences and affects that touched psychoanalysts amidst one of the most destructive and darkest experiences in human history. From Budapest to Paris, the Nazi scourge invaded the work of this seminal group of thinkers and clinicians, a century that belonged as much to Freud as it did to Hitler. How were these analysts professionally affected by a context of creativity and death?

I begin with the year 1938. After Hitler marched into Vienna, the Freud family, along with other Central European colleagues, found refuge and Melanie Klein's dominant voice in London, a situation not altogether pleasing to any of them. Sigmund Freud died less than a year later, and Anna, already a prominent child analyst, took up his standard as heir apparent. The year 1940 marked the beginning of the London "blitz" – the Nazi's lightning war of relentless aerial bombing – but the Viennese *émigrés* were at this point classified as "enemy aliens," not permitted to escape to the countryside nor to join the army, as so many of their English colleagues had done. A sudden majority at Institute meetings, they became bent upon identifying the "true" psychoanalysis to be taught and practiced. Friction only intensified when Klein and her British followers returned in 1941 as attacks on the city eased.

Can the student of psychoanalytic history prove that these circumstances influenced what fast evolved into the infamous Freud–Klein controversies, discussions filled with rancor and innuendo that nearly tore the British Psychoanalytic Institute to pieces? Documentation is not easy to find, and official versions of history often omit a more private reality. However, the recorded minutes of the "extraordinary business meetings" at the organization survive, and what the analysts say and don't say provide hints of their responses to war and terror. In a variety of ways, the hostile and destructive atmosphere at the meetings mimicked the carnage literally outside the institute's doorstep, and made actual theoretical differences between the British and the newly arrived Austrian *émigrés* more pitched and heavy-handed. Moreover, while the British and the Austrians were both touched by the war's murderousness, my reading of the available documents suggests that the Viennese refugees' relationships to their homeland had a distinct influence on their rigid discourse and their clinical work, particularly regarding the very nature of human destructiveness.[1]

To examine this possibility, we first have to turn the clock back to 20 years earlier. After witnessing the unprecedented carnage of World War I, Freud began to question the primacy of libido in psychic life. He also began to challenge the seeming triumph of sublimation of urges evident in the German *Kultur* of his upbringing, i.e., the art, science, and liberal politics that nurtured and sustained him. In 1920, he first mentioned a drive "beyond" the pleasure principle, evidenced in the human compulsion to repeat painful experiences. This drive to go backwards, as it were, came to be equated to Thanatos, or an urge toward death, in Freud's revised metapsychology. This inherently destructive thrust then became a staple of Melanie Klein's theorizing. Freud's view, however, was that a death drive is typically fused with such libidinous aims as mastery via repetition, for example, or in the ego's adaptive defenses. His awareness of this "overdetermined" quality in motivation led him to postulate that a death drive did not make itself plain in the consulting room. It was instead left to metapsychological theorizing. Klein went another direction. As Hinshelwood puts it, Freud's death instinct is clinically quiet, while Klein's is "noisy" (Kuriloff, 2014, p. 58).

For Klein, the death instinct presents as an irreducible instinctual hate readily observed in the aggressive play of her child patients. Furthermore, if Freud's Oedipal child's moral compass is set when he identifies, rather than wishes to destroy, his erstwhile rival (the same-sex parent), Klein's infant and toddler are not only possessed of a severe, if rudimentary, hate and love towards the object, but also of some sense of right and wrong. Klein's data is from her young patients (who play, according to Klein), and exhibited destructive fantasies towards their parents that were then met with introjected counter-aggression. This counter-aggression was evidenced in guilt-ridden self-punishment in response to the urge to devastate their loved ones.

These theoretical distinctions between the "quiet" and "noisy" presence of destructiveness impacted – and continue to impact – praxis. Anna Freud, following her father's developmental schema, did not emphasize the presence of spoiling hate, envy, and guilt in the young child's play, or link such presences to the death drive. She instead worked more supportively, preparing her patient to form an alliance with the analyst. The goal was to fortify the child's adaptive capacities as he or she began to take on the later developmental conflicts between desire, aggression, competition, guilt, and, finally, identification and introjection of parental ideals. Put differently, Anna Freud wished to shore up a nascent superego, while Klein attempted to tone down an extreme, self-punishing version of the child's guilt-ridden murderousness (see Liekerman, 2001, who elaborates on this point). Moreover, Anna Freud, like many of her colleagues, was never enthusiastic about even the Freudian version of the death drive, and, according to Steiner (2000), mentions it only once in her public statements and writings. Coles (1992) sums up Anna's mien when describing her work with World War II orphans:

> For her, child analysts were watchful students, anxious to explore and be taught, to extend themselves with interest and concern and unflinching attention, and in so doing, to be, directly or indirectly, the one who helps mend, repair, nourish, restore.
>
> (p. 21)

In sharp contrast, Klein (1932, quoted in Hinshelwood, 1994, p. 41) provides clinical examples wherein direct interpretations of instinctual aggression are the only means towards forming a therapeutic alliance with a child. Perhaps because Sigmund Freud's initial (1927) introduction of the death drive was primarily theoretical and did not in the main appeal to phenomena that were clinically observable, many analytic clinicians felt neither inspired nor compelled to embrace it.

However, Freud's tone towards the death drive shifted somewhat when he revisited it in 1930, during a time of mounting anti-Semitism and extremist, militaristic challenges to moderate government in central Europe. As if anticipating what was soon to happen in his own city, he writes rather emphatically of the ubiquity of a destructive instinct directed outward, rather than towards the self:

> Anyone who calls to mind the atrocities committed during the racial migrations or the invasions of the Huns, or by the people known as Mongols under Jenghiz Khan and Tamerlane, or at the capture of Jerusalem by the pious Crusaders, or even, indeed, the horrors of the recent World War – anyone who calls these things to mind will have to bow humbly before the truth of this view.
>
> (Freud, 1930, p. 111)

> Yet bow humbly they did not, and the concept of an innate drive toward death or destructiveness became a point of distinction between analysts' for years to come. Why would this be so? The Freudian scholar and clinician Martin Bergmann (personal interview, 2010) states that he was in the minority among New York Freudians for embracing what he believes would have been Freud's sentiments. As Bergmann states "I believe in the death instinct because it's the only possible explanation for the Holocaust." Nothing else we thought could have prepared us for it. In our youths we thought anti-Semitism was decreasing, and we were very idealistic about new ideas, and new forms of government helping in this.
>
> (Kuriloff, 2014, p. 59)

Asked why he thought the concept of Thanatos was unpopular among many of his teachers and colleagues, Bergmann replied that, when psychoanalysis was exported from its homeland, it was "sanitized" by Freud's followers. An awareness of the dark and destructive urges confronting human beings was avoided, according to Bergmann, in favor of a more "optimistic" view. This is in keeping with Bergmann's contention that refugees in the U.S. identified themselves with the prevailing American optimism. The psychoanalyst and Holocaust survivor Dori Laub (personal interview, 2010) identifies the same linkage more pointedly: "Post war psychoanalysts, even émigrés, have a difficult time with the Holocaust. They used theory as an armor against it" (Kuriloff, 2014).

While the notion of a death instinct has been modified in a variety of ways and understood through a variety of lenses over the years, it has remained controversial among analysts. Some modern theorists, such as André Green (2001) and Kernberg (2000), understand the life-and-death drives as existing in dynamic conflict with one another. But what of the debate prior to this time? There are complex factors contributing to any analytic sensibility, far beyond the scope of this discussion. Furthermore, fascism and genocide did not suddenly refocus the English analysts on an *a priori* primitive or murderous psyche, for they had already begun espousing an elemental fantasy life of the infant before Hitler was a known entity, let alone a world figure. When the Nazis reigned, the Freudians and Kleinians were forced to share the same city, institute, and students, all of which highlighted, and perhaps even valorized, the theoretical differences between them. Fighting intensified, and they held ever faster to their sensibilities, as is so often the case with group dynamics.

Yet the distinctions between the Freudians and the Kleinians during the era of the Third Reich are also contextualized by their proximity to the horrors of the war and its aftermath. Consider for a moment that when Freud wrote and published *Civilization and its Discontents*, he still enjoyed freedom and prestige in Vienna, and social and geographic distance from the full brunt of human destructiveness. Did this perhaps allow him more psychic space to explore a darker realm, a psychic region that arguably proved too close for comfort for his compatriots only a few years later? Distances matter: they can mean life or death; they can mean insight or trauma. Rescued from the center of a deadly fascist whirlwind, Freud and his fellow refugees were now adjusting to a strange, not altogether welcoming environment. Those who took up the psychoanalytic cause in the ensuing years became heirs to the hope that with determination and discipline it would be possible to repair what was damaged and to revive some of what was lost, even if this vision came at the partial expense of innovation and expansion.

British Kleinians, on the other hand, less preoccupied by preservation or adaptation, developed a more dialectical if elemental notion of psychic life, one in which love and repair must live alongside an *a priori* hate and destruction. Rather than stressing the supremacy of the ego, they assumed that access to visceral desires could inform and balance thinking. In this balance, love is, ideally, stronger than hate. Love's accompanying gratitude and guilt prompt the drive to restore and cherish oneself and one's people, while hate galvanizes and protects the individual from the destructive fantasies, urges, and actions of others. Mindfulness in this respect is expanded consciousness, rather than self-awareness in its socialized, vernacular meaning. The Kleinians were, so to speak, at home, and as such were free to roam wherever their thoughts took them. The *émigrés*, in contrast, had available to them a theory that would have provided an avenue for understanding the terrible ordeal they had undergone. Yet they did not take it. They had weathered directly an experience of such overwhelming human cruelty that some experience-near conceptualization of a death instinct, some identification of a basic root of human destructiveness, clearly invited. Yet, this theoretical opening was determinedly refused.

Consider now a most troubling story – one that goes beyond the chafing between individual and group psychoanalytic ideas. I refer to the non-Jewish analysts who remained in Berlin after Hitler assumed power in Germany, expelled the mostly Jewish members, and placed Matthias Göring – cousin of the infamous Fieldmarshal – at the helm of the former Berlin Institute.

Reports suggest that a modicum of autonomy at what became known as The Göring Institute afforded some psychoanalysts a space to practice and even popularize their method (see Cocks, 1997, for more detail). There were, to be sure, distinctions between analysts regarding their enthusiasm for, and participation in, Nazi psychoanalysis, which demanded that psychiatrists no longer administer to a single patient, but instead to the corpus of the German *Volk*. Patients, that is, who did not fit within the standard were essentialized as threats – carriers of disease who would contaminate the larger organism. They required healing or, in its absence, killing. By the end of the war, the British analyst Alan Rickman, who traveled to Berlin after the war in 1946, reported that many of the German psychoanalysts he found there were, as he put it, "deteriorated" (Goggin & Goggin, 2001, p. 135), whether or not they were enthusiastic Nazi doctors. Prominent analysts such as Carl Müller-Braunschweig, who had been analyzed by members of Freud's inner circle – Karl Abraham and later Hanns Sachs – at first attempted to preserve Freudian ideals, but later began teaching candidates the work of Herbert Linden, the director of the euthanasia program for the untreatable mentally ill (Antonovsky, 1988, p. 228).

Carl Gustav Jung, perhaps the most famous non-Jewish analyst, often came to Nazi Berlin to give lectures and seminars, and in one instance an interview for German radio, during which he highlighted "racial" differences between Aryan and Jewish psychoanalysis, the latter of which he deemed too intellectual and materialistic for more authentic German sensibilities. This, and other analysts' complicity with such views, certainly disposes of the conceit of the neutral and transcendent professional, possessed of an unassailable analytic identity across culture and circumstance. Rather, it's a cautionary tale for all of us. As Bernd Von Nitzchke (Goggin & Goggin, 2001) argues, positivist ideals of transcendence – and thus objectivity – may have only helped some of the German analysts who remained in the Reich to rationalize going along with, and even embracing, National Socialism.

What traction, then, does the analyst of any historical era have to resist the pull of context? What, after all, is the "cash value" in Freud's mapping of the regressive pull of the group or the archaic fantasies and identifications associated with group leaders if the analyst and the dyad are invariably influenced, seduced, or conquered by their milieu? Consider here Frosh's (2005) insight regarding the irony in both Müller-Braunschweig's and Jung's decision to remove the Freudian Jewish "taint" from psychoanalysis. As he puts it, in doing so, these "Aryans":

> jettisoned many of the elements of Freudian thought that might have protected them from conforming to Nazi demands . . . Freud (1930) famously theorized the individual as always opposed to society, always discontented within it; on a personal level, and despite considerable ambivalence, he identified his own Jewishness as a major, even necessary, spur to achievement precisely because it set him outside the social norm. "To profess belief in this new theory," he wrote, called for "a certain degree of readiness to accept a situation of solitary opposition – a situation with which no one is more familiar than a Jew."
>
> (Freud, 1925, p. 222, full quote in Frosh, 2005, p. 268)

This capacity is lost to totalitarianism. Can we limit this kind of loss to German or self-proclaimed "Aryan" analysts who chose to remain or to publicly associate themselves with Nazi Germany? Chasseguet-Smirgel (1987) turns what may seem an academic question to a more urgent, existential one by considering a post-war context, thereby alerting us that we are all in perpetual danger of behaving as German-identified analysts did in the 1940s, particularly in the midst of tyranny. Consider her depiction of what happened in Eastern Europe within the decade after Hitler's demise:

> When the Communists came to power in an eastern European country, they asked the analysts to declare that psychoanalysis was a "piece of capitalist putridity," after which they would be allowed to work and retain their Party membership. Quite a number signed this declaration. The authorities then said: "You see, they say so themselves," and decided to dissolve the Society. The interesting thing is that apart from a few émigrés, no one remembers this story any longer.
>
> (p. 435)

As the Interpersonal psychoanalyst Edgar Levenson (1989) would put it, perhaps what defines the psychoanalytic process – either in theory making or professional behavior – is not only the centrality of the question, "What does it mean?," but moreover the opportunity and willingness to ask, always and repeatedly, "What's going on around here?"

Note

1 My recently published book, *Contemporary Psychoanalysis and the Legacy of the Third Reich. History, Memory, Tradition* (2014), reveals in greater detail the relationship between the destructiveness of the war informed by the ferocity of the battles housed inside the British Institute.

References

Antonovsky, A. (1988). Aryan analysts in Nazi Germany: questions of adaptation, desymbolization, and betrayal. *Psychoanalysis and Contemporary Thought*, 11, 213–231.

Chasseguet-Smirgel, J. (1987). Time's white hair we ruffle: reflections on the Hamburg Congress. *International Review of Psycho-Analysis*, 14(3), 433–444.

Cocks, G. (1997). *Psychotherapy in the Third Reich* (2nd ed.). Oxford: University Press.

Coles, R. (1992). Anna Freud. *The Dream of Psychoanalysis*. New York: Addison-Wesley.

Freud, S. (1920). Beyond the pleasure principle. *The Standard Edition of* the *Complete Psychological Works of Sigmund Freud,* Volume XVII. London: Hogarth Press.

Freud, S. (1927). Civilization and discontents. *The Standard Edition of the Complete Psychological Works of Sigmund Freud,* Volume XXI (1927–1931). *The Future of an Illusion, Civilization and Its Discontents, and Other Works*, pp. 57–146. London: Hogarth Press.

Freud, S. (1930). Civilization and its discontents. *The Standard Edition of the Complete Psychological Works of Sigmund Freud*, Volume XXI. London: Hogarth Press.

Frosh, S. (2005). Jung and the Nazis: some implications for psychoanalysis. *Psychoanalysis and History*, 7(2), 253–271.

Goggin, E. and Goggin, E. (2001). *Death of a Jewish Science: Psychoanalysis in the Third Reich.* West Lafayette, IN: Perdue University Press.

Green, A. (2001). *Life Narcissism, Death Narcissism.* London: Free Association Press.

Kernberg, O. (2000). *Borderline Conditions and Pathological Narcissism: The Master Works.* New York: Jason Aronson.

Kuriloff, E. A. (2014). *Contemporary Psychoanalysis and the Legacy of the Third Reich: History, Memory, Tradition.* New York: Routledge.

Levenson, E. A. (1989). Whatever happened to the cat? Interpersonal perspectives on the self. *Contemporary Psychoanalysis*, 25(4), 537–553.

Liekerman, M. (2001). *Melanie Klein: Her Work in Context.* New York: Continuum.

Steiner, R. (2000). *Tradition, Change, and Creativity. Repercussions of the New Diaspora on Aspects of British Psychoanalysis.* London: Karnac Books.

Stern, D. B. (2010). *Partners in Thought.* New York: Routledge.

Chapter 24

Diversifying psychoanalysis

Reasons and resistances

Anton Hart

Despite our collective recognition of its importance, entering into conversation about racial and ethnic diversity is inherently risky. There are all kinds of potential losses in play. We could lose "the other," the one from whom we thought we could clearly distinguish ourselves and this, in turn, would occasion loss of self, at least as self had been previously constituted. We could lose our position of privilege, or of victimization. We could lose the repository of all things about ourselves that are unwanted and disavowed. And we could lose the powerful forms of escape from freedom (cf., Fromm, 1941, 1969) that being other affords. Dialogue about diversity, particularly when it involves that which is personal, is scary because it threatens to reveal those aspects of ourselves that are most unformulated and unknown. It is almost guaranteed that all parties in a cross-racial dialogue will have occasion to experience, at least unconsciously, deep levels of shame.

Everyone seems to have trouble talking with each other about issues of race, diversity, difference, otherness. The prevailing contemporary approach to this trouble seems to be *training* rather than unbounded dialogue. Experts in "multicultural competency" teach people what they should and should not say about racial difference. The matter of racial difference is so fraught, it seems as if people cannot be trusted to talk with each other about it. Instead they learn to repeat the lines that have been supplied by diversity experts.

But there are participants in the psychoanalytic dialogue, both "of color" and white, who are not satisfied with speaking from scripted words about racial, ethnic, or cultural difference, and also not satisfied with leaving such aspects of otherness out of the process of clinical work.

The U3 panel on otherness and diversity from which several ideas in this chapter were drawn involved psychoanalysts and students of psychoanalysis who took matters into their own hands and came forward to describe personal experiences that pertained to racial otherness in the consulting room and in the world.

It seems fair to state the obvious: psychoanalytically oriented thinkers and practitioners want diversity in our field. *And, also, we don't.* After all, if we really weren't ambivalent about seeing our numbers transformed into a larger group reflective of the racial and ethnic diversity of our country, such transformation of the psychoanalytic landscape would be much further along than it presently is. Of course, the reasons – for both our ambivalence and our lack of sufficient progress – are complicated, and I will not attempt to sort them all out here. Rather, I will try, in this brief paper, to focus our attention on some of the particular issues – the anxieties and the obstacles – that require elaboration if the goal of a more racially, culturally and socioeconomically diverse psychoanalysis is to be attained.

It may be tempting to attribute the *absence of influx* of underrepresented others to a lack of interest on their part. Those who make the effort and sacrifice to pursue psychoanalytic education and treatment are a special, self-selected group. After all, psychoanalytic thought has always been ambivalently received in the broader culture, and this is even more the case today, when ambivalence is often weighted toward more negative perceptions and caricatures. Nicholas Samstag (2013) argues that psychoanalysis is a "tough sell" in a contemporary cultural context where many would rather *not* look into things, not be in touch with the significance of their histories, their investments, their thoughts and their moods, their preferences and their prejudices. We psychoanalysts already often feel like a beleaguered minority ourselves. On top of this, should we feel responsible for the fact that people of diverse race, class, and culture don't seem to want what we have to offer? Still, Samstag argues that psychoanalysts must do more, much reach outside of their comfort zones in order to invite the indifferent or ambivalent others in.

Yet we must not fail to see the extent to which the other, through disengagement, is not just deprived of what we have to offer but also *deprives us* of enriching, pollinating ideas, principles, and sensibilities. We would do well to wonder how, if everyone with whom we are in psychoanalytic dialogue is like "us" (the royal psychoanalytic – all too often white – *we*), how likely is it that anything dramatically new will enter into the conversation?

And it is particularly important that initiation of dialogue around diversity not simply be the burden of the "usual suspects," those people who are in the (obvious) minority who stand out and are compelled to speak on behalf of their own kind. The panel on diversifying psychoanalysis to which the present discussion refers exemplifies multiple efforts from authors who are not necessarily the usual suspects. They (Fong-Hodges, Fronstein, Kwawer, Samstag, and White) are analysts of multiple races and ethnicities who felt called upon to expand the dialogue on obstacles to diversifying psychoanalysis.

When considering all of the relative silence around diversity-related topics in the psychoanalytic community, the notion of culturally "taboo" subjects comes to mind. Sex was, ostensibly, the original taboo addressed by analysis, the hardest thing for patients to be fully open about. Then, in more recent times, money seemed to take over the top forbidden spot. The majority of patients shifted toward being open about their sexual intimacies to a degree unanticipated by our psychoanalytic forebears, while often remaining closed about their bank balances. Does talking about racial and ethnic material, similarities and differences, the harmonies and the tensions between the groups of which we each are either members or outsiders represent an insufficiently appreciated taboo for psychoanalysis? If so, we need to repeatedly ask ourselves – and our interlocutors – what is making the conversation so off limits? Taboos usually have a role in guarding against some collectively recognized threat. What might the threat be in this case?

We need, particularly, to attend to those moments when being able to speak seems to break down. When we try to talk about race such breakdowns happen all the time. We must observe when issues of race enter the analytic dialogue. And we must observe when they conspicuously (and also subtly) do not. And we must be particularly curious about those transitions between engagement of racial issues and the disappearance of such engagement.

With some notable exceptions, I find that there is a readily observable divide in my own psychoanalytic practice. People of color talk in treatment about issues pertaining to race with some regularity; white people, however, usually do not. The black and multiracial people that I have seen have often reported previous treatments – ordinarily with white therapists – in which both members of the dyad refrained from bringing up race at all. In those pairs, unwittingly bound together by whiteness and, perhaps also, blindness of such, race did not seem to emerge as an issue worthy of attention.

There are many times that I, a part-black, part-white psychoanalyst have been sought out by patients who are black because they "need" a black analyst and I, being as black as our nation's president, will suffice. They have the idea that only someone who is also black will be able to understand certain things about their stories. While I consider such a perspective to probably contain some of the very prejudice that such people are running from, this perspective is also completely understandable, one that, I believe, needs to be treaded upon lightly, at least in the beginning. But I find it worthwhile to be mindful of the fact that one does not have to be white to be prejudiced, and one does not have to be black to have a deep, empathic understanding of prejudice's traumatic impact. I dare say, my own loving, white, progressive, Jewish, psychoanalytic psychologist mother came more profoundly to my periodically racially traumatized aid than did my often-moralistic, self-abnegating, empathically unreliable, African-American father. For me, in many respects, my white mother was "blacker" than my black father, in that she made me feel understood and affirmed in my black experience in ways that my father never did.

It is clear that psychoanalysis needs more psychoanalysts who are of color, those who can be available to prospective analysands who need the semblance of safety that only the fact of that shared racial background can provide. Also needed are more psychoanalysts from all backgrounds who *care* about color and understand that it must be addressed in conversations between colleagues and analytic dyads alike. These can be born among us; we need more opportunities to learn – both didactic and clinical – in which white analysts can access their own and their dialogic partners' experience of marginalization and prejudice. Dr. Motoni Fong-Hodges (2013) provided an engaging account of her experience in an ethnicity-focused process group she was part of during the course of her graduate training. She showed how her professor's commitment to cross-cultural and cross-racial dialogue helped overcome students' hesitations and inhibitions about such dialogue, leading to opportunities for personal growth that were both unpredicted and enduring. Dr. Helen Fronstein (2013) drew on details of her experience as a Russian-Jewish *émigré* to show how access to outsider status, discrimination, and otherness may be readily available for one and all. She made a strong case for psychoanalytic institutes' needing to actively add diversity matters to their required curricula.

Dr. Fong-Hodges, in her description of an experiential group experience that attempted to help participants recognize their own prejudices and promote "multicultural competence," reveals the ways that a *training* emphasis may creep into even the very thoughtful and committed attempts to address issues of diversity. While I understand that multicultural competence is a currently prevalent term, embraced by mainstream psychology, I would suggest that her described group's more primary purpose was promoting multicultural *curiosity* and *openness*, not competence. To my ear competence implies a kind of objectification and distance that stands in contrast to our psychoanalytic aspirations toward authentic contact, deconstructive recognition, and engagement.

Such engagement, it must be underscored, *ain't easy*. As Dr. Cleonie White (2013) illustrated in her courageous and vivid personal account of one such instance of engagement of race and class issues in a psychoanalytic dyad, the analyst may be forced to tolerate being spoken to – or, more aptly, *spoken at* – in ways that can make the skin crawl, whatever complexion such skin may be. She, the black psychoanalyst, was bombarded with a hypersexualized, objectifying, overtly racist and classist assault on her humanity by a deeply traumatized and disturbed white male patient, one whose hurt was expressed in sadistic and rageful forms. She demonstrated how much an analyst who has evoked, in a given patient, issues of race, class, or both, may have to endure, indeed suffer, these issues' divisive power. Any analyst who aspires to address issues of race, as Dr. White does, is opening herself up to potentially staggering layers of objectification, hatred, and shame comprising the bedrock of our sociocultural world. Yet accounts like hers may help us both look at ourselves in the mirror, and see our own ambivalence about taking up matters of race, class, and culture in our work – and to cast, as well, an empathic glance.

Dr. Jay Kwawer (2013), in his discussion of psychoanalytic training and treatment and their lack of availability to people of diverse backgrounds, foregrounded socioeconomic class as a crucial hub of discriminatory inaction in the psychoanalytic field. He argued that psychoanalytic institutes, and also individual practitioners, have not gone far enough to make themselves available to non-traditional, diverse groups of candidates and analysands. Kwawer's conception of psychoanalysis as an ethical calling and social responsibility challenges the ensconced upper-middle-class analyst seeing only patients who can pay high fees.

Arguably, psychoanalysts originally worked in the *field*; subsequently, they made their way into the *house.* We may wonder what has become of our souls as we cling to staying inside while failing to find ways to invite those with lesser, *darker* status in. And, of course, we must also consider that psychoanalysis, with its current diminution of both status- and income-generating potential, is not the destination it used to be. The work of diversifying psychoanalysis is contributed to by giving account of experiences around race and other forms of difference and otherness. The members of this U3 panel were not race scholars; they were psychoanalytic practitioners engaging with issues of diversity in response to a call to do so. They bore witness to their whiteness, their blackness, and their other forms of otherness, and in so doing they expanded the horizon for dialogue across multiple divides. This is how I think psychoanalysts should work toward diversity, through their own personal testimony, not through didactic mastery of the subject (if such mastery could ever be a real thing).

Transcending obstacles to racial diversity within psychoanalysis itself is best thought of as a psychoanalytic task. We have to start with saying what comes to mind. We have to be prepared to listen to thoughts and feelings that are foreign, strange, illogical, and unwanted. We have to be prepared to be responsive to all, yet not reactive. And we have to listen attentively for the moment when the saying of what comes to mind starts to break down. And, in parallel, in the analytic role, we must listen for the moments when open, associative listening starts to break down. Only through such psychoanalytic inquiry into the repressions and dissociations of difference will psychoanalysis have any hope of moving toward being something more than just homogeneous and white.

References

Fong-Hodges, M. (2013). Building multicultural competence from within. Paper presented as part of a panel entitled, "Diversifying Psychoanalysis: Reasons and Resistances," at the Spring Meeting of the Division of Psychoanalysis (39) of the American Psychological Association, April 25th, Boston, Massachusetts.

Fromm, E. (1941, 1969). *Escape from Freedom*. New York: Henry Holt.

Fronstein, H. (2013). The phenomenon of the marginalization of persons of color in psychoanalysis: a candidate's perspective. Paper presented as part of a panel entitled, "Diversifying Psychoanalysis: Reasons and Resistances," at the Spring Meeting of the Division of Psychoanalysis (39) of the American Psychological Association, April 25th, Boston, Massachusetts.

Kwawer, J. S. (2013). Discussion. Paper presented as part of a panel entitled, "Diversifying Psychoanalysis: Reasons and Resistances," at the Spring Meeting of the Division of

Psychoanalysis (39) of the American Psychological Association, April 25th, Boston, Massachusetts.

Samstag, N. (2013). Marketing, magnanimity, and maintenance: considering the lack of diversity in psychoanalysis. Paper presented as part of a panel entitled, "Diversifying Psychoanalysis: Reasons and Resistances," at the Spring Meeting of the Division of Psychoanalysis (39) of the American Psychological Association, April 25th, Boston, Massachusetts.

White, C. (2013). Inside/out: the analyst's prejudices. Paper presented as part of a panel entitled, "Diversifying Psychoanalysis: Reasons and Resistances," at the Spring Meeting of the Division of Psychoanalysis (39) of the American Psychological Association, April 25th, Boston, Massachusetts.

Part VIII

Silence and privacy

Negotiating boundaries between public and private – in and out of the consulting room

Chapter 25

Silence in adolescent psychotherapy[1]

Daniel Gensler

In this paper I am not describing teenagers who assume I am interested in what they have to say, or who are interested in what I have to say, or who are ready to talk about what is on their mind. Nor am I describing narcissistic teens who talk expecting an audience; or teens who talk histrionically in order to avoid something more central; or teens who go on and on compulsively to make sure they get it just right. I am not even describing the many teenagers in therapy who resent being there and withhold passively and aggressively in a demonstration of their anger.

The adolescent patients described in this paper do not naturally talk, open up, or express themselves, neither with their parents nor with their therapists. Though they might like to be able to speak up, and might try, they are not good at it or cannot find a way for it to feel comfortable in therapy. Answering questions is easier, but the answers are usually brief. Initiating conversations, with a therapist or with their parents, is hard. They do not usually resent having to be in therapy, though it would have been easier not to come. They are not on the autistic spectrum. They just do not know what to say or how to get into a conversation. They might know how to talk with their friends more easily.

When I am the therapist with one of these teenagers, after a while I am tempted to break out my Scrabble board or playing cards to make something happen. Sometimes I do, but I try not to for a while. At the beginning of therapy I make other things happen. I ask teenagers about the presenting problems that the parents have told me about, and learn very little. I ask if I can be of any use to them separately from what the parents want me to do, and learn nothing. I get them to join in with me in making a sociogram of their friends and acquaintances, and I learn a little or a lot about the structure of their social lives, but they stay guarded. I have them join me in making out other visual aids that I often make with children and teenagers, such as a family tree, a timeline of their life, and charts of their school day describing classes and teachers. Once I learn all this, I ask who and what they like and dislike. I get curious about their favorite websites and sometimes they show these to me on their smart phones or on my laptop. I learn more, there is some conversation, the atmosphere lightens up, and maybe the session ends with a feeling that at least we did something together. But the next session starts with the same feeling, bringing to mind the metaphors of pulling teeth, or of lighting a fire with wet matches or wet kindling, where again I have to work hard to get something going.

This is often the presenting problem ("my son or daughter talks with friends but not with us") and the parents want me to change this.

Little has been written about working with shy, silent, or withdrawn teenage patients. Briggs (2000) described timid and withdrawn children (not teens). He describes their attunement and concern about others' emotional state, their limited involvement with peers, reluctance to take the initiative, fear of expression of feelings and impulses, sometimes compulsive activities, active inner life of fantasy, self-devaluation, and excessive anxiety in at least one of the parents. Typical countertransferences include impatience, inadequacy, withdrawal, or irritation when attempts to intervene are rebuffed. In treatment, when a therapist can convey liveliness and interest in the child and actively try to extend the interaction between them without pressing too hard, the child realizes that the setting is safe. The therapist continues to improvise and participate spontaneously, modeling and eliciting greater vitality in the child without intruding excessively.

With silent teenagers I have learned not to stay silent. Leading with curiosity, I inquire. I respond to the scant material that the teenage patient has put out, using my own associations to it. I note my own reactions and feelings. Sometimes I think I am being played with, controlled, or manipulated, and I feel resentful. When I do, I note to the teenage patient that she or he would probably rather not be there. Usually the patient agrees; I raise the question of how to get out of having to go to therapy. The teenage patient suggests I tell the parents that therapy isn't really needed. I reply that the parents would think me a fool if I endorsed this opinion to them, and that they would fire me and find someone else. Then I raise the question of the teen's opinion of the parents' concerns and we get into some genuine (usually angry) topics.